Drama and Feeling continues Richard Courtney's examination of the role of dramatic acts – from children's play through social ritual and creative drama to theatre – in human development. A leading figure in the world of drama education, Courtney looks at how feelings are generated, attended to, and deepened through dramatic acts and shows that feelings are an intrinsic part of how and why we learn.

Courtney describes dramatic acts that generate deep and significant feelings that cannot be expressed directly but can only be elicited through metaphoric acts. He argues that the purpose of drama is to transmit feelings to others through metaphor, thus creating consciousness and self-consciousness. To show that this is the case, he dissects the feeling and emotion inherent in dramatic acts and examines them through a semiotic lens. He also looks at problems facing those who study cognition, feeling, and dramatic action and considers research methods that address these areas.

Drama and Feeling makes a case for placing educational drama firmly within the curriculum and provides drama educators with new insight into the dramatic art form and process.

RICHARD COURTNEY is professor emeritus, Forum for Arts and Media Education, Ontario Institute for Studies in Education.

Drama and Feeling

An Aesthetic Theory

RICHARD COURTNEY

McGill-Queen's University Press
Montreal & Kingston • London • Buffalo

© McGill-Queen's University Press 1995
ISBN 0-7735-1228-4

Legal deposit first quarter 1995
Bibliothèque nationale du Québec

Printed in Canada on acid-free paper

This book has been published with the help of a grant from the Canadian
Federation for the Humanities, using funds provided by the Social Sciences
and Humanities Research Council of Canada. Publication has also been
supported by the Canada Council through its block grant program.

Canadian Cataloguing in Publication Data

Courtney, Richard
    Drama and feeling: an aesthetic theory
    Includes bibliographical references and index.
    ISBN 0-7735-1228-4
    1. Theatre – Psychological aspects. 2. Theatre – Philosophy.
    3. Emotions. 4. Drama in education. I. Title.
    PN2039.C67 1995   152.4   C94-900803-6

This book was typeset by Typo Litho Composition Inc.
in 10/12 Sabon.

for David

and those who have devoted themselves to spontaneous drama and its remarkable effects upon others – with love and respect

Contents

Illustrations

Preface

This book is written as a companion to my *Drama and Intelligence: A Cognitive Theory* (Montreal & Kingston: McGill-Queen's University Press, 1990). In that volume, spontaneous dramatic acts were examined through a specific lens: a cognitive perspective was taken upon them.

In Part 1 of this book I address the reverse side of the coin, an affective and aesthetic view of spontaneous drama. My first notes on this theme were written over forty years ago. Then the emotional qualities of drama – the effects of educational drama upon students' emotional expression – were paramount. In the past twenty years, the issues of intellectual attainment have been stressed. Today, however, we see that spontaneous drama has a holistic effect. It simultaneously transforms the cognitive, affective, aesthetic, and psychomotor aspects of our thought. One of these mental aspects may be emphasized at a particular moment, it is true, but all other aspects are contained within it.

In Part 2 we extrapolate this to examine the nature of inquiry: in the creative arts as a whole in chapter 7; as a projected research method based on the hologram in chapter 8; and in universities in chapter 9.

Parts of some chapters have been rewritten from some of my earlier work, to whose editors I am grateful. I am also grateful to the Social Science and Humanities Research Council of Canada for a grant with which I developed certain aspects of the aesthetic theory.

As this book has been in gestation for many years, I owe much to a great many people. I do not wish to implicate them in what is contentious in this book, but I am extremely grateful to them for honing my ideas:

John Allen, Dr Métin And, Michael Ardenne;

Dr Sharon Bailin, Dr Judith Barnard, Zina Barnieh, the late Alec Baron, Dr Gisèle Barret, the late Dr Bernard Beckerman, the late Dr Daniel Berlyne, Dr Bradley Bernstein, Dr David Best, Dr Adam Blatner, David W. Booth, Derek Boughton, Dr Kathy Browning, Isabel Burger, Dr Shehla Burney, Rt Rev. E. J. Burton;

Robert Campbell, Louise Chamers, Dr David A. Child, Micki Clemens, the late Dr George Clutesi, OC, Dr Amir Cohen, Sarina Condello, Nina Consunji, Dr Donald Cordell, Dr Mary Coros, Jeanette Cox, the late Edward Gordon Craig;

Alec Davison, the late Ron Danielson, Dr Elizabeth Dickens, the late Dr Bonamy Dobrée, Joyce Doolittle, Helen Dunlop; Dr Susan Eden, John Ellis, John Emerson, Dr H.C. (Bobby) Emery, William (John) Emms, Dr Renée Emunah, Stanley Evernden; Dr Oliver Fiala;

Barbara Gans (née Severin), Dr Robert Gardner, Peter and Ken Giles, Bernard Goss, Mary Green (née Titerle), Dr Poranee Gurutayana, the late Sir Tyrone Guthrie;

Agnes Haaga, Sr Georgiana Hannigan, Carl Hare, Dr David Hawkins, Dorothy Heathcote, the late Barbara M. Hedgeland (née Coombe), the late John Hirsh, OC, John Hobday, W.A. Hodges, John Hodgson, Dr James Hoffman, Dr David E. Hunt;

Dr Ronald Irving; Barbara Jefford, CBE, Sue Jennings, Dr David Read Johnson, Keith Johnstone, Leonard Jones; Dr Judith Kase-Polisini, Sandra L. Katz, David Kemp, Barbara Kennedy, the late G. Wilson Knight, CBE, Judith Koltai, Dr Virginia Glasgow Koste, Natalie Kuzmich;

the late Rudolf Laban, Carole and David Lander, Dr Robert J. Landy, Dr Robert Lane, the late Fabian Lemieux, Dr Trevor Lennam, the late John Linstrum, Mark Long and The People Show;

Don MacLean, Dr Stanley S. Madeja, Mwai Magondu, Dr Norah Maier, Dr Ksana Maraire, Sybil Marshall, Sr Kathryn Martin, Dr Sue Martin, Dr Alistair Martin-Smith, Lord Redcliffe Maud, the late Frederick May, Dr Nellie McCaslin, Dr Colla Jean McDonald, Deborah McDonald, Dr John McInnes, Dr John McLeod, Dr Peter McLaren, the late Dr H. Marshall McLuhan, Peter McWhir, Dr Geoffrey Milburn, Victor E. Mitchell, Dr Penina Mlama, Gwilym Morris, Dr Jack Morrison, Dr Dennis Mulcahy;

Dr Hiroko Noro; Dr Harold Oaks, Betty O'Brien, Lawrence O'Farrell, the late Ruth Wynn Owen; Paul Park, Brenda Parres, Rose Pavlow, Dr Vance Peavey, Jay Peng, Walter Pitman, Gary Pogrow, the late Dr Peter Prouse;

Dr Frederick S. Rainsberry, Dr Natalie Rewa, Joseph Ribiero, Dr John Ripley, Dr Pamela Ritch, Dr Hélane S. Rosenberg, Dr Bernard Rosenblatt, Dr Christopher Ross, Dr H. Howard Russell; Dr Ann Saddlemyer, Dr Diane Saint Jacques, Gertrud Schattner, Graham Scott, Dr Paul Schafer, Dr John Sharpham, Dr Sandra Shiner, Dr Judith A. Silver (Baird), Rina Singha, Geraldine Brain Siks, Colin Skinner, Peter Slade, Dr Helen E.H. Smith, Lawrence Sparling, Dr Robert E. Stake, Michael Stephen, Paul Stephenson, Dr Elizabeth Straus, Dr Pamela Sturgess, Takako Suga (née Shimizu), Larry Swartz;

Dr Alan Thomas, oc, Katherine Thurston-Perret, Dr Audley Timothy, John Trinder, the late Dr Helen Tulk, Dr Christine Turkewych, Michael Turner, the late T.E. (Gerald) Tyler;

David Upson; Frances and Arie Vander-Reyden; Dr Anton Wagner, Dr Bernie Warren, Brian Way, Dr Bronwen Weaver, the late Dr Wilfred Wees, Dr Otto Weininger, Nadia Weisenberg, the late Dr Aurelieu Weiss, the late Don Wetmore, Dr Barbara Salisbury Wills, Dr Joyce A. Wilkinson, Dr Michael and Nikki Wilson, Dr Ian Winchester, Dr Robert W. Witkin, Ton Witsell, Peter H. Wright, the late Sir Donald Wolfit, Dr Lin Wright; and Dr Belarie Hyman Zatman.

My grateful thanks go to my secretary, Sandra Burroughs, for her forbearance and her skills. As always I owe much to my wife, Rosemary Courtney, particularly for her support, her editing skills, and the index.

R.C.
Toronto and
Jackson's Point, Ontario
1993

Drama and Feeling

"As she laughed I was aware
of becoming involved with her laughter"
                              T.S. Eliot

"My spirit has as much need
of emotions as my senses"
                        Pablo Picasso

Introduction:
Feeling and Intelligence in
Dramatic Acts

The close relationship of drama and intelligence[1] is strongly influenced by human feeling.

Dramatic acts generate deep and significant feelings. G. Wilson Knight once said that a player's experience in the theatre was, to him, like his time as a soldier in World War I. A feeling of great cameraderie was built that went far beyond that given by team sports and games: performing before an audience felt like "going over the top" of the trenches in Flanders[2] – a deeply felt and extreme form of human performance.

In a similar way, people in life acts who are *in extremis* can experience two deep and related feelings. First, they can create a remarkable unity in their mutual relations. For example, someone who is kidnapped can become very attached to the kidnappers, even identifying with them – as happened to Patty Hearst. Second, their joint acts can be on the knife-edge between fear and exhilaration. This has been described in a number of cases by both hijackers and their victims.

In other words, the metaphor for *theatrical* performance is the tip of an iceberg; it applies with equal force to *dramatic* performance. "Theatre" refers to a performance before an audience. *"Drama" is a spontaneous human process whereby we think and act in an "as if" fiction while, simultaneously, we are engaged in the living process.* Theatre codifies into an art form the kinds of feelings created in all human spontaneous and dramatic acts. However, this happens in varying degrees between the most absorbed and the most distanced. Generally, however, when adults use the roles of "parent" or "child," or young

Figure 1
Aspects of Drama and Theatre

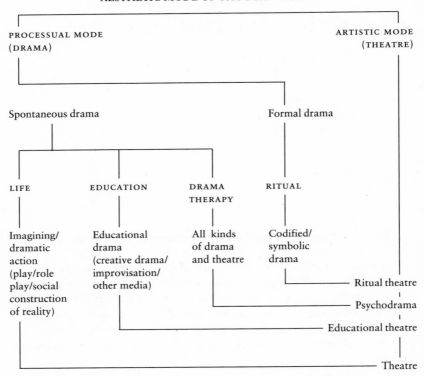

AESTHETIC MODE OF THOUGHT-ACTION

children play at mothers or fathers, or school students improvise a story from history, they generate strong feelings of social cohesion, empathy with others, and both commitment and dedication to their joint tasks. (See figure 1.)

DRAMA LEADERS

Feelings of deep devotion and commitment occur among people working in improvisation, creative drama, play, educational drama, drama therapy, simulation, role play, and theatre. This is most obvious among the players: all drama leaders tell "green-room stories" about groups of their players whose commitment was extraordinary. Most generalize this feeling to all such groups, and they are probably right.

But it also happens among the leaders, teachers, and directors themselves. It may be less obvious among these leaders than the players, but it is of equal significance. For over forty years I have worked alongside a great many people whose deep feelings have led them to dedicate themselves and their energies to promoting spontaneous play and drama with others. Often they have done so to the point of exhaustion and usually with no thought of reward. This is well known in the field, and is best illustrated in a number of examples.

In the late 1950s two brothers, Peter and Ken Giles, were young men working in Smethwick, a borough near Birmingham in England. At that time, Smethwick was a solid square mile of back-to-back slums, many without running water – a depressing and depriving cultural desert. Peter and Ken came to a two-day training course for potential youth drama leaders. They had no previous drama experience, but, by the end of only one weekend, they were so enthusiastic that they went out on their own to obtain all kinds of theatrical skills. For many years in the 1950s and 1960s in Smethwick, they ran a drama and theatre club for teenagers and young adults with an extraordinary dedication – night after night, using all their spare time including holidays. They may well be still doing so ...

Mark Long, Sid Palmer, and John Dowding gave up their careers as drama teachers in the early 1960s to form *The People Show*, then the most avant-garde improvisational theatre company in London. They were liable to appear anywhere – in the street, parks, shopping centres, conferences – in their seemingly haphazard surrealist events. They starved for so many years that Sid and John eventually gave up and went to earn "normal" livings. But the last I heard, Mark was still leading the troupe in performance ...

Dr Helen Tulk and her husband were the medical practitioners at Grand Falls, Newfoundland, from the end of World War II for over twenty years. Because no one else was available, she voluntarily ran a Saturday improvisational drama club for children, satisfying their real needs to stretch their imaginative capacities, social relationships, and practical creativity, and to express their feelings. With her medical and family duties, she could not obtain training. So she did the next best thing. She organized the First National Conference for the Canadian Child and Youth Drama Association (CCYDA) at St John's in 1967, inviting international experts to conduct workshops or seminars alongside Newfoundlanders. It was a gigantic task because it became a high-profile event with the last "Father of Confederation," Joey Smallwood, premier of Newfoundland, in attendance. It had great value for the country and the province, but even more for Helen. When it was over, she confessed to me: "Only now do I think I know what I'm doing on a

Saturday morning!" And she continued to work with the children until, shortly, her health prevented her. She died a little later.

While I was president of the CCYDA (1971 – 73) I spent virtually every evening and most weekends answering letters from communities as
remote as Buffalo Breath, North Saskatchewan. Most of these letters
were from isolated adults who, with no (or minimal) training and little
help from anyone, had been conducting spontaneous drama work all
their lives. Their requests to me for help revealed both a deeply felt
dedication and a need to be assured that they were not alone – that
there was a community of like-minded people who cared about them
and supported what they were doing.

Sister Georgiana at sixty-four came from Nova Scotia for a year's
graduate study with me and, as she completed it, she also retired as a
teacher. "But now I can really start work," she said as she returned to
Halifax and Dartmouth to begin pastoral work through drama in the
community, particularly around the docks. The last I heard she was in
her mid-eighties and she was still working there ...

A thirty year-old Quebecker, Renée, with a massive shock of bright
red hair, took a summer course with me, wanting to learn how to conduct drama work in schools and with the Inuit children. Two months
after she returned to the north, they made her a shaman! She was so
committed to their lives that in 1969 she went to live in the arctic
wastes with them. I have not heard from her since ...

An Indian chief on the Pacific Northwest Coast was also the janitor
at a local school. His white employers did not know that, for forty
years, he spent every spare minute travelling the coast, teaching Indian
dance and ritual drama to children of many villages of his people. He
continued to do so even when he retired as a janitor and became a famous actor on TV and in films.

In Australia, a beautiful young woman who had earned a great deal
of money by being a famous television personality threw this up to direct participational theatre with very young children. Nine years later
she was penniless and returned to TV part-time to keep the theatre running. It may still be ...

Talking of Feeling

I have worked or corresponded with hundreds of such devoted people,
or talked with them in both casual conversations and through a research study. We have talked in Canada, in rural and slum areas of Britain, in Holland and Belgium, on the bomb-sites of London and
Nuremberg after World War II, in the hot dry deserts of the American
Southwest and the high-rise deserts of New York and Los Angeles, on

the lush peaceful islands of the South Seas, across the dry, hot, and red island of Australia, in the cafés of Bulgaria, and many other places.

I talked with my colleague Brian Way, for example. This famous pioneer of spontaneous creative drama and participational theatre for children, who was the first to insist that his adult performers were "actor-teachers," regularly had to grab a few hours' sleep on the floor of his Theatre Centre in London in order to keep his troupes out touring the schools. And for the whole time he was director there – greeting people from all over the world who had heard of his work – he was scraping for money, both professionally and personally. When I asked him why he committed himself to drama in such a way, he shrugged and humbly said: "Well, it just *has* to be done!" What businessmen with similar reputations in their own field would be so dedicated to their work as to put themselves through almost a lifetime of such agony?

Most of the leaders, teachers, and directors I spoke to said that dramatic activity led them to commit themselves and their deepest feelings to it. One person laughingly exclaimed, "It's not so much a way of working, it's more a way of life!" In talking casually with them, I discovered that many, when they were younger, had a play or spontaneous drama experience which, in their words, "changed my life" for the better. There was an extraordinary unanimity among them about this. Dr Helen Tulk said that she was "never the same again." Renée, before she went to work with the Inuit, put it thus: "I felt so good about myself I had to help others to have the same kind of experience." The Indian chief said that, when his family and tribe conducted a *potlatch* (a ritual drama) for him as a child, it so affected his feelings that it never left him: "I became one with all people – and I still *live* it. I wanted our young people, so depressed in the white man's world, to feel like that."

To see if my casual observations had any validity, I conducted a research project over several years with some thirty-seven expert leaders and teachers and eleven directors of drama and theatre[3]. To the questions, Why do you do it? and, Why do you do it with such commitment? they implied that they did not know explicitly or cognitively. Rather, they said, they responded to a deep inner need – to their feelings. This study confirmed my initial observations and specifically showed that *drama leaders, teachers and directors commit their feelings both to the activity and to other people, presuming that their lives, too, can be changed in such a highly positive way.*

Primary Feelings

I also asked whether their feelings for the activity or their feelings for the people involved were more important to them. This was because two master teachers of drama have explicitly stated that their primary focus is the learner: Brian Way said that he is concerned more with people than with drama,[4] and Dorothy Heathcote commented that she is a teacher first and a teacher of drama second – and that she sees herself as midwife to others.[5] Her vivid metaphor was not replicated in the research study.

The overwhelming majority of respondents said that *the primary feelings* activated by dramatic acts clustered as follows:

- *empathy* for others – which is best expressed in the Italian as "sympatico";
- *identification* with and *trust* in others as players;
- *trust* in spontaneous dramatic activity (drama is fictional so it is "safe" for all kinds of practical experiment);
- *significance* of dramatic action (valuing);
- *enjoyment*, satisfaction, and exhilaration in the activity;
- *confidence* that they can achieve their purposes.

Although this primary cluster of feelings was agreed upon by all respondents, they also said that by far the most significant were, first, feelings *for* others and, second, the feelings within dramatic acts.

It is difficult to talk of these drama leaders, teachers, and directors without using the word "*love*." They have a genuine love for other people, an identification with and an empathy for them. All in their own way – which is sometimes not my way – so commit themselves to the spontaneous drama of others that words like altruism or high-mindedness are quite insufficient. So are devotion, attachment, affection, affinity, friendship, liking, and similar terms. Only *love for humanity* seems applicable. Expressed so, this may appear trite. The respondents used phrases that included:

- "a loving relationship";
- "togetherness";
- being one with them: "We are as one";
- "trusting and sharing together";
- feeling *for* them/on their behalf/from their perspective;
- reciprocal feelings: "Our joint/mutual/shared feelings."

Secondary Feelings

Leaders, teachers, and directors also commented on many other feelings they experienced while working with others. These *secondary feelings* were not common to all respondents but they were shared by many.

It is a commonplace that there is high correlation between good learners and their feeling that their life was changed by *identification with a highly influential teacher earlier in life*. About the same correlation exists with drama leaders, teachers, and directors. Although it was not common to them all, among those who did not share this feeling, many strongly identified with one or both of their parents.

Most of the respondents had a *strong bonding with other drama workers*. This could either be in direct face-to-face contacts or an indirect bonding – at a distance with a major writer in the field, or by correspondence with others, or through telephone calls. About the same high proportion felt that they and others like them were *bonded by a value system* promoted by dramatic activities. This value system is positive about dramatic and aesthetic activities, similarities, negotiation, peace, reciprocity, co-operation, and the quality of life. It opposes the dominant values in modern Western society of aggressiveness, opposition, competition, quantity, and the desire for money and material objects.

This particularly applied to drama teachers in schools, colleges, and universities. *Some of them felt strongly that Western societies not only did not value spontaneous drama but actively worked against what it stood for.* They cited many examples, but we will use only one here.

Bronwen Harris (not her real name) was a trained drama teacher with deep concerns about the dropouts and marginal people among adolescents and young adults. With them, her work was highly successful and she received many commendations. After marriage and three children, she returned to teach in the mid-1960s at a residential school for disturbed adolescent girls in England, using spontaneous drama as a basis for their learning, and devoting herself to the work and the students far beyond normal requirements. I was amazed at the difference between her class and some others in social awareness, thinking on the feet, concern for others, and reading and writing. But the administrators of the school, who wanted the young women to sit in rows of desks working silently ("children should be seen and not heard"), disliked Bronwen's teaching methods and, despite my objections, fired her. The result was that she could not obtain further employment. A year later she had lost her self-confidence and she said, "I'm no use anymore – I don't count. Those kids are going to be lost – and I want to help them so much!" She became increasingly depressed, her marriage broke up, and she died shortly thereafter in her mid-thirties.

A few drama practitioners quoted the adage "Just because I'm paranoid doesn't mean there's nobody chasing me" to express their feelings in this regard. Other equally concrete examples, and in all Western societies, could be cited.

As to their *working to exhaustion*, the responses of the directors, leaders, and teachers showed that this was common – so much so that I was reminded of Bernard Shaw's remark that when he died he hoped he would be thoroughly worn out in the service of humanity.

Revealing Metaphors

We discovered that the use of metaphors (either spoken or expressed in other media) can reveal significant meanings about people's unconscious feelings. Where Dorothy Heathcote feels herself to be a midwife to others, the respondents to the study also expressed their feelings about themselves in metaphors.

The most common metaphoric self-descriptor of the drama practitioners was as *a gardener*. One intriguing implication of the feelings behind this metaphor was that it was used differently by those working in the United States compared with those in Canada, Britain, and Australia. The difference can be related to Aristotle's two alternating views:

- that life can be seen as an acorn growing into an oak – from the bottom up (as in Canada, Britain and Australia); and
- that the ideal nature of the oak is inherent in the acorn – from the top down (the United States).

In simplistic terms, Americans saw themselves as gardeners *ensuring* that acorns become oaks, while the others saw themselves as gardeners *helping* acorns to fulfil their *potential* as oaks. The difference is subtle, but it indicates variations in the underlying assumptions of drama workers in different contexts. It also accounts, to an extent, for differences in the methods that they use.

A tangential issue was a comparison of the metaphors used by drama and non-drama teachers in schools. There were three main differences:

- Drama teachers never used negative metaphors of themselves or students. Non-drama teachers used such verbal metaphors as "With this class I'm a policeman at times," "I have to baby-sit this lot," "I must get the whip out occasionally," "they're not 'little darlings', you know," and "I sometimes wonder what rock they've crawled out from."
- A similar difference was found among teachers' metaphors in body language and gesture.
- Drama teachers understood Heathcote's "thresholds"[6] – often in a metaphoric way – but most non-drama teachers did not.

Usually when we discuss the deep and significant feelings generated by spontaneous dramatic acts, we do so from the perspective of the players. This is almost universally the case in the literature. Here, however, we have seen the importance of the issue for teachers, leaders, and directors.

PLAYERS

When we return to the perspective of the players we discover that their feelings are part of a whole thought process. As players, we experience thought (imagination and feeling) and action as one entity. Thought + action = dramatic acts. Together they create meaning. We can only separate them in abstraction, and in the past tense; we cannot do so as we live through them in the present tense. Artists specifically are aware of this distinction between expressing feeling in immediate action and abstract expression. Picasso said, "Art *is*," while Isadora Duncan put it: "If I could tell you what I mean, there would be no point in dancing." All artistic and dramatic acts express and convey imagination and feeling in particulars and in the present tense.

Imagination asks "what if?" Feeling asks "does it feel right?" And dramatic acts function "as if." Drama *is* transformation. When we engage in mental dramatization or external dramatic acts we transform things, ideas, other people, ourselves and the world around us. When we change we learn. Through "re-play"[7] and a feeling of trust in others, when we act we use specific mental structures (similarity, whole/part, continua, and metaphor) and dynamics (transformation, spontaneity, and substitution). These, like feelings, are mostly unconscious. They are part of what we *tacitly* know; often, when we try to put them into words, they change – as Michael Polanyi says, "We know more than we can tell."[8] Mental structures, dynamics, and feelings are important parts of our practical knowledge, the "know-how" whereby we operate efficiently in the world.

We create a dramatic world (a fiction) that exists in parallel with the actual world. Although we ground meaning in actuality, we check it against our dramatic world to see if it feels right. We try things out dramatically, make mistakes and correct them. Truth, thus, is not absolute but resides in the player *as an existing felt reality*, and in the playing as *an emerging felt reality*. These two felt realities coexist when we operate in the "here and now."

Dramatic acts are signifiers that stand for the player's imaginings and feelings (the signified). Observers and/or audiences must make inferences from the signifiers to discover what the player signifies. This interaction is a reversible process:

- Thought and feeling are mentally metaphoric.
- When expressed by players in dramatic acts they become symbolic. They take their meanings from the symbolic systems of the social world.
- Observers and audiences turn them into their own internal metaphors to understand them.

This is often seen as "turning the world upside down."[9]

The relationship of players is both dialogic and dramatic. These modes underlie all interpretation: we put ourself in the other's shoes to see and feel things from her/his point of view (or *felt*-reality). There is, thus, a feeling basis for resisting stereotypical thinking and bigotry, and this is specifically learned through spontaneous dramatic action.

Feeling and Power

Drama activates our feelings in a powerful way. This is most obvious in the playhouse. Lee J. Cobb as Willy Loman, Laurence Olivier as Archie Rice, Frederick Valk as John Gabriel Borkman, Edith Evans as Cleopatra, Marcel Marceau as Bip, Jean-Louis Barrault and Madeleine Renaud in a Claudel play – these are moments from the past which remain with us as extremely powerful icons.

Our feelings are no less activated when we are a player or a leader in improvisation. The active process of thinking on the feet provides a feeling of tension that, at best, can be electrifying. When used comically, it can result in improvisations, such as those directed by Keith Johnstone,[10] so outrageously hilarious that we can be helpless with laughter.

The drama of life can generate equally powerful feelings. For example, my mother insisted on playing her mother role, while placing me in the role of a small child, even when I was a grandfather! For forty years I have been allergic to onions, and for twenty years I have not eaten potatoes as a way to reduce my carbohydrate intake. She understood this *consciously*, but when I ate at her house and she was serving onions, I was given them too. And she never put a dinner plate in front of me without a pile of potatoes. She played her mother role *unconsciously*, but the reader can readily understand that mealtimes with my mother generated powerful emotions and feelings.

Children at play often experience strong feelings. They can be so immersed in their dramatic acts that they do not wish to stop when their mother calls them in for a meal. The loss of an "imaginary companion" can be traumatic to them. And often the feeling of completion experienced by the child at play can lead to a lifelong search to re-experience it. Feeling in dramatic acts can powerfully affect our lives in many ways.

Modes of Thought

Human thought is a complex of modes. The nature of these modes is the subject of some disagreement, but it is commonly said that there are four: the cognitive, the affective, the psychomotor, and the aesthetic. These modes are abstractions. They do not actually exist in the brain or mind. They are maps which provide a perspective on the territory of experience; they show the ways that thoughts often (but not always) cluster.

Cognitive thought ranges from the acquisition of knowledge of specifics to higher-level abilities, such as classification, comprehension, application, synthesis, etc. We emphasize this mode when we think in specific items ("the facts"), in abstractions like beauty or morality, or with a specified logic.

Affective thought ranges from basic emotions like fear and anger to moods, which include a degree of acceptance or rejection. We emphasize this mode when we are frightened, angry, etc.

Psychomotor thought ranges from muscular or motor skills to those that require neuro-muscular co-ordination. We emphasize this mode when engaging in such activities as walking, running, or bicycling.

Aesthetic thought is based on feeling. We emphasize this mode when we imagine, choose, judge, distinguish what we like from what we appreciate, and use intuition, insights, and hunches.

These four modes of thought are closely related. They are not separate and independent entities like soap and dogs. They overlap and mingle. All are present in our thinking – there is no thought that is entirely cognitive or entirely affective. It is the emphasis that we give to a thought that varies (see figure 2).

Cognition is concerned with knowing. In ordinary everyday terms we make little if any distinction between knowing and believing. When we say such-and-such is the case we usually mean that it is the common consensus that it is so. Learning is a cognitive process based on transformation so that the state of "coming to know" leads us from virtualizing to actualizing.

Cognition overlaps with the aesthetic mode in intuition and insight; we acquire knowledge through both, although, as insights appear suddenly ("like a flash"), we do not know their inner workings. We can accept them, so they become part of our store of knowledge, or reject them.

If we make an abstract distinction between emotions (the affective) and feelings (the aesthetic), emotions are seen as undifferentiated and come upon us quickly – as when Sartre asks, What happens when a tiger walks into a room?[11] His answer is that we have an immediate

Figure 2
Modes of Thought

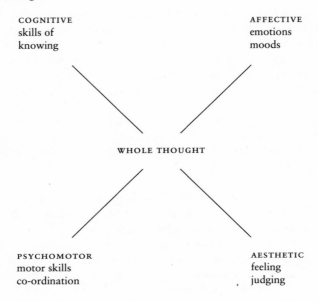

COGNITIVE
skills of
knowing

AFFECTIVE
emotions
moods

WHOLE THOUGHT

PSYCHOMOTOR
motor skills
co-ordination

AESTHETIC
feeling
judging

bodily reaction – metaphorically we either "tremble or faint." Emotions are always particular: they are about some *thing* – fear of a tiger, say, or love of a person – and (in an extreme case) even the generalized fear or anger of some depressives is *about* fear or anger.

Feelings, on the other hand, are reflexive. The feeling when we contemplate a sunset, for example, is a more discriminating response than an emotion. Nor are feelings always focused on one thing.

Emotions and feelings function like poles on a continuum; there are degrees between them that cannot be categorized one way or the other. (Do we, for example, choose to fall in love?) This also applies to moods, but these tend to be more affective than aesthetic.

Modes of Action

Modes of thought and action are interwoven: they are the weft and warp of who we are. All thinking has the potential of action within it. Every action is impelled by thought, conscious or not.

The unity of thought and action is not a one-to-one relation. On the contrary, the meaning carried by a thought is somewhat different from the meaning carried by an action. We discover this when, for example, we try to describe a dream to someone else. The character of our dream becomes somewhat different when we put it into verbal actions – words alter its *feeling*. This occurs similarly when we transform our imaginings into dramatic actions. Yet, even though the relation of thought to action is not a direct copy, *in our experience* it is virtually homologous.

Our acts always occur in interaction, either actually or in our assumption. This interaction can be with the physical world or with other people.

Yet there is a genuine sense that the model for all interaction is that of *person-to-person feelings*. We make an identification *of*, and then we can make an identification *with* another; we must re-cognize who the other person is *for us* and then we can empathize with him or her. We make the first identifications mainly on the basis of signifiers: facial expressions, posture, gesture, clothing, and the like establish the other person *for us*. We empathize with them when we put ourself in their place – mentally in dramatization, or physically in dramatic action – and think and feel on their behalf. In action this becomes the "Vaunt" of the assumed "I am," followed by the initial proposition that begins the drama between two people.[12] We are then two protagonists acting reciprocally to move the action forward. The feeling we share is one of mutuality – "we do it together."

THE SOCIAL WORLD

As our mutual felt-meanings are established from our reciprocal actions and our feeling of unity with others, they construct our social world. We create meaning through our normal activities with and feelings for others.

Although felt-meanings can be codified into conventions, they are not carved in stone. Felt-meanings, even when functioning in the social world, can be transformed: they change with the context and use we make of them. The meaning of an object in our social world depends on the function we give it there: a piece of paper can be written on as a manuscript, folded as a paper airplane, crushed as a ball or as a "mouse" for my cat. Often in educational drama an object is used in a way different from its normal meaning; an improvisational group may use a short stick, say, as a billiard cue, a ceiling handle of a subway car, a sword, a bar in a prison window, and so forth. The object's meaning depends on the context, its use, and the feeling with which it is endowed. Improvising students experiment with the practical possibilities of felt-meaning in fictional contexts which become the basis for their construction of social reality.

Feelings in the social world are in continual flux. Although they are *played* in reciprocity with others, when feelings are *re-played* they differ, if only slightly, from when they were first played. This is because who we are, who the other is, and what the context is are never exactly the same. Moreover, both players activate their own values and the values of the other, and so each particular act becomes pregnant with many dimensions of meaning and feeling – some old, some new. Feelings are inherent in dramatic acts. In fact, an act could not be dramatic unless it was infused by feeling.

These are the kinds of issues we will address in part 1, where our major focus will be the player. We shall be concerned with the kind of dramatic felt-experiences that people undergo in the present tense – in the "here and now."

In part 2, however, we will examine similar issues, but from a different perspective – the academic *study* of drama and feeling. This is not to examine things from the inside – from the viewpoint of the player, as it were – but from outside and the past tense. In part 2 we will address what happens in dramatic acts in the "there and then."

PART ONE

Drama and Feeling

1 Feeling and the Aesthetic Mode

"Aesthetic" is a term with two main meanings. It was first coined in 1750 for the search for beauty, *a philosophic inquiry* about perception that has occupied thinkers from ancient times. Second, as used by Kant, the term described *a mode of thought* of a particular style. Kant's great influence – from Coleridge to Dostoevsky, Heidegger to Gadamer, and Husserl to Sartre – has made this usage a critical commonplace. It is this second meaning that we will use here. Thus we are not concerned with "a theory *of* aesthetics," which would be about aesthetic perception, but with *an aesthetic theory about drama and feeling as modes of thought.*[1]

We must also make a distinction between aesthetic thought, which is the genus, and artistic thinking, which is a species. That is, while all thought (including that of artists creating art) includes elements of the aesthetic, these same artists additionally focus on artistic thinking, which codifies aesthetic thought into an artistic form.

FEELING

The focus of the aesthetic mode of thought is feeling. Feeling is difficult to define, as it is not wholly responsive to language. Any linguistic expression of feeling is more ambiguous than of a cognitive expression; e.g., poetry is more ambiguous than history. Language is not capable of capturing the whole of feeling because human feelings are less tangible than linguistic expressions.

Feeling is a partly conscious, partly unconscious mental activity that is mostly imprecise and can be ambiguous, even paradoxical. In com-

Figure 3
Feeling and the Aesthetic Mode

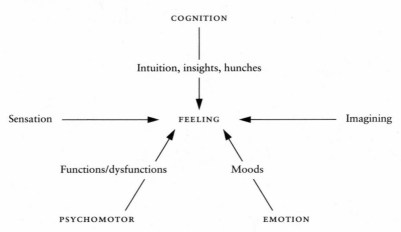

mon parlance, the term "feeling(s)" is falsely used for a variety of other states and activities (such as emotion, perception, touching, etc.) from which it will be distinguished here.

As the ground for aesthetic thought, feeling is nicely balanced between:

- emotion and moods;
- intuition, insights, and hunches (aspects of cognition); and
- psychomotor thinking in so far as dysfunctions disturb it. (See figure 3.)

Imagining appears to be central to all *aesthetic* thoughts and actions. Yet, simultaneously, it is also inherent to some degree in *all* mental processes. This is a paradox.

Imagining is the mode of possibility. It opens up a variety of avenues for action in any idea, situation, or context; we then make a judgment between them and activate one.

In everyday life, we emphasize feeling when we choose and make judgments. Initially when very young we do so between what we like and dislike; with maturation, however, we can distinguish what we *like* from what we *appreciate*. Alternatively, science and social science ask us to make judgments by objective criteria and reason. In reality, however, criteria are chosen by a great many scientists and social scientists because "they feel right." It is feeling that makes the aesthetic mode *qualitative*; the aesthetic criteria we use to make assessments are those of quality.

FEELING AND RESPONSE

We experience ideas, people, things, and the world as perception. Perception gives us sensations which we respond to first through feeling. It is our feeling response that results in action. Robert W. Witkin's influential book *The Intelligence of Feeling*[2] shows that there appear to be twin poles to our feeling response:

- *Subject responses*
  These are stimulated by internal events and are entirely of internal activity that only the player knows. But should the player turn the internal activity into external action (I am so happy that I throw my hat in the air), it is *subject reactive*.
- *Object responses*
  These are stimulated by external events and are internal acts that are generated by objective changes. But should the player turn the internal activity into external action (as I cross the road the traffic lights change, so I quicken my pace), this response is *object reactive*.

Witkin says that if I itch (subject response) and then I scratch (object response), my action is reciprocal and, therefore, *subject reflexive*. But if I cup my hands to catch a ball, my action is *object reflexive*.[3]

Both kinds of feeling can result in internal or external actions. In Witkin's words, I act in the world because my Being is disturbed in the world. Twin poles of action result: expressive and impressive. *Expressive action* occurs when subject response dominates my feeling and my actions result in *feeling-form*: feelings are projected through a medium to externalize my subject response. But *impressive action* occurs when object response dominates my feeling, and my actions result in *object-form*: feelings are projected through my actions onto objects (actual or assumed).

THE FUNCTIONS OF FEELING

Feelings characteristically operate in three major styles:

- *Comparative*
  We compare feelings one to another, mostly unconsciously. Thus if we expect to enjoy a party, but our enjoyment is not as much as at a party the week before, we are likely to judge this party a poor one

and so we leave early. Or if our apprehension of going to the dentist lessens with each visit, we are liable to keep our appointments more regularly.

- *Emergent*
  Feelings emerge from a context and they are in constant change. As we enter a house we may feel its atmosphere is pleasant or unpleasant; the longer we stay, the more this feeling will emerge – or the first feeling will change and another feeling will appear.
- *Dramatic*
  Feelings are dramatic in that they are double: two feelings oscillate back and forth when one is emphasized. It is often said that love and hate are much akin. We tend to experience one in terms of another; that is, we experience one in the perspective of another, and vice versa. This gestalt is precisely an operation with a dramatic character. Feelings oscillate (between, say, joy and anger) until one dominates. My feeling in expressive action, when projected through a medium, initially externalizes my subject response through such an oscillation. But my feeling in impressive action, when projected through my actions onto objects, oscillates between my subjectivity and the object.

We can say that *a dramatic act is thinking and feeling in a practical way*. That is, inherent within all dramatic action are feelings of a practical everyday kind with which we function. Moreover, an internal thought and an external act are felt by us to be a unity. They are not a separable duality. We do *not* mean that an act *demonstrates* thinking, or that thinking *produces* an act, or that an act is *the result* of our thought. In our living experience (that is, as we *feel* it to be) when we act we simultaneously think. As we do so, we may not be able to put our thought into words accurately, even if we can do so at all. In such instances, the map *is not* the territory.[4] Indeed, if we could externalize thought-action adequately in words, we would probably do so, and we would not need to use dramatic acts at all.

The kind of feeling carried by dramatic acts is usually beyond the reach of language. This is because it is powerfully charged with feeling. All media, as they carry meaning, are charged with feeling. But this feeling provides meaning that is in excess of the capabilities of language. Thus our task in this book is difficult because often we cannot use written examples; they so distort the felt-meaning of the thought-action that meaning cannot be adequately conveyed to the reader.

Media vary in their ability to carry feelings and thus to transmit meanings.[5] The purpose of dramatic acts is to convey fecund felt-meaning to others. Words and language in writing convey more precise meanings than drama, but feelings that are less rich. Numbers convey even more precise meanings and much less feeling.

FEELING AND METAPHOR

Metaphors and symbols are charged with feelings. These feelings specifically convey significant meaning – more than, say, ordinary language. Metaphors, popularly thought of as only linguistic, can be embodied in any medium, as can symbols; both can be inherent in speech, dramatic or theatrical action, dance, literature (myths, fables, poetry, etc.), visual arts, music, and other media. Moreover, while the meanings of metaphor are mostly subjective, when they are expressed they meet with the figurative properties of the social world and can take on symbolic meaning. That is, when players use metaphors in spontaneous drama to express their felt-meaning, they are already powerful; but when they meet the society's symbol systems within the performance, they take on symbolic qualities and assume even more feeling power.

We realize this power of metaphor when, as Ricoeur has said,[6] we see it as the solution of an enigma: it creates a change whereby two events are re-created into a whole (e.g., "the roses in her cheeks" is a unity whose felt-meaning goes beyond "the roses" and "her cheeks"). This is precisely what happens in improvisation: my metaphor meets with yours in the "here and now" and an increase in meaning is felt by us both. Thus if I metaphorize (imagine) myself as an evil policeman and you create a metaphor of yourself as a good thief, in our joint improvisation we create more felt-meaning than either of us would in isolation.

When we distinguish our present self from our past self, we feel that together they metaphorize us. This involves two specific transformations:

- *Temporal* – there is a change in the self; and
- *Spatial* – there is a change in our mental space.

This is to feel the power of the "here and now" compared with the "there and then." Of this, Floyd Merrell says, "We come to possess awareness of the self, which is at once inside itself and beside itself."[7] *It is the feeling power of the dramatic metaphor that creates consciousness and self-consciousness.* Thereafter, our conscious self oscillates between here and there, and now and then, as a sign. We become a metaphor of ourself – *we feel ourself to be "a costumed player."* This occurs in play, in improvisation, in social life, in ritual, and in theatre.

The play of a child is a self-contained and self-sustaining world: by being "as if," the child lives in a fictional world of thought and action. This world exists alongside and informs the mundane world (through comparison, emergents, and dramatizations). Children feel that this fictional world functions as a metaphor of the actual world; they use one to test the other. Upon the felt reality of this play world, the adult builds aesthetic or cultural worlds each of which has a sign structure based on a "root metaphor."

Root metaphors are signs by which human beings understand the cosmos and their place within it. They are also known by other names, such as paradigms, world hypotheses, conceptual archetypes, *eidios*, world views, and mental templates.[8] Root metaphors can become so powerful, so embedded in feeling, that the original meaning of the metaphor becomes lost; but its new meaning has great explanatory power. The classic example of this was Descartes's view that both the cosmos and the human being were machines.[9] In due course this metaphor became so powerful in the West that the universe was not viewed "as if" it was a machine but became seen "as" a machine.[10] When human beings were also seen "as" machines, a school was intended to provide students with input and they were expected to produce output; and spontaneous dramatic activity, not being responsive to such treatment, was denigrated. (This was the philosophy of Mr Squeers at Do-the-boys Hall.) To explain this phenomenon, Anthony Wilden says that root metaphors "are supposed to be models of basic aspects of reality ... but often model reality after themselves,"[11] and Victor W. Turner shows that "the more persuasive the root metaphor or archetype, the more chance it has of becoming a self-certifying myth, sealed off from empirical disproof."[12]

The feelings upon which root metaphors are built become highly active in spontaneous drama, although they are often tacit. They are usually implicit assumptions "about what sorts of things make up the world, how they act, how they hang together and, usually by implication, how they may be known."[13] These feelings become focused on a "fundamental image of the world"[14] that can remain unconscious. With such a focus, other metaphors and models emerge that are often conscious.[15] These can become, within the spontaneous drama, "conceptual lenses," or "epistemic codes."[16]

Thus in spontaneous drama our imagined signs become actual: our feelings evolve into what we see and believe. When we perform spontaneously in role, we construct a fictional world that parallels the actual world – we feel that one is a metaphor of the other. Then the implicit assumptions of one world inform the other world: we view the actual world through the lens of the fictional world, and vice versa.

It is important to realize that this occurs whenever dramatic action is used. It happens as much in everyday life as in improvisation.

FEELING AND SYMBOL

Symbols are a more complex form of signification than metaphors. Thus the feelings they produce are also more complex. Metaphors are doubles: the "as if" makes $1 + 1 = 3$ (e.g., "roses" + "cheeks" = "the roses in her cheeks"). While symbols may originate in metaphors, they signify more. They can mean various things at the same time; or different things to different people; or a received symbolic meaning may not be a replica of an intended meaning. Symbols activated by spontaneous drama are multifaceted, imprecise, ambiguous, and feeling-giving.

When we talk of the feelings within dramatic acts as symbolic, they are so to each person in the interchange. What I do establishes who I am for you (and thus for me), and what you do establishes who you are for me (and thus for you). Between us, our felt-meanings are dialogic:

- they interrelate like a set of Chinese boxes;
- they are steadily progressive – we move the action forward;
- they are multiform – their complex significance is symbolic and, possibly, ambiguous and paradoxical.

Because these feelings are inherent in dramatic action, they allow improvisers to *reconstitute social reality for them*. That is, dramatic action encourages the players not only to adjust to social reality but also to change it progressively. This is suddenly seen as obvious when we realize that improvisational groups constantly create new fictional realities. Then spontaneous drama activates specific kinds of feelings:

- *The feeling of perceptual continuity*
  This is specifically an aesthetic quality: there is a "likeness" between symbolic form and its meanings that patterns the relationship.
- *The feeling that symbols have external existence*
  The shared cultural code gives an assumed objective quality to symbols.[17] They feel real to us.

Dramatic acts of all types increase their meaning from these two kinds of feelings. The projection of perceptual continuity into the world results in feedback; thought then includes the assumed objective quality of symbols. The players feel that the symbolic meaning of their actions has the power of external reality. But by changing the spontaneous drama, and thus its symbolic felt-meaning, the players attempt to re-create the social reality in which they live.

Not only can the depth of feeling within symbolic ambiguity lead us to create and re-create social reality, but it also supplies dramatic acts with a considerable *ideological effect*. We can see this in a number of dramatic forms.

Examples

Symbolic ambiguity in the playhouse can stir very strong feelings in audiences. This is the case, for example, in the ideological impact when Valverde enters carrying an immense wooden Christ in act 1 of *The Royal Hunt of the Sun*. Other examples are not so simple. Thus in *Hamlet* the initial appearance of Claudius in his crown ("a crown for a king") would have had great ideological effect upon an Elizabethan audience, most of whom did not know the story beforehand; they would have endowed Claudius with true royalty and the grace of God. But the later revelation that he was the murderer of his brother, the king, would make them feel ambiguous, about him and about the crown, when he next appeared wearing it. The ambiguity in the Lear-Fool relationship, and "the innocent guilt" of Oedipus, are other cases in point.

Even more significant, perhaps, are the ambiguous feelings generated by the Western playhouse itself. The inherent ambiguity of the actual audience juxtaposed with players in the performance of the play, and then with the play-within-the-play – symbolically, the illusion within the illusion – can entrap the feelings of the spectators. This is particularly so when it is re-created by masters like Shakespeare, Cervantes, or Pirandello. When allied to specific ideologies (religious by Claudel, political by Brecht), the impact can be considerable. In improvisation, similar effects upon feelings can be achieved by related symbols – the mirror, the envelope in the pocket, the mask and the face, and so forth.

Culture is structured around symbols because ambiguity makes their felt-meaning socially useful. When their ambiguities are activated by spontaneous drama, they have a great potential to encourage either order or disorder. Politicians can manipulate them to control society and, when they are placed within quasi-dramatic acts (like Hitler's rallies and the use of the swastika), the emotional effect can be devastating. Similarly, those who want to control freedom in education often use the ambiguous feeling of symbols to do so; e.g., gold stars, the "house" system, prizes, etc. More extreme are those schools that use symbols which ritualize behaviour;[18] there spontaneous drama is normally not encouraged unless it uses the symbols that underpin required feelings and behaviours. This is often observable in schools which have a foundation in a particular religion.

Political oppositions can also manipulate the ambiguity of symbols. Those in political power often fear the effect of theatrical symbols, specifically those that are spontaneous. The history of the twentieth century is littered with opposition theatre groups destroyed by fascist governments, and two of this century's most famous political prisoners have been dramatists – Wole Soyinka in Nigeria and Vaclav Havel in Czechoslovakia. From the 1960s, groups of improvisers using the symbols of freedom travelled through Europe, Africa, and Central and South America, and they quickly engaged the feelings of their audiences. This had considerable effect on totalitarian regimes, and it partially accounted for the sudden success of the freedom movement in 1989 – 90. Social activists, like Ed Berman in London, have their greatest impact when they unite the feelings that arise in symbolic ambiguity and spontaneous drama; thus when, one Christmas, Berman took out on strike all the Santa Clauses from the London stores, it was the focus of everyone's attention immediately.

When spontaneous drama combines symbolic ambiguity and a carnivalesque atmosphere, as with Rio's Carnival or New Orleans's Mardi Gras, it can result in sharply contrasted feelings. If it does so with the symbols of anti-structures (as with the medieval Feast of Fools), it can swiftly propagate disorder by producing feelings that insult the establishment, the status quo, normal standards of behaviour, or the powers that be, through a surplus of contrasting symbols. But simultaneously it gives rise to feelings of celebration, praise, and rejoicing on behalf of those symbols which ambiguously encourage order.

Christianity is full of ambiguous symbols: the Virgin Birth, the God who was a Man, and so forth. When it raises up the downcast, it is a revolutionary faith; but when it turns the other cheek and renders unto Caesar, it is also counter-revolutionary.[19] Symbolic ambiguity dramatized in ritual – say, the bread and wine as the body and blood of Christ – carries very powerful feelings.

The depth of feeling aroused in circumstances such as these may be accounted for, at least partially, because *the ambiguous power of symbols has action potentially within it*. The felt-meaning of symbols goes far beyond what can be pointed to or seen; it is not shown directly in concrete experience. Indeed, when we dramatize symbols we find no object or action directly referred to, except as ideas of the relationship. The qualities of that relationship are things which cannot be simply or directly seen, described, or enacted. Thus Gilbert Lewis can say: "Human ideals and values and counter-values are pre-eminently the sort of things for which people require symbols, because they are insubstantial and abstract. They are hard to grasp and apprehend. But the values and ideals are felt as real, they have personal validity for the people who hold them."[20]

The dramas within which symbols are embodied can also be taken for the reality they stand for. That is, instead of being a symbol they can mistakenly become a substitute for the action; then, an observer from outside the culture might consider these things ambiguous symbols, but "for the actors they are not any longer."[21]

Feeling and Symbolic Learning

Learning is related to the feelings generated by symbols. The ideal model of the act of learning is the "Aha!" moment when we feel we are changed in a highly significant way. This does not necessarily mean that our personality structure is radically altered, which is the view of dialectical materialists[22] and social determinists,[23] although it is gradually changed. Nor is learning the amassing of information which can be recalled with ease, as is popularly thought.

Significant learning is aesthetic, a change in the *quality* of thought. There is an alteration in *how* we think more than in *what* we think; by changing the *how*, we can deal more efficiently with the *what*. This is commonly called "learning to learn," which rests on feeling, imagining, self-consciousness, complex conceptual frameworks, and the use of both information and meta-perspectives. These are exactly the characteristics of the aesthetic mode of thought.

Any complex symbol system functions as feeling: it operates as a style of thought. It does so by permitting the clarification, systemization, and comprehension of events,[24] although these are more tacit than in cognition. In dramatic activities, the felt-meaning of symbols not only elaborates one's own perceptual knowledge, it also constructs autonomous symbolic representations.[25] In spontaneous drama, symbols may be manipulated, examined, and organized in their own right so that they have their own feeling power. This is particularly the case when metonymy becomes dramatized: "a crown for a king" and "a sail for a ship" develop towards theatre where they are the essence of the scene designer's art.

To think adequately (that is, to be intelligent) is to be skilful in dealing with the feelings inherent in symbols – to emphasize the feeling quality that promotes the required value system. This kind of learning goes beyond the perceptual world and improves the mastery of symbolic systems and their application to actuality.

Feeling and Key Symbols

Just as there are root metaphors, so there are key symbols – those around which others cluster and by which they are dominated. They express two fundamental feelings in a culture:

- *Integration* of the cultural meanings in a society. The use of key symbols is a movement towards unity.
- *Belonging* of the individual to the culture. The dramatic use of key symbols improves the cohesion of groups.

These two feelings provide cultural models, or pervasive frames, for a wide range of diverse symbolic systems. They also provide crucial clues to the dominating feelings and themes inherent in a culture.[26] Thus the symbolic systems in the plays of Ibsen and Strindberg are vital indicators of the major felt-meaning and themes in late-nineteenth-century Norway on the one hand, and Sweden on the other.

Key symbols (such as the Cross in the West, Shiva in India, Wolf on the Canadian Pacific Northwest Coast, etc.) are grounded in feeling. They are mainly understood in an intuitive way by members of the culture as part of each person's tacit and felt knowledge, and they can appear in many different contexts and symbolic domains. People's feeling response to them is strong. Rarely are people indifferent to them – it is more likely that they respond in a highly positive or negative way.

When they are expressed in dramatic acts, key symbols are liable to be surrounded by a greater number of cultural rules than other symbolic acts. They also tend to be more highly elaborated – extended vocabulary and ornamentation in language, and more detailed gesture and movement.[27] In terms of function, key symbols operate from two poles on a continuum:

- *Synthesizing*
  Some key symbols synthesize, condense, or collapse experience. Thus the Statue of Liberty implies feelings about democracy, free enterprise, competition, progress, freedom, and so forth. These symbols are clearly related to root metaphors.[28]
- *Elaborating*
  These largely work in a double manner by using analogues of previous experience to provide felt-meaning. The Horatio Alger myth (the poor boy who works hard and becomes successful) is a modern American example where the symbolic content is comparatively

clear, orderly, and articulate. These symbols relate to dramatic action in two ways:
– as categories and orientations players can use; and
– as strategies for social action.

Symbols and the Self

Symbols strongly relate to the feeling of Selfhood – the unity of a person. Yet, paradoxically, we constantly perform roles where only parts of our personality are involved. Two fundamental feelings are involved:

- *The wholeness of the interior self*
  In our dramatic self-presentation we feel we are a whole person, a unified personality, as we interact with others with the total self. "Symbolic action is by definition action involving the totality of the self. Symbols vary in their potency. The more potent the symbol, the more total the involvement of the self."[29]
- *The fragmentation of roles*
  The performance of roles such as husband/wife, son/daughter, worker/boss, etc., increases with maturation. Others encounter our roles and reflect these back to us – and this is who we feel ourselves to be.

Normal social life asks that we balance these two feelings – that our roles are integrated into the self. But the modern world tends to be increasingly compartmentalized and to require more roles of us. As we know ourselves as others know us, and because we have reflected back to us more and more roles, we can feel that our personality is increasingly fragmented and we resist further roles. Then when a bureaucrat performs his tasks to the letter but no further, he stereotypes: he cannot deal with people flexibly his role entails.[30]

The nature of the self is a matter of considerable disagreement among scholars, and so too is the nature of the symbols which affect feelings of the self. There is a considerable difference, for example, between the various major European traditions. Althusser[31] follows Hegel, Marx, and Lenin in seeing the self as formed through socioeconomic and historical processes. On the other hand Lacan,[32] in following Freud, says that there are three orders of Selfhood:

- *The symbolic self*
  This begins in "the mirror phase" between six and eighteen months when the child experiences an imaginary feeling of unity. It occurs "by means of identification with the image of the counterpart as total

Gestalt; it is exemplified concretely by the experience in which the child perceives its own reflection in a mirror."[33] Symbols like mirrors and other forms of reflection become highly significant and filled with feeling. This self leads to two others:

- *The imaginary self*
  This is based on early identification with others.
- *The real self*
  This satisfies basic needs.

In the terms used in this book, Lacan's imaginary self is the focus of the fictional, or dramatic worlds, and the real self is the focus of the actual world.

In American scholarship, symbolic interactionism is a particularly influential trend. The dominant symbols in a society create a social self, say Kenneth Burke and other scholars,[34] but they do so in a particular way. The self creates a drama whereby we interact with the world, and specifically with other people. Feelings of the personal self are primarily embodied in symbols of the actor, forms of presentation, the scene, costume, and so forth. These create "master symbols" of political, economic, religious, educational and other spheres, which, in a kind of feeling feedback, form the social self.

Somewhat differently, Anthony Wilden considers that mind works by both analogue and digital systems; that although social symbols affect the nature of the self, "the subject is immanent in the unit of mind."[35] Thus feelings of the self are primarily personal and thereafter social. In this he agrees with Gregory Bateson and much of contemporary thinking in biology.[36] It is clear, however, that contemporary scholars in many disciplines, whatever their differences, regard symbols as having great significance in feelings and other mental operations.

IMAGINING AND DRAMATIC ACTION

Although symbols are structured by culture and generate social feelings, they are also strongly felt by an individual because they have a unique relation to imagination. We have seen that imagining conceives possibility. It asks, "What if?" In doing so, it creates some symbols and uses others that pre-exist. These are realized through covert or overt acts.

In the aesthetic mode, feelings based on imaginings are increased when they are transformed into acts – particularly the spontaneous dramatic act which, because it is a medium between each of the players who are thinking on their feet, has a very high energy level. The chief effects of imagining and spontaneous dramatic acts upon feeling are as follows:

- *Memory*
  These acts activate memories and, by setting them in new contexts, recharge them with feeling.
- *Unconscious*
  They activate unconscious feelings and metaphors, while increasing their power in relation to symbols. These reveal and clarify both the fictional and actual worlds.
- *Structures and Dynamics*
  They revivify the feelings inherent in old mental structures and dynamics, and create new ones. Realizing possibilities in spontaneous dramatic acts, these feelings become fecund and they strengthen their own structures and dynamics.
- *Frames*
  They provide practical and social mental frameworks within which feelings can work.[37] Drama specifically activates frames (e.g., the play-within-the-play) and has a particular significance for feelings of reality and illusion (fiction).
- *Practical Knowledge*
  Players have practical knowledge ("know-how"), with its unique combination of tacit and explicit elements, of moving dramatic action onwards. They always do so in the "here and now" whereby they engage in self-presentation on the knife-edge of the future. This has two major effects on feeling:
  – it keeps feeling uppermost in the players' attention;
  – it generates in any audience the feeling that the acts are tokens (symbols) of other feelings beyond the action (the subtext).
- *Self-concept*
  They have a major effect upon the feelings from which self-concept is formed: The self and role inter-act so that the self is continuously in the making because it must guard against using a partial role.

SUMMARY

In improvisation, when our imaginings are performed they become infused with feeling. A dramatic act is thinking and feeling in a practical way. Its purpose is to transmit felt-meanings to others and it does so metaphorically; we feel ourself to be a metaphor ("a costumed player"), and that the act is metaphorically powerful – drama creates consciousness and self-consciousness. Aesthetic feeling in spontaneous drama reiterates the improvisers' Selfhood.

This is important to education today. The stronger the pressure of society upon us to conform to its norms, the more we must use roles that are merely a fragment of the self. In order to involve more of the self, we must extend our social roles; then we can develop, maintain, and improve our feelings of confidence and self-worth. This has genuinely practical significance for those populations whose self-worth is attacked by being alienated from others and society. These include women, young children, adolescents, members of minority cultures, the emotionally or physically handicapped, the deprived, the disadvantaged, the highly creative, and borderline people generally. Dramatic action provides the players with real choice, judgment, and responsibility for the lives of themselves and others.

Spontaneous drama in life, in improvisation, in education, and in therapy generates a highly energetic feeling and attachment to the activity. It externalizes imagining in a hypothesis that is active, forward moving, feeling, and practical. The dramatic hypothesis is a symbolic dynamic of aesthetic quality. Such symbols, as Rollo May tells us,[38] are central to the creation of each person's self-image.

Drama also leads to the construction of social reality. Paradoxically, dramatic actions create root metaphors – signs of world-views that operate as templates – which become embedded in society. They then give further meaning to later dramatic acts. Through drama,

- our feelings evolve into what we see and believe;
- we feel there is a perceptual continuity;
- we feel that symbols have external existence;
- we feel that the ambiguous power of symbols has action inherent within it;
- we socially construct reality.

We will examine the latter further in chapter 2.

2 Feeling and Ritual

Feeling is part of all social acts, including ritual acts. In this chapter we will examine social and ritual acts, overt expressions of thoughts and feelings that affect others. Yet a thought *is* also a *covert* action: it implies symbolic action even if it does not take place. In other words, *thoughts are acts of mind; but when they are externalized they become the signs of social life.* How can we characterize such signs?

THE NATURE OF SOCIAL ACTS

The major signs of society are acts of self-presentation – the significant dramatic performances of people in everyday life. The focus of social behaviour is on actions where the felt-meaning (the signified) is inherent in the social performance (the signifier).

Key social acts are important for each person involved. Personal intelligence for Howard Gardner is twofold: the understanding of the Self, and the understanding of the Self in relation to others. These are so intimately connected that the interpersonal and intrapersonal signs affect both ourselves and others. Theoretically we can conceive social acts as *dramatic, symbolic,* and *ritualized,* as follows.

The social process is as dramatic as children's play, improvisation, and theatre. This is because we understand the environment through our drama of self-presentation. Social life is created when we see ourselves as "costumed players." The Self is the protagonist, while others are the antagonist and/or chorus for us. Paradoxically, we too are the antagonist and/or chorus for others who are their own protagonists.

The human social drama, thus, is a complexity of (seemingly) simultaneous performances. Each of us alternates between protagonist, antagonist, and chorus in a multiplicity of shared performances. Yet we *feel* we exist as a protagonist in the present tense, the dramatic moment.

Understanding social life has been influenced by the dramatism of Kenneth Burke. For him, language and thought are modes of dramatic action. Key social performances are called "sociodramas" by sociologist Hugh Duncan and "social dramas" by anthropologist Victor W. Turner, for whom they "induce and contain reflexive processes and generate cultural frames in which reflexivity can find a legitimate place."[1] Such a perspective parallels what happens in human thought. To view both thought and social life as dramatic is to think metaphorically, as with the *Theatrum Mundi*. It is to work by analogy which is "the stuff and fibre of social relations, and the very substance of the sociological perspective invites consideration in dramatistic terms."[2] In which case, as Abner Cohen shows, the social drama unifies the symbolic and political worlds.

Human life generates a particular kind of fiction. *A symbolic performance is a complex sign that is dynamic, ongoing, and social; it transforms the mundane into the significant – the symbolically significant.* Social dramas are forms of symbolic action. Dilthey, Cassirer, Mannheim, Collingwood, Whorf, and others conceive symbolic experience as mental activity which works as a form of action in society. The dramaturgical model indicates that human beings live in a word of symbols.[3] Human existence has need of the symbolic: "There is no person whose life does not need to unfold in a coherent symbolic system ... Symbolic boundaries are necessary for the private organizing of experience."[4] Symbolic actions enable people to experience the group and culture of which they are part in more than mundane terms: "Taken together [symbols] constitute an expressive system – almost another language – of the culture."[5] This is the case in both tribal and industrial societies.[6]

Metaphor gives felt-meaning to social actions. The culture in which these social actions occur is oriented through the cumulative effects of its symbolic performances – what Victor W. Turner calls "root paradigms." In other words, *root metaphors are given flesh by "root paradigms."* These are systems of symbolic felt-meaning that are "the fundamental codes of a culture";[7] they give to social action a symbolic form by the metaphors and paradigms in the mind of the actor. Culture is viewed as a system of symbols from the perspective of "symbolic anthropology"; it unifies many disparate meanings, even paradoxes and ambiguities.[8]

To put this more simply, the way we think and feel is structured by metaphor so that we understand two things at the same time:

- the mundane and the habitual, and
- the fictional world we create.

The fictional provides the mundane world with felt-meaning. Our thought is always double. When we act in the world (a world that includes other people),

- We externalize in action the metaphors of our thought.
- Our metaphors meet with the externalized metaphors of others to create symbols in the social world.
- At the same time they meet with our cultural world: the inherited metaphors of our ancestors which, accumulated over time, have become symbolic.

Some highly significant actions in social life are rituals.

THE NATURE OF RITUAL

Rituals are "special experiences," signifiers that re-present, synthesize, and circulate symbols in complex sociocultural felt-meaning.[9] It can be supposed that rituals are always religious actions, but contemporary scholars do not relate rituals only to liturgy and worship (although this may be the case in certain instances). Rather, *rituals are social and symbolic actions performed in imitation of models*. They have, thus, a dramatic and feeling character.

Rituals as Felt-Signs

Ritual is a formal type of dramatic sign that is *felt*. Whereas some dramatic actions (like play) are less formal, two kinds are highly formal: theatre and ritual. Theatre codifies dramatic action into an art form, whereas ritual codifies it another way, by repetition for social and cultural purposes. Both are grounded in feeling.

The performer of the ritual act brings about a heightened intensity of feeling through the unification of time. A ritual act, by repetition, coincides with its archetype. Act and model fuse so that time is abolished: the model act (past) and the ritual act (present) unify in the contemporary performance and collapse time; past and present become one. This act is a felt-sign. The ritual actor breaks with the everyday world; he emphasizes the fictional which is grasped as a heightened reality.

The unity of play, drama, and ritual actions lies in the highly significant feeling given to fictional thought and action by the performer. The difference is that the ritualist does so by dramatizing a model in a unique and highly formal manner.

Definitions of ritual are exceptionally diverse. The contemporary study of ritology, as this new field of study is called, has begun to provide definitions that are viable in the modern world. For Ronald Grimes, a ritual is a form of symbolic action that evokes two things: gestures – the enactment of evocative rhythms which constitute dynamic symbolic acts; and postures – a symbolic stilling of action. Ritual is, thus, "enacted metaphor and embodied rhythm."[10]

Within a ritual, the relation between a sign and a referent may be indexical or self-referential.[11] Moreover, rituals do not merely reflect felt-meaning; *they articulate felt-meaning*[12] *and bring states of affairs into being.*[13] Rituals can be distinguished from habits or routines by the way in which they use symbols; while rituals may accompany routines, they also possess a felt-meaning beyond the information they transmit.[14]

This felt-significance can be examined in terms of its properties and functions, as indicated by Peter McLaren as follows:

- *Properties*. Rituals have the following properties:
  - a form where the medium is part of the message;
  - a content of clusters of symbols;
  - a dramatic quality;
  - a psycho-social integration towards personality development;
  - a language which, as text, may have authority;
  - a formal quality of repetition, a "special behaviour" or stylization, and an evocative presentational style;
  - a repertoire of choices centred on specific rules;
  - codes that may relate to family structures and/or class;
  - six modes (ritualization, decorum, ceremony, liturgy, magic, celebration); one generally dominates at one time.
- *Functions*. Rituals are functional in that they:
  - serve as a framework (as centre/periphery or figure/ ground relation) which functions as a meta-language;
  - encourage "the willing suspension of disbelief";
  - communicate by classifying information in different contexts;
  - transform participants into a different social status or state of consciousness;
  - negotiate or articulate felt-meaning by distinctive rhythms;
  - provoke an aura of sanctity;
  - give a participant a unique type of "ritual knowledge";
  - possess performative force giving conventional effects;

- reify the sociocultural world where they are embedded;
- may invert the values of the dominant social order;
- enable participants to reflect on their own processes of interpretation and their location in the dominant culture;
- fuse binary experience (e.g., physical/moral)[15] into quaternities.

The felt-significance of rituals become particular cultural codes that:

- contain symbolic signs for understanding, interpreting, and negotiating events of life;
- unify signified and signifier by creating the world for the social actor; and
- have complex relationships with symbols.

Rituals as Felt-Symbols

Root metaphors cluster around connected symbols[16] that are the focus of the social drama. This expands the root metaphor and, thus, the clusters of symbols that are codified in a ritual. Symbolic meaning and feeling are more tightly interconnected in ritual than in social drama, where symbolic relations are more open-ended.

A ritual's symbolic power effectively constructs world views. It creates ideas of "the way things are" and legitimizes the cultural order, at least partially, because symbols create an important part of a person's self-image.[17] When symbols are re-created in rituals, therefore, they reinforce feelings of confidence and self-worth.

It is this symbolic power possessed by ritual that accounts for the feeling of devotion that many celebrants have to ritual,[18] although the ambiguity of the symbol also increases its degree of persuasiveness.[19] *The symbolic power of ritual lies in the feeling it generates, and that is due to its dramatic character.* But once symbols lose their relevance, the rituals with which they are associated generate less feeling.[20]

Ritual in Early Societies

In archaic societies, rituals and myths were one entity. Rituals were practical dramatic imitations of the myths: "We must do what the gods did in the beginning," say the ancient Indian scriptures. Myths were the stories that had to be enacted in rituals. Thus we can speak of "ritual-myths": myth (story) + ritual (action) = ritual myths. Thus the signifier = the power of enactment, and the signified = mythological power.

Origin myths in all cultures were enacted as death-and-resurrection rituals in which the use of water implied death and rebirth: "Contact with water always brings a regeneration."[21] In many cultures, generation and childbirth were microcosmic versions of a paradigmatic act performed by the earth. Thus earth was the Earth Mother, often represented on her knees, while Egyptian texts have the expression "to sit on the ground" – meaning "to give birth." Among Christians, Sunday is a festival to celebrate the resurrection while the Jewish festivals of Matzoth and the Passover are signifiers of renewal and rebirth.

Similar performances occur in contemporary tribal cultures. Australian aboriginals still enact "the other reality" by creating or refreshing magical rock illustrations (petroglyphs and pictographs), by chanting the myths, and, particularly, by performing what took place in the Dreamtime (myth). The re-creation of the Dreamtime occurs at a sacred place where each actor re-enacts (reincarnates) an ancestor-spirit. Also, a chorus of old men "chant those verses of the traditional song which commemorate the original scene in the life of the ancestor which has been dramatized in the ceremony witnessed by them."[22] Past time (myth), present time (ritual action "here and now"), and future time (what will happen) are collapsed into "a perpetual present" (the total performance) – a common factor in many ritual-myths. Similar performances occur today among the Coast Salish in their spirit dances on Vancouver Island, among the Ainu of northern Japan in their bear rituals, and among others.

Alongside these communal ritual-myths, all hunting cultures had the performances of the shamans, the magician-priests who worked for the welfare of their society. In their initiation performances, the old personality of the initiate had to be "killed" and the new, powerful personality of the shaman had to be "reborn." All such ceremonies celebrated the idea of death-and-resurrection.

In the ritual world, the human being as actor ("the costumed player") becomes transformed into a supernatural being, a spirit or a god. In extreme cases, possession occurs: actor and role become one. Later the actor continues as the self. The double of the metaphorical relationship is felt to be present in what the ritual performer thinks. At the same time, what he does (the performance) takes on symbolic qualities. Metaphor and symbol are felt to be the heart of the enacted ritual-myth.

Such complex signs are also transferred to objects within the ritual myth. A stone which is a sacred stone is two things, its mundane self and its supernatural reality. There is a parallel here with the learning of the young child through play in all societies. He or she in dramatic play is felt to be both metaphor and symbol; and, at the same time, objects used in dramatic play (e.g., toys) take on both qualities.

The first agricultural civilizations of Mesopotamia, Egypt, India, China, and the Americas changed the primordial hunting rituals. For farmers the crops were vital to existence. The seed grew into corn in the renewal of spring despite the "death" of winter; thus vegetation was "resurrected." The historic change in these ritual-myth traditions is exemplified in today's Hopi and Pueblo Indians of the American Southwest, where hunting was changing to farming when the first Europeans arrived.

In the ancient Near East, once farming was fully established, the death-and-resurrection rituals were felt to affect the crops, human and all other forms of life, the cosmos, and the supernatural (the gods). Each was felt to die and be resurrected when the actor-king in the role of the god went through a ritualized death-and-resurrection. This one powerful ritual affected all life. Great festivals of many days arose at which the king acted the god (Damuzzi in Sumer, Marduk in Babylon, Osiris/Horus in Egypt) as an exemplary model for the people. In such performances, the archetypal act was dramatized and time was abolished. The actor, although existing in the mundane present, performed in the mythological time that had created life and would do so annually again. In other words, dramatic re-creation brought about creation once more.

Thus, although agrarian societies have far more complex rituals than those of hunting cultures, the fundamental effects of their ritual actions are similar:

- they are felt as both metaphorical and symbolic;
- they regenerate existence, giving it a codified, ordered, and synthesized feeling; and
- they achieve this by collapsing time through dramatized signs that make models actual.

Rites of Passage and Intensification

Rites of passage and intensification are two major forms of ritual. Although we can distinguish between them in abstraction, many ritual performances include both. Rites of intensification have more or less great depths of feeling. They are attempts to unify, with as much intensity as possible, human beings and the divinity – supernatural beings, the gods, or God. The ancient tribal ritual-myths were performances where the actor/dancers did not consider themselves truly human unless they imitated the divine model so as to become one with it. The actor can be possessed by a spirit today in the shamanic areas of the Americas, Siberia, Australia, Southeast Asia, and elsewhere. In a parallel case, Christ is the model for all Christians.

Rites of passage mark the social change of an individual from one societal state to another: birth, adulthood, marriage, death. All have three major phases:

- the *separation* of an individual from the group to which he or she belongs, usually in a symbolic "death";
- the *liminal*, or the symbolic hiatus, an ambiguous situation where the person is between groups; and
- the *aggregation* of the individual to the new group, usually through a symbolic "resurrection."[23]

The classic instance here (and possibly the historic prototype) is the initiation of a shaman. This tripartite structure became generalized to many rituals and today can be found in performances as diverse as the first communion of Catholics and academic ceremonies to indicate passage to a new scholarly status. In all cases, the successful initiate is expected to act according to the signs or models of the new status.

The liminal period, as Turner and others have shown, is the period when extraordinary dramatic acts are permissible. As a symbolic hiatus, it is felt to be "in between" and, therefore, is "neither one thing nor another." In various cultures, the liminal period is intercalary: those times after the Old Year has ceased but before the New Year has begun and, therefore, felt to be highly magical and powerful. These are the times when "topsyturvydom" occurs, ceremonies and dramatic acts that "turn the world upside down," as in the medieval Feast of Fools when social status was inverted. In tribal initiations, it is the time when the spirits are about and many rituals display the most colourful costumes and masks.

Each society has its own signs of ritual structures of intensification and/or passage in relation to which the individual acts.

Contemporary Rituals

The actor's performance is based on metaphor: that is, the actor thinks "as if" he or she is the model. But while theatre and ritual acts are similar, they are not the same. Within a ritual structure, a performance takes on a more symbolic feeling with a less diffuse meaning than in theatre.[24] Both can be distinguished from habitual action, which has meaning for itself alone. It exists in the mundane world and its signification lies in simpler codes. Theatre and ritual acts, however, make the actor into a living metaphor within a symbolic context that has heightened felt-meaning beyond the simple level of the information transmitted.[25] Ritual, for Durkheim and others, is a form of symbolic action in which the signifier is the performed sign while the signified is the symbolic felt-meaning. This felt-meaning is more open than the act of theatre. Yet the symbolic importance of a ritual varies between excessive randomness or high entropy, and rigid structure or high redundancy. Thus, "Nascent rituals are more idiosyncratic and less static than formal liturgies."[26]

It has wisely been said that ritual functions in a modern society as a form of "artwork."[27] It has both manifest and latent content[28] so that it contains aesthetic felt-meaning; and this has been shown also in the analysis of theatre events.[29] Ritual is "ethnographic drama":[30] metaphor and symbol unite in a form that provides metaphysical felt-meaning.

Rituals pervade all that we do. They provide a felt-reality for us[31] through their underlying structures as a symbol system.[32] Our acts work within them as they do in dramatic play[33] but through aesthetic forms.[34]

Some modern rituals are remnants and residues of earlier ritual-myths: bullfights, athletic contests, games, racing, the laying of ceremonial stones, and the like. These still concentrate time by unifying the present act with that of the "beginnings." While this may be obvious with the Olympic Games, in other instances their origins may be forgotten by the practitioners.

Other public acts are more obviously rituals based on historic precedent. The crowning of a monarch, the opening of parliaments, the inauguration of a president, the May Day parade – these and others all over the world are ceremonial rituals intended to stabilize the state by imitating the first of such rituals. That they all evoke strong feelings is known to all who take part in them.

There are other modern rituals which are based on the myths of the secular media. Theatre, radio, tape, film, and television directly affect our feelings. Each form provides a heightened intensity to ordinary life and also works with models, signs that are the subject of imitation. As a result, people tend to imitate the behaviour and fashions of media heroes and heroines. They attempt to fuse the reality of the model with their own reality – a profane act, it is true, but one that can provide intense felt-meaning in an industrial society, as the use of religious signs and models did in pre-industrial cultures.

The ritualist relates his or her inner thought and feeling to the external world through ritual. He or she attempts to re-create the elements of the environment into a heightened pattern that brings about a new and significant level of felt-meaning. This is dramatic in that it is based on the processes of empathy, identification, and impersonation. *The ritual action has two levels of felt-meaning:*

- *Actual felt-meaning*
  The actor and his action exist on the plane of everyday life: he feels it in the "here and now."
- *Fictional felt-meaning*
  The actor and his action exist on a symbolic level: he feels it within a fictional plane that has become ritualized; it evokes intense feelings and is significant.

In this sense, while there is a difference in content between ancient and modern rituals, there is much less difference in their levels of felt-meaning. Thus *in today's industrial societies we can distinguish:*

- A ritual that is an operative act becomes formalized. This is a formula which marks out what is done, such as sticking a pin in an effigy, or modelling oneself on a pop star in order to impress others.
- A ceremony whose elaborateness heightens the occasion and gives it aesthetic expression, such as cutting a ribbon to open a road.
- The sacraments, where matter and form are indispensable for the efficacy of the act.

In each case, the dramatic quality of the act is based on the logic of the operative action; it results in heightening the function of the ceremonial within which it is set. Yet, at the same time, rituals encapsulate the norms of the culture within an aesthetic matrix. Modern rituals create a variety of sub-worlds, whereas tribal rituals create one consistent universe.[35]

Ritual saturates modern life and specifically provides the social construction of reality.[36] In this sense, ritual and aesthetic felt-meaning are closely parallel. There are many modern myths to ritualize. Real and imaginary heroes and heroines still play an important part in human life, whether they come from history, tales of adventure, pop music, films, or television. In fact, mythological images are to be found almost everywhere, even if they are fragmented and disguised in rituals.

Both secular and religious rituals have their origins in religious worship. This appears in what we can call political religions; e.g., the ritual trials of the French Revolution, or the "life festivals" of Nazi Germany. The place in life which should naturally be occupied by real festivity cannot remain empty. When real festivals are no longer celebrated, for whatever reasons, the tendency to artificial ones grows.

Ritual and Theatre

The aesthetic quality of ritual also outcrops in theatrical form. The origin of theatre lies in ritual drama. Whereas generalized action is important in social ceremonies, the rituals of social life themselves can be codified into an art form through theatre. This view is shared by theatre scholars of different persuasions.[37] The theatre director Richard Schechner explored the relation of ritual to theatre in a variety of practical situations.[38] In his view, ritual and theatre relate in these ways:

- the efficacy of performance to change life relates to the appreciation of performance for entertainment and critical ends; and
- the transformation of performers into a different state (as with initiation rites) relates to the transformation of performers into a fictional world.

Yet ritual and theatre are to be distinguished. Ritual does not separate performers and audience like theatre.[39] In ritual, performers are surrounded by "witnesses" in the biblical sense; for example, all those who attend a potlatch of Canadian Indians on the Northwest Coast (whatever its theatrical qualities) "witness" a particular ritual event and thereby validate it. Commercial theatre in the West, however, is attended by an audience for the purposes of enjoyment and appreciation. The fact that many theatre performances of the contemporary avant garde[40] are ritualized does not alter this fundamental distinction. Yet both ritual and theatre are aesthetic in terms of signifier and signified.

Ritual and Drama

In other words, *ritual is a particular kind of dramatic action that is related to the aesthetic.* Indeed, there is a close family resemblance between play, aesthetic, artistic, and ritual actions. This resemblance lies in their dramatic qualities; they originate in the metaphoric mental structures of the actors, and, in addition, each occurs within a cultural form of symbolic quality. In all cases the performers are "costumed players." Each type of act has:

- the power to create important ideas (root metaphors and world views) because of its double structure;
- a mythological component ("the story line");
- a component of action – the embodied or performed felt-meaning.

All carry symbolic feeling. While these similarities are most obvious when we consider the origin of theatre as an art form, they are also present in religious and secular, ancient and modern rituals, in all types of human play, and in all aesthetic creations. Put simply, *play, aesthetic, artistic, and ritual actions are signs that have ontological and epistemo-logical felt-meaning in human life.*

RITUAL AND LEARNING

What is the connection between ritual and learning? Learning occurs through mediation: that is, the dynamic of the inner and outer centres upon a medium which is charged with feeling. Sufficient feeling creates a change in us and, as we have seen in *Drama and Intelligence*, when we transform ourselves we learn.

With young children, the prime medium is play. As we mature, we increasingly use the media of language, the arts, and the sciences. As ritual is also a medium, it has close ties to learning in two ways:

- Our ritual actions help us to learn about the ritual and its implications.
- Our actions with any media, if they are pregnant with felt-meaning, have a ritual quality and, thus, we learn about both the medium and the message.

Schooling

Peter McLaren shows that ritual is a significant variable in classroom interaction in two important ways:

- It affects learning through the messages embedded in metaphors, symbols, and the structural patterns employed by teachers and schools.
- It acts as a conceptual model to illuminate both instruction and learning. Everyday rituals in school life tacitly shape the learning process by means of their dominant symbols and metaphors.

Ritual with felt-meaning is a "psychosocial vessel" in which we, as social actors, find the balance between our inner needs and the demands of our culture. It has been said that these feelings can be ritualized in a host of ways that vary as poles on a continuum:

- They can be external structures, semantic networks or labyrinths, through which we learn; and
- They can include symbolic gestures, e.g., metaphors of the body, in that they signify the identifications of the performer.[41]

Each is performed within a ritual structure which embodies the dominant metaphors of the society. The two meet – and we learn. In other words, through ritualizing our metaphorical acts within cultural symbols we can learn to create an aesthetic world.

The rituals of schooling are felt-processes that may include the following:

- The traditional framing devices of an institution – school assemblies, teachers' repeated routines, and the like.
- Cultural structures for schooling processes as determined by the society; e.g., systems of meaning, taste, attitudes, and norms that legitimate an existing social order.
- The symbolic actions of students as living metaphors within existing ritual frameworks. "Students assign meaning to their transactions and interactions"[42] and, in doing so, reinforce and/or alter existing feelings and ritual frames. Students' acts determine how well or how badly they learn.

Thus McLaren can say that rituals are:

- *implicated* in the day-to-day interactions of the hidden curriculum that tacitly teach important norms and values;
- *related* to the organization and deployment of the formal curriculum which is planned and found in various materials, ideologies, and texts actively filtered through teachers;
- *linked* to fundamental perspectives that educators use to plan, organize, and evaluate what happens in schools.

These qualities are made effective through feeling. McLaren's description of the ritual of schooling affords us a broad background against which we can ask how feeling, in ritual, relates to such questions as:

- what do we know?
- how do we learn what we know? and
- what is the relationship of aesthetic knowledge to aesthetic learning?

Maturation

The evolving use of ritual signifies a learning *style*. As children's rituals develop, learning matures – both personal and social learning.

The close connection between ritual and the growth of personal intelligence has been shown by Erik Erikson. Human ritualization is based on the pre-verbal experience of infants that provides "the groundwork for the lasting mutual identifications between adult and child from generation to generation." The fundamental feelings of identification and empathy, learned by the baby in relation to the mother, become ritualized in infantile acts. For Erikson, however, ritualization must "consist of an agreed-upon interplay between at least two persons who repeat it at meaningful intervals and in recurring contexts; and this interplay should have adaptive value for both participants."[43]

Early ritualization is important to the growth of confidence and self-worth. Ritualized learning builds a strong ego, without which the learnings of personal intelligence are vitiated. This applies to both interpersonal and intrapersonal growth. Upon this basis, Erikson explicates a life cycle of human learning that traces ritualization from infancy to adolescence and beyond.[44] This ritualization is framed in the "as if" of aesthetic learning which is fundamental to the complex process of psycho-social integration.[45] Based on empathy and identification, Erikson says, maturing individuals learn the patterns (rituals) that they encounter and how they can share them with members of the group. In other words, through rituals they learn

- how to communicate with others;
- how to channel their raw emotions into feelings; and
- how communal bonding links groups together.

The importance of dramatic action in establishing these learnings can hardly be overestimated; they are necessary for all other forms of learning.

Through ritual we gain three kinds of social learning:

- we adjust to the social order,
- we establish it, and
- we maintain it.[46]

We act within the social order, using the rituals available to us. We learn to subordinate ourselves to social order and ritual structure. If we do so within religious ritual, this entails our acceptance and therefore obligation because the sacred is the most invariant ritual: "Thus, by performing a liturgical order the performer accepts, and indicates to himself as well as to others that he accepts, whatever is encoded in the canons of liturgical order in which he is participating."[47]

Acceptance of this framework for action is intrinsic to all performances, sacred or not. Thus:

Rituals are innately rhetorical. Doing is believing, and as Mircea Eliade puts it so well, one may become what one performs. Rituals call for belief, but not through the cognitive mechanisms that allow critical thinking to interfere with conviction.[48]

Rather, this belief is founded on felt-meaning. Yet, simultaneously, what the individual does helps to establish the social order; e.g., in the secular rituals of schooling the acts of both teacher and student within the ritual framework affect that framework by either maintaining or altering it.

The ground for these acts is feeling. We maintain a ritual framework based on felt-meaning we know and wish to continue; we alter such a framework when the feelings we currently have are not satisfying to us. The signifiers (the actions) in the classroom are the effects of the interactions of many signifieds, all of which are grounded on felt-meaning and bring force to bear upon the action. That is, ritual is a powerful method in all forms of maturational learning because of its inherent level of feeling.

Learning How to Think

Ritualization provides us with practical examples of metaphoric thinking in action. It enables us to learn such thinking by experience. Liturgy, for example, is an expressive and communicative event which embraces both verbal and embodied metaphors. When we re-play them in action, we re-learn a forgotten way of doing things which generates the felt-meaning associated with both insight and commitment.

What is learned is the feeling power of similarity and ambiguity, because ritual is both present and elusive, understandable and enigmatic, personal and impersonal. It teaches us interaction, the power to bring two separate domains into a cognitive and emotional relationship. It also teaches us the power of disclosure, the value of the sudden insight or the dawning realization, the hunch or intuition, that reveals reality in its wholeness, the ground of our being.

By working with the embodied metaphors of ritual, we learn how to work with feelings rather than with analysis. We learn to discover meaning and feeling within both what is *done* and what is *implied* in what is done. The metaphors and symbols of ritual all point beyond their literal meaning and, by working with them, we learn how to disclose tacit feelings. This allows us to assimilate the cognitive qualities of experience in a holistic manner so that they are built into our insights.

Ritual helps us deal with uncertainty. From the metaphoric and ambiguous feelings inherent in ritual we learn that there is no one answer but various possible answers. Thus we learn to go beyond stereotypical and categorical thinking and accept ambiguities – to see things from different points of view – to think and feel perspectively. This is the case in the Catholic mass where group participation is initiated and the value of group cohesion is learned. The performance of the Catholic priest is focused on group identity. But at the same time, he has ambiguity in his role: he is himself and he is God; he both addresses and represents the divine and the congregation; and, by ascending the altar steps, he physically moves from the level of the people to "a higher plane" and then returns. What he feels and performs (the felt-meaning that he gives), and what we feel and learn, is the metaphorical and ambiguous relationship between mortals and the divine.

From ritual we also learn the fundamental nature of symbolism and how to think and feel with it. This symbolic felt-learning always occurs on two interlinked levels:

- the conventional and objective meaning that is derived from culture and tradition; and
- the personal and subjective meaning that is related to both emotions and feeling.

This felt-learning transfers to the symbolic nature of general intelligence and to discrete intelligences: the linguistic, the spatial, the logico-mathematical, and so on.

Aesthetic Learning

One function of ritual, as with all media, is to link inner and outer. This is specifically a felt-relation: it functions well or not according to the effectiveness of feelings. It is, thus, a major factor in our learning how to create aesthetic and fictional worlds. Through both ritual and art we learn to transform experience into symbolic truths.

Whether sacred or secular, ritual maintains its power to instruct us in learning to learn. In the medieval mass, the ritual performance was addressed to God, and the learned symbolic truths were both aesthetic and metaphysical. But when the Church ritual of the middle ages began to be secularized (c.900 AD), theatre as an artistic form emerged. Over the centuries, as secularization increased, theatrical forms multiplied. Today performances in playhouses, on film, on television, and in contemporary media in general, also provide learned truths and feelings that are symbolic, aesthetic, and ontological. In both sacred and secular ritual performances, we learn to create and develop the aesthetic world.

We learn to transform experience in such ways by externalizing our imaginings. The development of imagination is the learning of possibility: openness to the imagination commits us to the future. It is the imaginative basis of performance that leads action in the present tense towards the future.

RITUAL AS PERFORMANCE

Ritual is a formalized kind of dramatic performance. It is a function of human performance to put a person in touch with the foundations of his or her existence, "to reconstruct continually a living and dynamic web [of existence]" in which a person can develop and grow. In other words: "The re-shaping of consciousness or experience that takes place in ritual is by definition a reorganization of the relationship between the subject and what may for convenience be called reality. Ritual symbolism always operates on both elements, reorganizing [representations of] 'reality,' and at the same time reorganizing representations of self."[49] Performance balances the development of personal and social learning.

It also enables us to learn through action on the basis of intuition and feeling. Our performance is a signifier, but what we learn through it is mostly tacit and felt; this becomes a new signified.[50] All performatives have felt-force, but rituals, in addition, can have explicit meanings: "Ritual ... not only ensures the correctness of the performative enactment; it also makes the performatives it carries explicit, and it generally makes them weighty as well. If a message is communicated by participation in ritual it is in its nature not vague."[51] Thus Olson argues that a written text has a performative authority in that it provides speech with a power it would not have if it was spoken;[52] yet Jacques Derrida says that speech has the performative power of life but writing, by putting speech into a fixed form, is "death."[53]

Significant human performances include several kinds of action, all interlinked: social interactions, dramas, and roles; rituals, sacred and profane; play; aesthetic actions; and artistic actions, including theatre. These kinds of performance share the following characteristics, each with its own emphasis:

- The focus is the action of "the costumed player," the presentation of the Self as signifier.
- Implicitly signified is the tacit knowledge of metaphor, symbol, and myth – the various kinds of knowing that are primarily felt. Discursive knowledge is not usually signified in the performance (except with some rituals) but may occur as the result of it.
- Imagined thought is expressed through its embodiment in "the costumed player" in significant time and space, with the possible additions of sound (voice and/or music), scenery, and lighting.
- All action is social; communication between participants is inherently implied.
- The degree of distinction between actor and role varies with the form of the performance.

• All exists in a concrete "aesthetic world," in the present tense, which parallels (and fuses with) the actual world.

Human performance with these characteristics leads to knowledge.

Performative Knowing and Feeling

Human performance is a way of knowing which is achieved in three ways:

• *By the performer*
  Knowledge occurs because performance transforms the world, or the place of the performer in the world. We re-play in the present tense what we have perceived or imagined; the act of performance transforms what we *think* into what *is*. But, in doing so, our performance changes the context in which it is made.
• *By the participants*
  Performance transmits knowledge to its participants.
• *By the witness (audience)*
  The observer gains knowledge by perception of the display.[54]

Whichever way performance knowledge is gained, the knowing that results gives us direct felt-meaning. It is only indirectly informative. *The knowledge gained* (i.e., what is signified and what we learn) *in a performance is experienced; it is specifically not discursive but tacit.* It is personal rather than explicit, corporeal rather than cerebral, active rather than contemplative, and transformative rather than speculative.

Performative knowledge gained by the player has a particular relation to spontaneity. As Moreno rightly indicates, *spontaneity exists in the readiness to act* rather than in the act itself.[55] But the performer does not think about the action and then perform it. Rather, the body "discovers" the fitting gesture within the performance. It is in and through the embodiment that we achieve felt-meaning and gain knowledge. This kind of knowledge is homologous with feeling, doing, and acting.

This does not mean that performative knowledge is devoid of intellectual meaning. On the contrary, although the knowledge gained may be primarily tacit, it also provides a feeling basis for cognition. Just as Sartre says that imagination brings about the cognitive-affective synthesis,[56] so Wallace says that performance constitutes a cognitive re-synthesis.[57] *Spontaneous drama allows us to re-play our knowing*, to test out our existing cognitive knowledge as a hypothesis within the external world and ask, Does it feel right?

The knowledge gained by the spectator of a performance is somewhat different. He or she, first, witnesses the experience of the performance and, second, comes to know reflectively what is known performatively – this is to re-cognize performative knowledge.

Yet the tacit and the explicit styles of knowing are unified in the dramatic nature of performance. Any performance exists in a double manner. In the aesthetic worlds, the performer takes what is already known and imagined in order to re-play it in the present tense of the performance, in the next context; in this sense, cognition is re-synthesized. But in the mundane and everyday world, the actor is the (assumed) witness: he gains reflective knowledge at a secondary level. As the actor is both the performer and the (assumed) witness of his own performance, he gains a whole kind of knowledge.

Embodiment and Morality

Performance is embodied. That is to say, what the actor does is with the total Self including the body. Then we know "in our bones": the dramatic character provides performative knowledge and learning with an incarnate quality. It works noetically, provides a pattern of doing, and has the power to create and transform the world.[58]

In these cases, the body is the signifier, but it incorporates "both consciousness and the body" and "gestures forth the world."[59] More is involved than simple movement: movements become gestures. But gestures emphasize the symbolic meaning and feeling of action, whereas simple movements are pre-symbolic. In other words, gestures not only "lead to, or reinforce, particular values, liabilities and lifestyles, they generate corresponding thought and feeling patterns."[60]

Performance establishes a state of affairs that is, within the act, assessed as good or bad. That is to say, *performance embodies morality.* To act is to make moral choices and judgments. The better our performances, the more we improve our moral learning. This is particularly the case in the dramatic play of young children who hypothesize the effects of moral action during their play: performance allows them to try out moral possibilities within their improvisations and choose between them. By discovering which types of choice are successful, and within what contexts, children improve their moral learning.

In a parallel way, the choices within aesthetic actions are always moral. Aesthetic performances are both aesthetic and moral signifiers.

Wholes

Through performance we learn to think in wholes, in quaternities rather than binary forms. It has been assumed by Lévi-Strauss[61] and others that thinking, knowledge, and learning are codified through sets of binary oppositions; e.g., black/white, raw/cooked, friend/enemy, etc.

But this view is an imaginary representation of a real relation: "It is not an opposition at a single level, but a distinction between levels in a hierarchy."[62] In fact, binary oppositions are simplistic distinctions based on the ontological "I" as distinct from the "non-I." Such distinctions are extensions of Descartes's machine metaphor, and the peculiar abstraction of mechanistic thought.

It is performance that teaches us the inadequacy of binary oppositions. Either/or within dramatic action leads to the stereotypical performance and two-dimensional playing that is characteristic of very young children. In older children it signifies regression. What is learned in performance is that binary structures are insufficient and that both the mundane and the aesthetic worlds require, if we are to function adequately within them, a more subtle mode of operation. As we have already seen, this mode is the quaternity.

The quaternity dynamic of dramatic action is specifically not binary. The two elements of dramatic actions are doubles – they are based on similarities not on oppositions. The double relation is itself doubled through the energetic oscillation of feeling.

SUMMARY

Our acts of self-presentation are social: they transform everyday life into events of dramatic, symbolic, and ritualized significance. Rituals are performed in imitation of models which range from liturgy to the ritualization of ordinary events. The unity of play, drama, and ritual lies in the highly significant feeling given to fictional thought and action by the performer. The ritualist creates a heightened feeling of intensity through the unification of time; s/he reflects and articulates felt-meaning and, through a ritual's symbolic and dramatic power, effectively constructs world views and brings states of affairs into being.

Ritual is a particular kind of dramatic action that is related to the aesthetic, but it also outcrops in artistic form in theatre. Indeed play, aesthetic, artistic, and ritual actions are signs that have ontological and epistemological felt-meaning in human life. Ritualization affects what we know and how we learn in schooling – our social learning, and our thinking. In practice, all dramatic acts have elements of ritual, some more than others.

Ritual also activates performative knowing, thinking, and learning in three ways: by the performer, by the participants, and by the witness (audience, if any). The knowledge gained in a performance is experienced; it is specifically not discursive but tacit. Performance embodies morality and teaches us the inadequacy of binary oppositions as a way to understand dramatic acts.

3 The Structures of Feeling

In this chapter I will examine dramatic acts and feeling in relation to the structures, first, of thought and, second, of meaning. *Feeling is the nub of all structures expressed in drama*; in fact, feeling lies at the core of all mental operations and external acts.

THOUGHT AND FEELING

Mental structures combine images into the working units of thought. They have their own dynamics, each with feeling qualities, and they affect the environment as signifieds. Their nature and purpose are complex. Scholars have striven to understand this difficult phenomenon for years. Even Roland Barthes saw his own human project as the discovery of the structure of "intellectual imagination in our time."[1] And it was Barthes who taught us that where there is meaning there is system.

Mental Structures

The energy of mental constructs creates what A.-J. Greimas calls conceptions of the world.[2] From what we perceive, images are formed which, combined as imaginings, become mental constructs. We try them out through signs. These are carried by various media into the environment by using action; we represent these mental constructs in the world, incorporating elements of the environment into our ideas and adapting them. Thus *we create mental worlds*. The most common media we use for this purpose are those of the Self (through the drama of self-presentation), language (through talk and writing), movement (gesture, posture, etc.), number, and the arts. These signify mental worlds: *each represents a felt-world.*

Our thoughts are based on actuality but our mental constructs operate in a quasi-independent way. We can represent a mental structure in the world by drawing the traditional philosopher's unicorn. But an actual unicorn does not exist, even though its elements are created out of our perceptions of other animals. In other words:

- the realities we create through media are entirely mental;
- they have no necessary content; the medium is the message;[3]
- through them we understand the world around us;[4] and
- from their signifiers, others infer our felt-thinking.

We create such constructs to order the chaos of the environment, to satisfy the feeling of unity in diversity. The primary mental structure is *differentiation*: the result of a gestalt process whereby one thing is seen in relation to another thing – as similar or different. This gestalt is the prime source of mental energy. Lying deep within all other structures and concepts, it is always felt to be double. We can, therefore, talk of *felt-concepts: those that parallel cognitive concepts but are based in feeling and are often tacit.*

The double concept (cognitive-aesthetic) is as old as *homo sapiens.* Even the Neanderthals spread red ochre (representing life-giving blood) and colourful flowers over human graves, indicating the presence of two worlds – the mundane and the spiritual. Paleolithic magicians and shamans in hunting cultures acted in coexisting worlds: in the mundane world as themselves and, when possessed, in the spiritual world as various enacted spirits. Today's shamans also work with this double structure.

This twofold energy underpins dramatic action. Being "as if" is to be two-in-one: "the mask and the face" – a metaphor of oneself. We are all "costumed players." This became the theatre metaphor ("All the world's a stage") of reality and illusion with Pythagoras, Augustus Caesar, Cervantes, Shakespeare, and Pirandello. It entered the study of mind with the unconscious of Freud and is now a commonplace in psychology. It is inherent in contemporary sociology with role theory, dramatism, and the social construction of reality. These are just the most obvious examples.

Fictional Worlds

From an early age, we learn to grasp a distinction between the actual (the real) and the representation of the actual (the not really "real"). As we think, we acknowledge that both exist; we may do so cognitively but feeling is the primary ground. The "as if" is what Plato called "the great lie," and what Ernest Becker said we create in order to fend off the fear of death.[5] It is the play world of Heraclitus and the pre-Socratics, as well as the aesthetic world of modern philosophers from Kant and Rousseau to Heidegger, Gadamer, Derrida, and others.

Mind dramatizes the actual in order to create the fiction of "the play world" (or "the aesthetic world"). Then *the drama process creates the world for us:* our spontaneous dramatizations bring symbolic actions that signify what is felt to be a double of reality. The structures of fictions correspond in a high degree to the external world. But as imagining is inherent in the drama process, the mental structures of fictions are also potentially capable of infinite variety. *Whereas feeling is the ground for the double, it is the creative imagination that is the ground for dramatization whereby the actual and the fictional worlds coexist and their operations overlap.* But it is the play-within-the-play that doubles the double – and that is a quaternity.

Signs of Constructs

Naming a mental structure – concepts like "blowing," "sitting," "running," and the like – is something else again: the name becomes a sign. By naming it, we see the manifestation of a mental structure in a specific way. Wittgenstein says that a name does not indicate content;[6] rather, it represents a particular perspective, or frame, on the world – an imaginary entity. But no perspective provides total knowledge about a represented object or event; it inevitably differs from other perspectives.[7]

Because our mental constructs and their names are perspectives on the world, there is always a degree of overlap between the meaning of words, language, concepts, and world-views, and between actual/fictional and mundane/aesthetic.[8]

These factors affect communication. Differences between perspectives, and between a mental construct and its sign, can lead to a breakdown in communication. But there can be communication when mental constructs overlap. As Floyd Merrell tells us, the reality we invent is bound to particular perspectives by convention; and yet we continuously generate mental structures at biological, cultural, and individual levels, "and with each successive level greater parameters of freedom are enjoyed."[9] At the same time, because our mental reality is constructed in such a way, it is possible to *see* what is there because we *believe* that it is *supposed* to be there.[10] Ambiguity, in other words, is an integral part of signification. And ambiguity, inherent in drama, is primarily *felt*.

DUALITY *VERSUS* THE DOUBLE

The nature of the two-ness in life has been developed as follows:

- as duality in a cognitive form, and
- as the double in aesthetic form.

Properly speaking, feeling is an inherent element of both. Mechanistic thinking in the West, however, has unfortunately tended to withdraw feeling from duality by trying to become clinically objective and binary.

Duality has been a fundamental Western concept over many centuries. For Plato there were two discrete levels of reality: the ideal and the real. In the Judaeo-Christian tradition there was a split between the soul and the material Self – the mind/body dichotomy. For centuries, duality and the double were in tension as poles on a continuum. Not until Descartes and Newton, however, did duality become binary, and from then on it dominated the Western world. This split rested upon the concept of opposition: Good/bad, right/wrong, intellect/emotion, conscious/unconscious, and so on. This split has permeated Western ideas in the last three hundred years.

In the nineteenth century, two forms of binarism predominated: determinism and the dialectical method.

- For *determinists*, there were two levels of mind: the covert determined the overt. Darwin said all life was determined by evolution. Marx thought overt human behaviour was determined by covert historico-economic forces. For Freud, the conscious was determined by the unconscious. For Frazer and other early anthropologists, contemporary actions were determined by themes and structures from the past. When dramatic acts are determined, the freedom of improvisation is denied. It is little wonder, then, that the plays of Ibsen, Strindberg, and Shaw, which denied determinism, were considered strange and avant-garde in their time.
- From the late eighteenth century, it was commonly assumed that cosmic and mental processes were *dialectical*. As expounded by Hegel, the duality of thesis and antithesis (opposition) led to a third process, synthesis – which was another thesis. This extended binarism into triangularity. Taken over by Marx, it came down to modern times. Scholars who deny the dialectic and advocate dialogism (Buber, Bakhtin, Burke, McLuhan, etc.), and dramatists like Samuel Beckett who exemplify it, can also be considered strange.

Duality or binarism, as determinism and/or dialectic, continues to underpin much popular thought. We perceive the objects in the envi-

Figure 4
Pepper's World Hypotheses

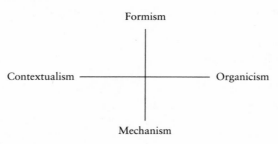

ronment in some order, as non-overlapping and uniquely identifiable things. This assumes a spatio-temporal, material, and objective (i.e., non-feeling) world-view. To many physicists, the quantitative aspect of number is of prime interest.[11] But, as Bertrand Russell remarked, mathematics is the only intellectual discipline with no content, that is entirely abstract. Many contemporary views about numbers, knowledge, and mind are still binary; they deprive mental structures of feeling.[12]

But the picture of human existence revealed by binarism does not fit with our experience of spontaneous drama. It is the view of this book, in contrast, that while dualistic thought structures exist, they are not primordial to mind. *The fundamental two-ness of thought is the double which, when doubled (the play-within-the-play) is the quaternity. This is basic to all spontaneous dramatic acts and it rests firmly on feeling.*

FEELING AND MENTAL STRUCTURES

The two-ness of mental structures might be seen simplistically as cognitive on the one hand and affective-aesthetic on the other. But the issue is so complex that this cannot be said with certainty. *Feeling is central to all mental structures.* This is best seen in the universality of the quaternity as a way of understanding mind, life, and the cosmos. The quaternity primarily represents the feeling of wholeness: unity in diversity, the transformation of energy into harmony – which is also the purpose of dramatic acts.

Among contemporary scholars, Stephen C. Pepper says that the mind, rather than having a binary structure, is structured around the double.[13] Two pairs make four world constructions, or root metaphors, to which individuals fit new knowledge (see figure 4). Two of these pairs, formism and mechanism, are analytic theories, while the other two, contextualism and organicism, are synthetic; formism and contextualism are dispersive constructs while mechanism and organicism are integrative. In its time, Pepper's view was seen as quite radical. But it was not new. In fact, the concept that there is a holistic fourfold structure to thinking appears to be as old as the human race. Universally it assumed that feeling was primordial and for millennia this idea was unrivalled as a way of understanding.

But once science was created by the Ionians, both duality and the double/quaternity coexisted in the Western world. This parallelism is best illustrated by Plato. On the one hand, in creating the idealist world of Forms (e.g., Beauty, Truth, etc.) of which mundane existence was an imitation (a dramatization of abstraction), his thinking was dualist. On the other hand, Plato also used the notion of the quaternity. In the *Timaeus*, the creation of the world soul (the law of the physical universe) is a mixture of four elements: same/different, and divisible/ indivisible. This scheme closely resembles the structure of Pepper.

Plato, however, went further. He said that both pairs meet in a middle term, as in figure 5. The fifth position is the quincunx, which is the unifier. In the same book (36B), Plato said that, in this arrangement, the fourth position "possesses generative powers" while the fifth makes them all one whole.[14] This has a close resemblance to Greimas's semiotic square.

The opposing ideas of dualism and the quaternity were the focus of fundamental intellectual disagreements for centuries. Today binarism and non-feeling objectivity have been maintained by technological thinkers who use quantifiable methods. In contrast, quaternity is maintained by holistic thinkers who acknowledge feeling in rational and qualitative methods; but they also recognize quantification as being of relative use. As we shall see, *quaternities form the basis for various views of mind that have great import for aesthetic thought, feeling, and dramatic action.* Because it is difficult to be explicit about feelings, in order to examine their relation to thought structures we must use examples rather than definitions.

Tribal Cultures

In modern hunting societies, as in Paleolithic cultures, all phenomena are thought of in twos and fours.[15] The fundamental idea of the four cardinal directions and the four winds (N/S/E/W) is a mental dramatization of the cosmos, a paradigm which in ritual drama is the signifier of all life.[16] The feeling of wholeness and unity is at its core, as in the sacred spaces among Australian aboriginals and the Balinese.

The qualitative felt-concept of number is inherent in the thought of the native peoples of North America. As for all shamanic peoples, the

Figure 5
The Quaternity of Plato

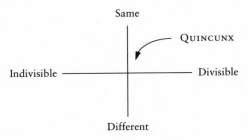

actual world is for them an illusion while the spiritual world is real; "the other reality" made popular by Carlos Casteneda is a classic example of the dramatic creation of a fictional world.[17] Nothing is what it seems to be in mundane existence. The retrograde, rhythmic, and repetitive character of numbers is known through the periodic structure of the elements and its parallels in animal life and in changes of the heavens. Similarly in atomic electron states, the modern physicist sees many recurring symmetries, and the artist finds recurrences of lower notes within higher frequencies in the octaves of music. In number, sequence appears part of correspondence, and vice versa. Actual and felt-concepts are really inseparable.[18]

In tribal cultures, the illusion and paradox of number exist in multiple signifiers of feeling, but two are primordial:

- *ONE = TWO, TWO = THREE, and THREE = FOUR*
The Tewa Indians of New Mexico feel that all things, animate and inanimate, are double. There are two elements: Essence/matter, spirit/form, reality/illusion.[19] The Southern Kwakiutl Indians on Canada's Northwest Coast think that a wolf is a spirit in the clothing of a wolf, and a man is a spirit in the clothing of a man.[20] *Two as a sign is the focus for metaphor.* Two is likeness between difference: the duality of sense; the pretence that the two senses are one.[21] The physicist Roger S. Jones says, "'The author and recipient of a metaphor connive, as it were, in agreeing to a tacit 'as if.'"[22] The "as if," the dramatic quality of thought, infuses two-ness among Amerindians who create the signs of the living metaphor in their ritual dramas.

Two becomes complicated into three cosmic levels: there is one everyday world but the spiritual is divided into two, an Upper World and a Netherworld.[23] Thus 2 = 3.

The three cosmic signs are also four: the three levels are linked by "the shamanic ladder" ("the cosmic tree," the *axis mundi*, the may-

Figure 6
The Quaternity of Southwest Hopi and Pueblo Indians

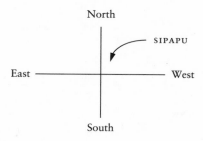

pole of Western folklore) whereby shamans can move across all three levels. *This action creates the fourth point*, the dynamism that both unifies the four and breaks them apart so that something new is created. (This has close parallels with Greimas's semiotic square.) In other words, 3 = 4.

• *FOUR = FIVE*

Amerindians stress that the four winds blow from the four directions to the community itself – the focus of four is five. Five is the quincunx: it is the sign of "the navel of the world." This existed among the Babylonians near the Tower of Babel. Today the sacred *kiva* of the Hopi and Pueblo Indians has its *sipapu* in the centre of the floor, as it had for their Anasasi ancestors of Chaco Canyon centuries ago. The *sipapu* is the sacred hole which is "the navel of the world": the contact point with Mother Earth containing the Great Snake of the Earth (see figure 6). This idea is generalized over the Southwest to include all sacred spaces.

Alfonso Ortiz tells us that the fourfold concept is the prime mental structure for all rituals among the Tewa. For them, mind is a felt-entity explicable through the quaternities. It was just as fundamental to the ancient cultures of Central America; e.g., it is commonly found in ancient mounds;[24] and Quetzalcoatl, the Mayan god for the higher self, wore an insignia, or cross, that represented the four cardinal directions.

This relationship to number exists also among the Plains Indians. To become part of the Great Powers of the Medicine Wheel is to perceive from all four directions simultaneously. For the Plains people, one who possesses the gift of only one direction will never feel close to or be touched by feeling (see figure 7).[25]

Among contemporary Amerindians who still think in traditional ways, therefore, number does not signify the digital, abstract, and discrete. Rather, any number is seen to overlap with other numbers. None

Figure 7
Plains Indian Quaternity

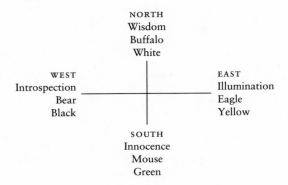

NORTH
Wisdom
Buffalo
White

WEST
Introspection
Bear
Black

EAST
Illumination
Eagle
Yellow

SOUTH
Innocence
Mouse
Green

of them are entirely separate. As in all their mental structures, feeling is primordial and unity is prior to diversity. The quaternities of tribal peoples are:

- built on feelings;
- generated by dramatic action;
- the deep structure of all subsequent mental structures;
- the underlying signifieds of all tribal thought;
- structures with an aesthetic quality.

Ritual drama is a primary signifier and all arts are created for such purposes. As the Balinese say, "We don't have any art – we just do everything very well!"

Quaternities in the West

Four in Occidental ideas is a sign of system and order in both the mundane and spiritual realms. Most antiquely, it occurred in the four phases of the moon, the four seasons, the four corners of the world, and the four planes – the buddhic, mental, astral, and physical – as cosmic order. The quaternity underlies most Western religious ideas of order. The Kabbala has order inherent in its four vital points. Religious stability for Jews was in the four-square form of the altar. Early Christianity has the Trinity, plus the fourth dark and feminine entity. Among the Egyptians, the four gods supporting the four corners of heaven were the offspring of Horus.[26] In Masonry, there are four points within "the still centre" – the altar; and the Installation of the Master pulls together the four "plus."

But order includes the cosmos and the community. In the Celtic thought of pre-Christian Ireland, Eire itself was a quaternity indicating an ordered cosmos: Ulster (N), Connacht (W), Munster (S), and Leinster (E), which fuse at the quincunx, Tara, Uisneach. Tara had its own quaternity – the four within the four. On its own small scale, Mull reproduced the same cosmic plan.[27] The ancient science of geomancy was also a fourfold drama.

Graphically, quaternities can be represented by a square (wholeness combined with passivity) or a diamond or pentagon shape (the active plane). The quaternities infused the ancient Near East and, later, the ideas and ritual dramas of Europe. Some examples follow.

Egypt

Two/four signified mind, life, and the cosmos. Units of measurement were based on the quaternity: the Great Pyramid's base is a square whose perimeter is equal to the circumference of a circle, the radius of which is the Pyramid's height – designed as a dramatization of squaring the circle. The Pyramid Text refers to four gods and four spirit souls.[28]

After the sun (Re) set in the west, he travelled the Netherworld to appear the following morning in the east, his journey being conceived in units of four. This was related to life-giving water, life and death, and the underground lake which the sun had to cross during the night.[29] At Karnak in the temple of the god Amon, a ritual drama enacted this fourfold journey; there was an artificial lake which the priests crossed in a procession of theatrical boats "as if" part of the sun's night-crossing. Number was an enacted metaphor.[30]

The power of four was inherent in the ritual drama of Osiris at Abydos,[31] and its huge festival play of Horus.[32] The myths had four originating gods, of whom one was supreme; and the ritual had four major characters (Osiris and Isis, with their offspring, Horus and Set). Below them was a structure of two-ness arranged as whole/part: order/reason was the whole while disorder/irrational was the part; Osiris the king (order) was overcome by Set (chaos), who was overcome by Horus (order), the new king. The staging of this cosmic drama signified feelings about earthly life (the seasonal change) and mental life (rational and irrational).

When Menes united the Upper and Lower Kingdoms, Egypt became two-in-one and remained a living and dramatic metaphor. There were two thrones, two crowns, two granaries, and so forth. One was thought of as the double of the other. Even when the pharaoh performed the ritual dance of the land he had to do so twice. This idea became more complex: a god had several roles (e.g., Re had one role when rising, another at midday, etc.) as well as roles as birds, animals, and other figures. Human beings had a number of souls. The Egyptians (like their shamanic Nubian ancestors) dramatized people, the cosmos, and life as a myriad illusions. They did so in terms of felt-meaning in ritual performance.

This idea focused on the god Thoth. One of the originator gods, his major role was the moon; the priest-actor wore a silver mask and was "slippery." But he also took the role of other gods[33] and was, in fact, a shape-changer (like the shaman), but now as a role-model. Thoth, as five, unified all through dramatization. Like Hermes, who had a similar position for the Greeks, Thoth personified (dramatized) a notional number based on felt-wholeness. In an accident of history, the Abydos ritual drama almost became theatre simultaneously with the first trage-dies of Aeschylus.

Mesopotamia

The double relation of mundane/spiritual in Mesopotamia was simpler in structure than in Egypt but it was conceptually more sophisticated. What was signified by number was the feeling of the human tragic con-dition, death-in-life – centuries before the Greeks performed it in the Theatre of Dionysos. Earthly and divine life were mirror images (a double) meeting in the temple at the top of the pyramid ("ziggurat"). There the god and the goddess had divine intercourse (myth) as enacted by the king and a priestess (ritual) in the annual "sacred marriage" rit-ual drama that unified the world. This echoed down the centuries to modern European folk traditions. The ritual drama unified various forces – the quaternities (directions, seasons, etc.) and the various dou-ble forces, to create a fourfold power (or intensity of feeling) that, in the performed ceremonial, renewed all of life.

Pythagoras

Pythagoras was reputedly the first to ascribe symbolic meaning to the quaternity; for him, it was second only to the One in importance: the feeling that the whole was greater than the parts. Three signified suffer-ing (the world of matter) but people could restore their psyche through the quaternity: "The sacred four, the roots and source of ever-flowing nature."[34] As an ecstatic shaman, Pythagoras had great power. He con-verted others by inducing an inner and dramatic change in them. He was said to have died underground and revived in death-and-resurrec-tion shamanic ritual drama. As a mathematician he controlled the magic of number, and, as a musician of genius, "like Orpheus, he had discovered the secret musical correspondences in the cosmos."[35]

Figure 8
Byzantine Ritual Quaternity

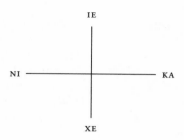

He was reputedly the first to state the *Theatrum Mundi* ("All the world's a stage"): actual life, where people lived by acting roles, was an illusion while reality existed only in the spiritual world (as with shamans). It was also Pythagoras who translated earth, air, fire, and water to the psyche in intelligence, knowledge, opinion, and sensation: "It is because of this that we are intelligent beings."[36] Pythagoras *consciously* united the four and five with the idea that life is a drama.

Christianity and Alchemy

The cross is an iconographic quaternity. Almost all crosses derive from the four directions and generate powerful feelings of unity in diversity. The Bible abounds with quaternities: the four winds of heaven[37] and the four angels of the Apocalypse who hold the four corners of the earth[38] are obvious examples. For St Gregory, people consist of body and soul with seven qualities. Three are spiritual while the four physical are hot, cold, moist, and dry matter – as with the psychological "humours."

The latter concept, an ancient one, was widely held by alchemists. They linked the quaternity/quincunx to the four stages of the world in their alchemic quest for "psychic gold." They gave the names of *nigredo* (black), *dealbatio* (white), *rubefactio* (red), and *citrinitas* (gold) to the colours that were the signs for the elements.[39] Control over these gave alchemists feelings of considerable power.

The mass signifies many quaternities and the feeling of unity with the divine. This is most obvious in the Byzantine ritual.[40] Here the host is broken into four pieces and marked as in figure 8. This means "Jesus Christ is victorious," and, by being arranged in a quaternity, it has felt-power and the character of wholeness. And the mass of Honorius, the fundamental form of the late middle ages, was consciously dramatic, speaking of the priest as "actor" and the church as "theatre."

The root metaphors of Pepper are parallel with the quaternities of alchemy, particularly in the interaction of the four elements. Heat and dryness were masculine and active while humidity and coldness were feminine and passive. "The Royal Art," or the Art of Alchemy (also known as "the spagyric art," the "spagyric" meaning "to take apart" and "to bring together")[41] was a combination of analytic and synthetic factors – in the same way that Pepper describes root metaphors.

In the Renaissance, alchemy found the opposition of both Church and State difficult to handle, yet "herms" were built everywhere. These square figures representing Mercury had only a head and a phallus – to dramatize the sun as the lord of the world and the sower of all things. The four sides of the square represented the four regions of the world and the four seasons.[42] Alchemy developed an elaborate semiotic system by means of metaphoric numbers which is as coherent as those we call scientific.[43]

After Descartes and Newton had used the machine metaphor, however, quaternity became twisted into magic, witchcraft, and "the black arts." Under this pressure it finally wilted to become mere folklore or part of the musings of "strange" artists, like Blake and Turner, and could therefore be safely ignored by mechanistic scientists. Yet the feelings dramatized in these felt-concepts remain with us, in artistic performances and products; as an integral part of our unconscious which outcrops as insights, hunches, and feelings that cannot be accounted for by mechanistic science; and as integral components of improvisation.

Asiatic Quaternities

Quaternities that represent the primordial feeling of unity in diversity are even stronger in the Orient, where felt-meaning is commonly a fourfold relationship. This relationship is communicated through signs, often those which have been dramatized in some way. Some brief Eastern examples follow.

In the ancient Hindu scriptures, the Sacred White Elephant is the Self (mind); the quaternity of its legs signifies mundane nature from which the soul is born. Anything complete and self-contained is dramatized standing firmly on its "four legs" (catuh-pada). The pantheon of the Hindu gods is excessively complicated, but Brahma, Vishnu, Shiva, and the female Shakti (each in their many roles) progress through cosmic cycles as a powerful quaternity. Brahma, the God-Creator, sits at the centre of the lotus, using four faces to control the universe,[44] including

Figure 9
The Tibetan Quaternity

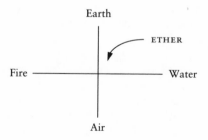

the four *yurgas* (or cyclic ages). Brahma's four faces resemble Renaissance "herms," the four Kumaras (angels in Persian tradition), the four fixed signs of the zodiac, and the four rivers of Paradise rising at the foot of the Tree of Life (or the world-axis).[45] The quincunx completes all: "Where there are five, there is God," and "The fifth is the fruition of the act."[46] These felt-concepts underpin Sanskrit plays and the contemporary Kathakali ritual dramas.

In ancient China the quaternity paralleled the quincunx. There were five elements (water, fire, wood, metal, earth) of which the last (like the *sipapu*) occupied the centre,[47] similar to the signs of alchemy. The square signifies the lower physical plane; at death there is a transition, or transformation, to a different plane of existence.[48]

The quaternities of Tibetan mysticism are related to those of India and China but also parallel the semiotics of alchemy. In Tibet, the sacred temple of the body is composed of Four Great elements (or four gates) (see figure 9). They represent vital psychic forces and laws.

In many Tibetan monasteries, these felt-concepts are linked to the fearful ritual dramas of Bompo shamanism. If the symbols of the five elements are placed upon one another in their three-dimensional forms, they constitute the essential structure of Tibetan *Chortens*, the extraordinary religious monuments that once served as receptacles for Buddhist relics. They are, however, purely symbolic structures, or plastic mandalas.[49]

The Mandala

The mandala is a religious art form, creating a sacred space of power through rites of intensification. It occurs everywhere. It results from an internal dramatization so that felt-concepts of the fictional world are externalized in a plastic form. While there are many mandalas with a host of different shapes, each is based on the quaternity.[50] But the mandala is more than just a sacred space. It is a dramatic map of the universe (and the way in which the mind understands it) that is also a ritual symbol, a multifaceted sign the performance of which reveals the structure of life.

The Tibetan mandala signifies both the potential unification of mind within a visual fourfold system, and the integration of parts within a whole. Two as a sign exists within a paradox: all people are already Buddhas, yet they must transcend delusion to become Buddhas; all is void, yet all is made up of entities; there are no achievements, yet people have limitless rich possibilities; and while there are harmonies and the unique unfolding of all beings, all is totally mutable with absolute freedom.[51] Thus opposition presupposes similarity and unity as a felt-concept.

The Hindu mandala, or *Yantra* (The Wheel of Siri), has a mid-point of "the mysterious matrix" (the *Bindu*, or quincunx). This has not merely cosmological signification but also groups the four around the focal point which indicates mental understanding, that "All is reflected in the Ego."[52]

There are many other forms of mandala. In the American Southwest, Navaho and Hopi sand paintings are mandalas providing ultimate meanings but in specific contexts. The mandala was a basic theme in early Christian, Byzantine, and Celtic beliefs and art. Over known history, West and East, the sign of the circle has surrounded the quaternity and the quincunx; this is reflected in the art forms of the great cathedrals of Europe and the work of Bosch, da Vinci, Raphael, Botticelli, and many others of the Renaissance. Earth, air, fire, and water signified the psychology of "humours" which, inherited by Shakespeare and Jonson, was the prime way personality was understood over many centuries. The unifying ritual theme is destructive energy transformed through the felt-harmony of difference.[53]

Number and Aesthetic Thought

We have seen that number as a sign has been universal in understanding mental structures – through both feeling and dramatization, either internal or external. As the signified in dramatic action, number structure has many meanings both within one culture and between cultures. We have also seen that number as metaphor is part of the signifier. That is, the dynamism in the relations between mental structures is predisposed towards metaphorical number; mind ensures that we have an imaginative, dramatic and feeling relation to metaphoric number, presumably through DNA and our physical inheritance. Among possible examples, number within aesthetic thought and dramatic action has two types of relation to metaphor:

- *It affects action*
  The metaphoric power of number can affect the way we work in the mundane world. Through beliefs of life, death, and the nature of existence, mind works with number as signifier and/or signified of our beliefs about human and divine; this fiction affects the everyday. A contemporary example in educational drama occurs when the theory of probability (itself a metaphor) is unconsciously used in improvisation but cannot be explained in words by the players.
- *It affects art*
  The metaphoric power of number can affect art. A painting or a poem can have metaphors of number within it (e.g., "the golden mean" or mandala structures in visual art). When we create or perceive a work of art, our mental metaphors of number interact with those in the art work, usually unconsciously. This specifically applies to drama and theatre.

STRUCTURES OF MEANING

"What are the meanings contained and conveyed in *this* improvisation, and how are they structured?" But the felt-structure of meaning is complex, ambiguous, and often paradoxical. It raises as many semantic as semiotic issues. It is often tacit, so it can be difficult to talk of. In dramatic action meaning is more a matter of showing, not telling. Thus, once more, we must resort to examples.

Labyrinth

Most semioticians find dictionaries unsatisfactory. Many signs (e.g., words and dramatic acts) are not codes with one-to-one meaning but have a plethora of meanings. Many consider encyclopedias almost equally inadequate and assume meaning to be like a labyrinth. Yet labyrinthine models are insufficient for Umberto Eco, who puts forward the net (as rhizome) as a model for the virtually infinite interpretation of meaning.[54] Labyrinths, mazes, and nets have many implied meanings that are imaginative, and are based on tacit and felt-knowledge. Because they are polydimensional, *they are a three-dimensional metaphor for the structures of felt-meaning*.

How does the labyrinth provide a model of felt-meaning? The earliest accounts of labyrinths ignore their function, but we know that ritual dramas were performed there. The oldest known was built around

1800 BC, in Egypt at Medinet el Fayum, some eight kilometres from the pharaoh Amenemhet III's pyramid tomb at Hawara. About 475 BC, Herodotus said it surpassed even the pyramids.[55] It had twelve covered courts with opposite doors; twelve intercommunicating courts; over three thousand rooms of two kinds – those above ground were open to visitors, and those below ground housed the tombs of embalmed kings and sacred crocodiles; and one wall surrounded them all. Much was built of white stone, quite possibly gypsum or alabaster. About 18 AD, Strabo found it in bad repair. It had a large palace composed of as many palaces as there were formerly *nomes* (districts); an equal number of courts surrounded by pillars and contiguous to one another – all in one line and forming one building; long and numerous covered ways; and winding intercommunicating passages so that no stranger could find his way out without a guide.[56] Excavations confirm the main descriptions of Herodotus and Strabo.[57] It was a structure of monstrous size.

The meaning structures implied by the Egyptian Labyrinth are better understood by comparison with the Cretan Labyrinth at Knossos, seat of the Minoan culture. Probably older than that in Egypt, it was built before 1364 BC.[58] Despite the speculations of Sir Arthur Evans,[59] Cretan civilization probably began when Mesopotamians went there in antique times, taking the Neolithic death cult of the bull which became the Minotaur. The Palace at Knossos was both a necropolis and a labyrinth (in comparison, Egypt separated the two). Made of very soft materials, particularly gypsum like that in Egypt, the floors could not have been walked on without immediate damage. Indeed, the buildings were never intended as a real palace. These labyrinths were signifiers of the Netherworld. Cretan specialists (*Keftiu*) supervised death rituals in Egypt, substituting embalming for dry mummification: they dramatized the Land of the Dead in mortuary ritual dramas.[60] The Cretan rituals began in natural caves during the earliest times, moved to artificial caves, then to crafted tombs, and, finally, to funerary palaces twenty thousand square metres in area. The dead of sufficient rank were taken care of "as if" they were living. The illustrations at Knossos display many of their entertainments. Linear B tablets indicate bequests for the payment of funeral costs and provisions for the souls of the dead, and they tell us that the presiding deity was the Earth Mother, Sito or Demeter, whose daughter Persephone became the symbol of resurrection at Eleusis. The Knossos labyrinth-necropolis included a theatre where ritual games and plays were performed for the dead, a small rectangular acting area enclosed by wide, ascending tiers of seats. At Phaistos, there was a second row of seats on the side with an even more generous space. A long paved road, the Sacred Way, led directly into the theatre.

In other words, *the Cretan labyrinth was a three-dimensional metaphor that dramatized the felt-meaning of death-and-resurrection*. The meanings it carried were meant to be complex: the dead acted "as if" they were living in ritual dramas about death-and-resurrection with sacrificial rituals.[61] Knossos mixed the architecture of the quaternity, the quincunx, and the circle, together with dead-ends, upper and lower chambers, long corridors, and huge courtyards. Reputedly, it represented "the secret of existence." Were the ritual dramas of the Earth Mother (like the Greek Mysteries) re-enacted there? It is impossible to tell. But Minoan coins indicate that it was likely. The coins bear the insignia of a labyrinth, a codified quaternity format with roses, crescent moons, bulls, or goddesses at their centre. The felt-meaning structure of the labyrinth was specifically polydimensional and capable of many interpretations.[62]

Roman descriptions of the Minotaur and labyrinth myth derived from the Greeks. Plutarch (XI) mentions that dancing took place there. Labyrinthine dances are performed today in Crete before wedding celebrations,[63] in other words, polydimensional felt-meaning structures derived from the most ancient traditions still function. The link between the dead and the labyrinth is also made by Pliny, who discusses a remarkable tomb built for an Etruscan general that contained a subterranean labyrinth of gigantic size.[64] A similar Etruscan construction, known as the tomb of the Horatii and the Curatii, existed in Albano as late as the nineteenth century AD.[65] As with alchemy and mandala rituals, those of the labyrinth were surrounded by secrecy. Labyrinthine medallions in simplified designs were carried over the Roman Empire and secrecy was attached to them.[66]

Although the full meaning of such creations must remain speculative, it is clear that *they emerge from thinking, feeling, and dramatization in the aesthetic mode* so that the oscillation between impulse and medium create a series of actions – in architecture, paint, sculpture, music, dance, and drama. Fundamentally their felt-meaning structures suggest answers to: "To be or not to be, that is the question ... "

There is an absence of labyrinths in early Christian iconography.[67] The earliest known Christian labyrinth is found at Orleansville (Algeria) and thought to date from the fourth century AD. It mixed Roman and Christian traditions: a central cryptogram (read in any direction except diagonally) spelled the words *Sancta Ecclesia*. Christian labyrinths continued the Cretan tradition of dramatization. They were a sign for "the secret of existence": they re-enacted the layout of the cosmic city, Jerusalem or Troy, in tangible form.[68] This tradition is continuous from Babylon to the Christian cathedral. Christian labyrinths ranged from the simple key-pattern square spiral at Thornton, Leicestershire, to the famous league at Chartres. Christian tradition said that to walk the labyrinthine paths was the spiritual equivalent of a pilgrimage to Jerusalem – a metaphoric signified that became a signifier through dramatization.

The labyrinth structure, therefore, was not a fixed form. It metaphorized existential meanings, and went beyond a simple code to an aesthetic, artistic, feeling, and moral (or religious) multiplicity. This same structure is precisely that of spontaneous dramatic acts.

Maze

The most common mazes were those of pavement and turf. At least forty-four turf mazes existed in England alone and dated from the Bronze Age or earlier, and hundreds of others are known from all over the world. They have a labyrinthine character and are closely associated with the quaternities and the quincunx as signifiers of existence. They were supposed to be walked upon, over forces in the earth below called *tourbillons* (vortices of energy, or transition places from the physical to the astral world) whose points of support were generated by the sacred dance on the sacred *omphalos*.[69] Given that turf mazes are constructed close to ancient sacred places, or on the tops of hills, it is no surprise that some of them bear a close resemblance to the pavement maze at Chartres. Mazes derivative from the labyrinth arose in late medieval and early Renaissance times. Christian buildings with floor mazes include cathedrals and churches.

Yet there are historical significances too. Welsh shepherds cut turf mazes which they referred to as *Caerdroia* (*Caer* being "walls" and *Droia* being "of Troy": thus, "Walls of Troy"), for, according to ancient legend, a great-grandson of Aeneas went to Wales to found a new city for liberated Trojan prisoners of war which was called *Caerdroia-Newydd* – the New City of Troy.[70] Even in Chaucer's time it was a common metaphor to compare Britain to Troy; and John Lydgate dramatized Britain "as if" it was Troy. The association of maze names with Roman lore, and Roman pottery and coins found in their vicinity, indicate that turf mazes shared similar origins. Thus *the felt-meaning structures of mazes are similar to those of labyrinths*, the difference being that mazes were adapted to the particular context in which they were created.

Ritual Dance and Games

Mazes in Elizabethan times were increasingly used for recreational purposes. But in rural areas they retained a pagan flavour by being traced by young couples of the village at certain seasons of the year; the "ritual marriage" as a network of felt-meaning was in the process of becoming folklore when Troy-town at Pimperne in Dorset was described as being "much used by the young people on Holydaies and by ye School-bois."[71] Sword and Morris dances, even today, are performed with meticulous attention to the quaternity and other patterns that are also common to the turf maze traditions. Hopscotch, a game that is (at least) as old as Pliny, is assumed by folklorists to be associated with the labyrinth or maze.[72] The patterns drawn on the ground are signs that are closely related to the quaternities, the quincunx, and the circle; the throwing of stones in some versions of the game is derived from the Babylonian ritual to forecast Destiny; and the skipping hop may have connections with the earliest known ritual dance by the pharaoh in the land ceremony, and as talked of in Samuel.[73] Ritual dance and game, now reduced to folklore, are networks of felt-meaning derived from the most ancient traditions.

On the surface it may seem a far cry from Crete to *Caerdroia*, and from the Labyrinth of Egypt to Chartres Cathedral and to hopscotch today. But is it? *Labyrinths, mazes, and nets each demonstrate structure clusters of felt-meaning focused on the fundamental question that faces all humanity: What is the meaning of life and death?* The fact that we cannot be precise about what these meaning structures are simply shows that they are aesthetic, tacit, and grounded in feeling. They do not respond to explicit language.

Early anthropologists like Sir James Frazer tried to make these felt-meaning structures explicit. For him, contemporary labyrinthine dances were symbolic of both the path of the sun through the sky (or the Netherworld), and of the awakening of spring after its winter sleep – analogous events in early times. But because events had specific meanings in ancient times does not mean that they have the same meanings in the "here and now." What is carried forward is the felt-meaning *structure*: the form the felt-meaning takes, not the meaning itself. *Both cognitive structures and felt-meaning structures are primarily significant not for their content but for their form.* Frazer himself demonstrated this when he also cited a practice of the Chilcotin Indians who, during an eclipse of the sun, walked around a circle, leaning on staves, as if to help the sun complete its journey through the heavens – or in the land of darkness. The similarities with the Night Journey of Re, the Egyptian sun god, and the universal drama of death-and-resurrection, are structural.[74]

Although the secret of the labyrinth cannot be directly found in games and entertainment, folklore and children's activities, there is a line of structural descent of felt-meaning from Knossos to the *lusus*

Troyae described in the *Aeneid*, and to the Troy Towns and the sports connected with them. Although these acts may contain felt-meanings due to particular historical events (such as the Roman occupation of Britain), their structures (quaternities, the quincunx, the circle, etc.) were associated with the question of life and death. *These structures were used by ritual dramas that signified both cosmic and human existence* – "the sacred marriage," the ritual battle, the Game of Destiny, the sun's travels through the Netherworld, and the games linked to ceremonies for the dead. Thus when these ritual dramas come down to us as folklore, it is their felt-meaning structures that are significant.

It is no coincidence that these fundamental human acts and the performance of plays in playhouses are both centred on the key issues of existence. What is life? what is death? is there life after death? The questions addressed by the death rituals at the labyrinth and by Hamlet as he holds a famous skull ("Alas, poor Yorick!") have a similar felt-meaning to labyrinthine structures.

But why cannot we explain them with cognitive precision, categorizing and labelling them? The labyrinth, like the ancient Mysteries, was secret. Both had a double function: to exclude, in order to protect, a sacred trust; and to admit those who were permitted entry.[75] But *they were secret because they had to be: they could not be explained in words.* That is, labyrinths, mysteries, ritual dramas, mandalas, crosses, and other expressions of great feeling (power) were signifiers that communicated far more meanings than simple signs. By performing them in highly significant actions, human beings gained a particular kind of meaning – a meaning of similar structure to that of *Hamlet*, which gives us a different experience each time it is performed.

Contemporary dramatic action of all kinds contains felt-meaning structures of similar types but with different content. This meaning structure is aesthetic. It is both of the mundane (the action to be done) and fictional (the imagined significance of the action). The felt-meaning structure gives a particular way of knowing – tacit and personal rather than discursive. This knowledge is of two kinds, both the everyday and the spiritual, which are, after all, a unity – and that is a paradox. It reveals existential concerns. In other words, the labyrinth, the maze, the mandala, the cross, the play in the playhouse, and the nature of our improvised self-presentation are each highly complex signifiers of an aesthetic and ambiguous signified. *They are physical and dramatic ways of representing the meaning of feeling.* Relying on the complex interrelations of the quaternities and the quincunx, they are multivalent sign systems – networks that are specifically over-coded with meaning. This might account, for example, for the dedication that most players have for the playing.

SUMMARY

Dramatic action has an aesthetic subtext of structures that express feeling and create our felt-worlds. To this end, the media we use are those of the Self (self-presentation), language (talk), and movement (gesture, posture, etc.). We create entirely mental realities with no necessary content; through them we understand the world around us; and from their signifiers others infer our felt-thoughts. We create such constructs to order the environment: to satisfy the feeling of unity in diversity.

The primary mental structure is differentiation, a gestalt where one thing is seen in relation to another thing – as similar or different. This gestalt, the prime source of mental energy, is as old as *homo sapiens*. It is always felt to be double and underlies all dramatic action. Being "as if" is to be two-in-one: "the mask and the face" – a metaphor of oneself.

From an early age, we learn to distinguish the actual (the real), and the representation of the actual (the not really "real"). Mind dramatizes the actual to create the fiction of "the play world" (or "the aesthetic world") which the drama process externalizes. Then the actual and the fictional worlds coexist and their operations overlap.

Feeling is inherent in both the cognitive duality and the aesthetic double. But Cartesian thinking has withdrawn feeling from duality by trying to be clinically objective and binary. Contrary to this, it is the play-within-the-play that doubles the double (quaternity), the basic structure of all dramatic acts. It rests firmly on feeling. Various views of mind claim that the quaternity is the structure of all thought, and not just aesthetic thinking. On this view, two (doubling) as a sign is the focus for metaphor; this becomes complicated into three cosmic levels; and the three levels are linked by "the shamanic ladder," the fourth point, which is created by action. The mid-point of the quaternity is the quincunx (five).

Various examples show that this mental structure is primordial. In tribal drama, unity is prior to diversity, and numbers have a symbolic as well as a literal meaning. These quaternity structures have an aesthetic (feeling) quality, and they are the deep structure of all subsequent (i.e., post-tribal) mental structures, including our own. This is indicated by many examples; e.g., labyrinths are three-dimensional metaphors for the structures of felt-meaning. Today dramatic action contains felt-meaning structures of similar types but with various kinds of content.

4 Holism and the Dynamics of Feeling

In the broad spectrum between feelings and emotions, there are many dynamics. So many, indeed, that no typology has been able to grasp them all.

Feeling as a mental dynamic is an activity, not an object or a state. It works between two or more aspects of mind, and its model is the metaphor. That is, between "the roses" and "her cheeks," a feeling is generated when we create the metaphor, "the roses in her cheeks." The energy that is generated by feeling is in constant oscillation. The dynamic oscillates back and forth between structures in three ways:

- between the ideas of the structures of objects in relation (e.g., roses, cheeks, and their interrelation);
- between the imaginative structures of what is possible; and
- through the extension of these possibilities into media by dramatic acts.

Further, we continually find that when the original metaphoric interrelation is re-played in improvisation and educational drama, it is so refurbished as to be virtually a new feeling.

As we have seen, it is the gestalt of differentiation that is the origin of both energy and feeling in human organisms. This is to talk of feelings and dynamics in holistic terms. Why does holism have explanatory power about feelings and dynamics?

HOLISM AND MIND

There are many views about holism. Some dictionary definitions are: whole entities that are fundamental components of reality; a coherent system of parts that fit or work together as one; entities that are more than the sum of their parts; and the organic and/or functional relation of parts and wholes. The model of mind that is used here is based on the view that holism sees the human being as an organismic whole rather than an aggregation of separate parts. It assumes that unity and similarity are prior to opposition, binarism, and the digital; thought and action are experienced as one whole; and feeling is inherent in all aspects of thought and action. This model of holism is grounded on the following notions:

- *The organism*
  Human and other forms of life are conceived as organisms characterized by purpose and intention. This is to emphasize human self-choice, self-government, and self-regulation.
- *Process*
  Life, the human and natural environment, and the cosmos, are viewed as processes. This is to collapse the subjective/objective dichotomy into one total ongoing movement.
- *Energy*
  The contemporary view of energy as the vital force of life is accepted. Thought, feeling, action, and learning are energetic: they are activated by dynamics that obviate the duality of body/mind; they work with the totality of Self (mind, brain, body) in energetic relation with the environment; and, in terms of language, they are primarily verbal rather than nominal. Holism focuses upon the energetic developmental process of the whole Self (the personal) within specific contexts or environments (the social).
- *The Gestalt of Whole/Part*
  Differentiation is not built on part/part but on the oscillation between whole/part; at one moment we can "see" the whole, at another the part; and we can reverse them.
- *Feeling*
  Feeling is integral to the dynamics of the organism, its thoughts and actions. It is generated by the oscillations between whole/part.
- *Dramatic Action*
  The double creation of actual/fictional worlds ensures that all the organism's acts are dramatic and dialogic. This arises from differentiation: the oscillation of energy between whole/part in imaginings becomes externalized in "as if" acts.
- *Perspectives*
  Putting oneself in someone else's shoes allows two perspectives and feelings (actual and fictional) to be gained on any event, which, through comparison, constitute the sense we make of it. The model assumes that the arts, the sciences, and the social sciences are per-

spectives on the holistic process and that all are of relative use. Mind, brain, ecology, ethology, society, and culture are viewed as abstractions that can lead to a perspective of value – a partial understanding of a whole entity.

The interdependence of these factors is one reason why a semiotic method of inquiry is useful in understanding both the whole/part relation and the nature of dramatic action. Semiotics is an analytic way of working, through signifier/signified, that permits the discernment of overlapping (but not necessarily discrete) parts within an organic, processual, and energetic whole. *In dramatic terms, an act is a whole signifier while thought and feeling are whole signifieds.*

Holistic Thought and Action

How can that which knows know itself? Any signifier of the known must include the knower. Models of mind are metaphors, signs that reflect our feeling, thinking, acting, and learning operations. They depend crucially upon values which, over history, have produced diverse points of view.

The Greeks saw mind, or soul, as part of the universe: a unified relationship existed between people, gods, cosmos, and nature. For Plato, the soul was a winged chariot drawn by two horses that symbolized the tension in human nature; one pulled up, the other down. Soul was also symbolized as the Cretan labyrinth where Theseus slew the Minotaur, like all heroes who killed monsters: metaphorically the irrational was overcome by reason. Civilized minds arose that were ruled by *sophrosyne* ("nothing to excess") and characterized by *harmonia* ("harmony"). Little wonder, then, that Plato objected to the irrational Dionysos and to tragedy. It was the tragic perspective that finally focused the human science on people as individuals working within a society.

Augustine said that harmony was destroyed by Adam's fall. Just as Adam's soul was divided against itself by sin, so human society was divided by selfishness. By prizing knowledge above unity and harmony, Adam upset the balance of the cosmos and his own soul. This breach was healed by the Crucifixion, the signification of salvation. Until this point, feeling was inherent in all models of mind in Western ideas.

But Descartes divided mind/body, subject/object, feeling/cognition, and knower/known so that, in the mechanistic root metaphor, the Observing Mind remained apart like "a ghost haunting a machine."[1] Hobbes even reduced mind to material causes, while Locke pictured it as a blank slate written upon by sensory information. By the nineteenth century mind was seen to be predetermined: Hegel said that it was shaped by abstract categories and the ideals of reason; Marx thought it was formed by economic relations; Jeremy Bentham saw it as social atoms, seeking pleasure and avoiding pain; and Darwin considered it was the result of "the survival of the fittest." With the advent of experimentalism, mind was totally a mechanism: it was "an assembled organic machine ready to run"[2] and "a completely self-sustaining robot,"[3] so that Skinner could say that man is not free.[4]

In contrast, the seeds of oscillating models had begun again, with Kant giving primacy to imagination, and with the emergence of the dialectic. With Hegel the latter was binary, but expanded into a triangularity. The dialectic was taken up by Marx and others, including Freud. Freud thought that the larger unconscious, created out of past experiences, determined the present consciousness. But in *the movement* between the two was the preconscious, which recalled mental events through the symbols of dreams, neurotic fantasies, hypnosis, and slips of the tongue. In other words, although Freud's model of mind was determinist, he also emphasized process and movement. It was not mere coincidence that, at the time he began writing, electric power was first harnessed for domestic and industrial use. From the seeds of Kant and Freud, the oscillation model grew.

While Jung borrowed Freud's concepts of the conscious and unconscious, as well as other incidental ideas, the differences between the two men were profound. Compared with Freud's model of mind, Jung's was more organic and expansive. For him, the mind was not just caused. It was purposeful, using the acausal principle of synchronicity – an effectance through synthesis or created wholes.[5] Unlike Freud, for whom processual movement was still triangular, Jung related oscillation to the quaternity. Oscillation was based on four axes: thinking/feeling and sensation/intuition. This quaternity was independent of content. Moreover, it was theoretically capable (through the quincunx) of infinite combinations.[6]

Oscillation became the fundamental model for existentialists who focused upon the inner life of the person. S/he was a union of more than one pair of opposites, "half angel and half beast" caught between freedom and restriction, living half in nature and half in dread of death – an idea that was deeply felt.[7] This paradox was unified by signifying the absurdity of being human in a dispassionate universe. Mind has the anxiety of oscillating between expectations and reality[8] while working with two kinds of reason: technical reason, which produces anxiety because it deals with cause and effect, and gives yes/no answers to dualistic questions; and encompassing reason, which develops Being because it deals with alternatives and gives both/and answers in a holistic way.[9]

Figure 10
The Neurological Quaternity

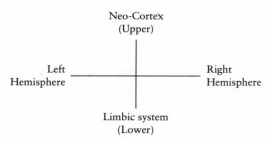

The cognitive, affective, aesthetic and psychomotor are a whole with oscillating dynamics; mind tends to see others as particular signs – as beings-in-themselves – so that interpersonal relationships are a perpetual struggle to assert the fluidity of our own existence against persistent attempts by others to objectify us.[10] These ideas were expressed with deep feelings, contrasting with the cold and distanced descriptions of experimentalists. In a similar way, Laing condemns contemporary psychiatry for falsely objectifying psychic states.[11] By giving others false labels (objectified signs), it encourages the creation of false selves.

Many contemporary thinkers, often not existentialists, also believe that mental structures are unified by the inherent dynamics of oscillation and that these are predominantly *felt*. For semioticians who follow this view, mind is in continuing process while signification is in constant change. Signifiers alter; acts indicate signifieds that are also in change. We catch glimpses of these events through the masks and roles used by players and by inference from the fictional worlds they create. Then both learning and the signs of learning indicate oscillating feelings.

Mind and Brain

Modern brain research highlights feeling, if only by implication. It presents a quaternity model based on the tensions of unity/diversity between two interlinked operations: the lateral (the left and right hemispheres), and the vertical (the lower and upper brain). Much research, unfortunately, deals with one or the other and only rarely synthesizes both (see figure 10).

Lateral operations are of two types. The left hemisphere works primarily in the verbal and rational mode, with logical and analytic thinking, and is connected to the right side of the body. The right hemisphere works primarily in the holistic mode, with simultaneous and relational thinking (spatial orientation, artistic endeavour, crafts, body images, recognition of faces, etc.), and is connected to the left side of the body.

These two lateral modes of mind are not dualities but doubles of each other which are dynamically related: the link between them (the *corpus callosum*) allows a unity that is more than a sum of the parts – like a metaphor. Contemporary research indicates considerable variation between individuals. But non-verbal responses from the right hemisphere are quicker than verbal and logical responses from the left. To rephrase this in terms of the current study, the two hemispheres are not digital structures. Rather, the right appears to be primordial; the verbal/logical appears to work in the context of the non-verbal/relational. The gestalt of hemispherical balance is essential for good mental development.

Vertical operations are different. The MacLean-Papez theory[12] says that there are fundamental differences in anatomy and function between the deep brain (limbic system), which controls instinctive and emotional behaviour – the archaic structures that humans share with reptiles and the lower animals – and the upper brain, or neocortex, which controls rational, linguistic, logical, and symbolic thought – the specifically human.

The horizontal and vertical operations of the brain are psycho-biological distinctions that closely parallel the quaternity. Mind simply cannot be explained by the dichotomy of dualities, by a mechanistic system of input and output, or as a chain of conditioned responses. Mind is a whole with dynamics between its parts whereby feelings infuse all of its operations. Indeed, the neurological model of mind indicates a close parallel with the double of metaphorization, the complexity of multivocal symbols, and the semiotic square (described in *Drama and Intelligence*).

Other Holistic Models

Contemporary thinkers are currently debating other models of mind, many of them holistic. Our concern with them here is to see whether they widen our perspective on the significance of feeling in dramatic action.

Many modern models centre on the mind as metaphor. Julian Jaynes has popularized such a model: mind works by metaphors or analogues of behaviour in the physical world. Consciousness is, therefore, metaphorical. It is a map of a territory – a dynamic, between the brain and its referents. Jaynes says that consciousness unifies mental operations through:

- spatialization – the dimensions of time and space;
- excerption – the maps of selected territories;
- the analogue of "I" and "me" – projected personification of our Self moving in time and space which anticipates doing and being done by;
- narration – selecting events for congruence or sequence;
- conciliation – the conscious assimilation of ideas to each other.[13]

This model, based on structuralism, derives from Jung and others. While popular, it has only tangential relations to dramatism.

More significant is the hologram model, notionally based on similarity and metaphor. Karl Pribram shows that cells in the sensory cortex (and others) encode holographically: each part knows what the whole knows. The open and intentional system of the total organism works with the environment through oscillation, while subjective experience, including feeling, alters *the structure* of the brain.[14] If so, it is significant for aesthetic thinking and learning: the more holographic relations are used, the stronger they become. We will examine these issues in chapter 8.

Importantly, a number of contemporary models link the metaphor with dialogue and paradox. Many follow Martin Buber, who uses the theatre metaphor for his model of mind.[15] For Buber, Bakhtin, and others, mind centres on dialogue not dialectic: it is not triangular in structure; *the form of dialogue is the double gestalt of two speakers* – a quaternity where the psychological and the social are interdependent. Dramatic feeling is the key to the emergence of mind: the human commitment must be to "I and Thou," a felt-processual relation, rather than "I and It," where persons are seen as objects. Although in objective concepts of truth (abstractions) only one of two contraries can be true, in the reality of life as we live and dramatize it they are inseparable. The unity of differences is a mystery at the innermost core of dialogue.[16]

Arthur Koestler says that the unity of action is a signifier of a double dynamic, the bi-sociation of two or more thought matrices (or frames of reference) so that two parts of a paradox are placed in conjunction; and this releases great energy, including considerable feeling power.[17] On this view, metaphors and dramas are heuristic devices. They review the likeness of unlike categories not only through contraries and the paradox but also in tangential thinking and intuitive leaps across boundaries. Paradox, according to Frank Barron,[18] is the crux of creativity: order/disorder, certainty/doubt, ego-strength/anxiety, closure/openness, and rational/ intuitive. Koestler postulates "holons" (double theoretic entities that synthesize "whole" and "atom") which occur at the junctions of bi-sociations and are the genesis of energy and feeling.

A major holistic idea extends oscillation to "synergy": two dynamics mutually enhance one another and progress spirally. This has influenced ideas in a variety of fields, the physical sciences[19] and psychology[20] among others. It is carried into biology through the General Systems Theory of Von Bertalanffy, which says that life unfolds at progressively higher rates of differentiation;[21] wholes are not reducible to their parts; their developed forms are qualitatively different from earlier forms; and all organisms, including mind, are dynamic and open in their interaction with the environment. Another biologist, Jonas Salk,[22] agrees with Buber, Barron, William Blake, and others about the paradox: life reconciles oppositions; mind combines physical, chemical, biological, and socio-biological systems to actualize this endowment. Gregory Bateson shows that the oscillation of synergy characterizes mind as a cybernetic system; problems occur, he says, through schismogenesis – "a growing split in the structure of ideas."[23] Similarity/harmony, not opposition/conflict, is the structural basis of such models. There is a close parallel between these models and contemporary information theory that a structural dynamic is independent of content where the medium itself is the message.[24] In this root metaphor, the quaternity is the foundation of the circuitry within which oscillation operates; but it is also capable of extension through the quincunx to infinity (at least theoretically).

The implications of contemporary holistic models are considerable. *The mind works with probability* (the foundation of contemporary information theory, science, and mathematics), *which functions in terms of hypothesis and estimation. It does so through imagination, which creates possibility.*

As we have already seen, imagining is metaphoric, is closely linked to action, is the basis for symbolization, and is aesthetic in quality. Thus when holists metaphorically conceive mind as a quaternity, they picture human life as a tragicomedy whereby it plays out, through dialogue and at a meta-level beyond the mundane, human feelings and understandings about thought, action, and learning. Linked to the model of the act of learning as a signifier, the quaternity becomes a powerful explanatory tool.

OSCILLATION AND ENERGY

Contemporary science shows that matter is finally reducible to energy, that energy itself has mass. In other words, energy is not something matter *does*, it is what matter *is*. Similarly, *energy is what drama is.* The relationship of the Self and the world, which includes the interrelation of selves in dramatic action, is a transaction in which energy modifies the relations of structures. The senses are active, interrelated, and interacting systems.[25] They actively co-operate with the experienced world, including other people, by interacting in integrated activity (both actual and fictional). The world affects our senses in natural rhythms – of light, sound, air, heat, weather, the seasons, and lived organic experience. We experience life as the modulating and endlessly pulsating rhythmic transaction of all beings with each other and with the whole.[26]

In one sense, feelings and emotions are experienced in a comparative manner. This is so in so far as they are similar to or different from such rhythmic transactions. If our fear occurs as a tiger walks into the room, the transaction in which we are engaged is very different from our experience when our cat walks into the room. The rhythm has changed and the transaction has altered; and we acknowledge that with a tiger we have different feelings and emotions from our normal experience with a cat.

As we engage in dramatic activity, we rhythmically transact energy; you and I act jointly in patterns and reflexes. *From a dramatic perspective, consciousness is to be both self-aware and aware of the other as an other.* The dynamic of the self and other-self establishes a variety of metaphoric relations: here-there, this-that, inside-outside, etc. – things are transformed into felt-meaning and purpose which we can (falsely) view as "a thing."[27] *Feeling is involved in transformation but in degrees.* Self-awareness specifically generates our felt-response and purpose. In spontaneous dramatic acts, in life or improvisation, our response leads to the purpose of moving the action onwards.

In other words, we should not think that mind and the world are merely objective things (or nominals), as analytic intelligence has taught us. We must accept the fact that process is as real as objects, that relations are as substantial as substance, and that rhythm is as much a part of our experience as the ordering of the muscles. This is specifically so in drama. From a dramatic perspective, there is no such thing as a separate Self, or a separate Nature. We are in constant interaction with the natural order, and the energetic and dramatic process wherein this occurs is metaphorical. We enact narratives and we ritualize myths that shape our understanding of the world. It is this process that is "culture." Culture is metaphor, a means for human transactions.[28] Metaphors are what we *do*, and, as has been wisely said, we live with their consequences.

Metaphor and Movement

Metaphorization begins from the double process. Once the baby functions with the double of actual/fictional, metaphorization is the next step. It is a fundamental act of mind. But, as we have seen, metaphor is a dynamic based on imagining: it has a dramatic character, is constantly in process, and is a continuous doubling activity. Using the example of "the roses in her cheeks" once more, cheeks = the actual, roses = the fictional, but when united as a new whole a metaphor occurs. Or, as we have also seen, $1 + 1 = 3$.

This, however, is to state the issue in a nominal way, cognitively. To restate it processually, the dynamic between "roses" and "cheeks" creates a further dynamic of their interrelation. This processual metaphor:

- exists in time as a process;
- is a movement not a form;
- creates felt-meaning; and
- functions as energy.

Parallel with this, it is the view of Victor W. Turner that culture and society itself are likewise processual.[29] The movement inherent in felt-dynamics is always purposive. It can, therefore, be sequential or comparative, but not necessarily so. It often has movement that oscillates or leaps from one frame of reference to another, thereby activating association, synaesthesia, and similar styles of felt-thought.

Spontaneous dramatic activity in all its forms has a similar dynamic:

- it exists in time (the present tense) as a process between people;
- it is in continual movement and is never static; and
- it functions as energy between players and, if there is an audience, also between players and spectators.

Players think and feel metaphorically while they act, so it is no surprise that their playing is grounded in felt-dynamics.

In a sense, all metaphors and dramatic acts are leaps between two energies. The metaphorical and dramatic structural systems make possible a leap between one logical class and another -- they energize human creative behaviour. At a specific moment, each player can select from a variety of signs that generate messages and, by chosing actions that relay signs, they construct a new world or reconstruct an old world; discontinuities are made continuous and continuities become discontinuous[30] – and feelings change. In other words, to play or replay with the feeling of inner relationships is the foundation for creative acts. Mental and/or dramatic play of this type results in an infinite number of possible creative acts including dreams, poetry, imaginings, spontaneous improvisation, mystical religious experiences, scientific creativity, and all analogical acts. At least potentially, all human acts have their origins in our play with feelings. Intriguingly, each of these acts has its own feeling. No metaphor, and no dramatic act, feels quite the same as another.

In the spontaneous drama of life and improvisation, feeling appears to have many variables, according to:

- the two sides of the action (e.g., "roses" and "cheeks");
- the created relation;
- the two or more persons in relation;
- the context;
- the need to continue the action;
- the plot, theme, and genre.

Yet such a typology cannot fully account for the uniqueness of feeling.

Floyd Merrell uses two examples that help to illustrate this. First, if we are converted to another religion, we have stepped from one mental structure to another; we have learned to exist in another realm where there are alternative feelings. Second, and more to our purpose, if we work within one artistic mental structure (say, the improvisational form of Viola Spolin) we tacitly hold particular conventions, modes of behaviour, and range of feelings. But should we change our artistic view (to, say, the improvisational style of Keith Johnstone),[31] or alter our creative behaviour in some way, then we step into another realm. In that realm there are other alternatives which are potentially infinite in number. We now have two different kinds of feelings and, in theory at least, potentially infinite sets of them. But in any one context the available number of feelings is theoretically limited. To play with metaphoric and dramatic processes is to create choice.[32]

What is creative about the metaphor and the dramatic act is that they are iconic: they create a parallel between two feelings in one – the double that is also a unity. This allows the player to intervene between them. Because they are a unity, the intervention affects both sides of the feeling. This is why we can talk of the "play" of metaphor. The player is given the choice to elaborate the parallel structure. When this happens, the act creates new feelings and the resulting dynamics function in new situations – new, that is, to the player. It was Aristotle who said that "a good metaphor implies an intuitive perception of the similarity in dissimulars."[33]

Dramatic play is a living metaphor. In metaphor we play with double meanings; we "see both sides of the question" or make a "flip" of ideas. This is to alternate, to "switch," continuously – between the actual and the fictional – where each resembles the other.[34] To act "as if" one is Napoleon is to do two things: to be Napoleon and also to be one's Self – to feel both. The resemblance lies in the fact that both live in the present – the Self in the actual present, Napoleon in the fictional present. The human actor (whether in life or in theatre) is a sign of metaphorical order that generates feeling of a particular quality: of success in achievement, stronger self-concept, and confidence in working with others.

Key Factors in Felt-Learning

From a holistic perspective, the oscillation of energy leads us to consider two prime factors in learning, each closely related to the other:

- *Intuition and skill are both required to be creative and to solve problems.*
  In Aristotle's terms, "epiphor" and "diaphor" are one: vision and construction coexist. The child at play learns that this is a paradox. This is what Jeanne Cohen calls "the semantic impertinence"[35] and what Ricoeur calls "the conceptual structure of resemblance that opposes and unites identity and difference."[36] The creativity of play has a specific feeling that resembles the creativity of the artist: "Perceiving the likeness between the multiple referents of a metaphor, a person thirsty for an aesthetic experience, and the poem permitting, makes an effort to include as many seeming-unlikelinesses as possible."[37]

  In play, children feel they make an effort to extend their created world as far as possible, uniting its diversities as far as the play permits. The feeling of success after making the effort becomes a way they understand their selves and the world. Once habitual, this satisfaction underpins the later need to pursue a task to completion – an invaluable generic skill in adult life.
- *The leap between frames can be transferred to the making and breaking of categories.*
  "The costumed player" learns how to make and break frames in two main ways. First, by thinking and acting metaphorically, the player learns that some things feel the same while others feel different – the actor begins to construct categories. Metaphor is primarily based on similarity and resemblance; on the unity of things despite their differences. Thus classes can be identified while learning and knowledge can occur through the concept of similarity.

  Second, by thinking and acting metaphorically, the player also learns that acting can break categories. When the player learns that acting can be logical, he or she can also be illogical, turning the cognitive into the aesthetic and vice versa. The resemblance and similarity inherent in metaphor incorporates difference: breaking boundaries, cutting loose from classes and categories. In the same way, inversions ("turning the world upside down," or topsy-turveydom) can result in feelings of great excitement and high creativity, as in festivity.

These two aspects of feelings, broadly stated here, can create processual relations of great complexity.

OSCILLATION AND FEELINGS

Feelings oscillate. This is the case in metaphor and dramatic acts – particular instances of the movement of energy within all mental processes. This energy is constantly in motion, oscillating between pole and pole. Indeed, "Everything, from sub-nuclear particles upward, oscillates between itself and the other, existence and non-existence. You cannot step into the same river twice."[38]

The comparison of brain waves to an oscillator was first made by Norbert Weiner.[39] The activity of the brain and all natural phenomena is governed by periodic wave functions: they give out wave pulses of different frequencies.[40] As Merrell has explained, the frequency of an oscillator can be changed by impulses of a different frequency and, therefore, its structure is non-linear.[41] The brain contains a number of oscillators with frequencies of nearly ten cycles per second; these frequencies can be attracted to one another – pulled together in clumps. This leads to a sharp drop in the generation of brain waves from other areas. Not only is the power of energy within feeling non-linear but also, as the oscillation returns to one pole, it is never quite the same as it was before – as any lover will tell you …

Thus we see that *oscillation is characteristic of all the dynamics of thought.* When we connect A to B, the oscillation carries the energy (message, information) from A to B and, in doing so, unites the contrasts of A/B while acknowledging the differences. Should the oscillation return the message from B to A, the energy is altered – and thus A is not the same as it was in the initial instance. This also describes the oscillation of feeling in metaphor and dramatic action.

Time

In metaphorization, one mental structure conceived at a specific instant is connected to a second mental structure conceived at another instant by a dynamic "leap." In much the same way, someone who is bilingual may assume that he or she operates simultaneously in English and French. But in actuality, the linked operation of two mental frameworks of whatever kind must be by a mental "flip," or "switch."

Similarly, thought and act may also falsely appear to be simultaneous. In fact, even though the unit of time may be extremely small, thought and act operate by alternate oscillation. The resulting units of time can be experienced as feelings, as a function of our brain wave rate.[42]

Dramatization has a double relation to time:

- It "stops time" like metaphor. As an analogue, the two parts of metaphor are parallel in time. To say that a man is a lion, or to act the role of a lion, is (seemingly) to reduce two things to one so that they appear to exist in one time frame whereas, in actuality, they do not.
- It exists in sequential time like metonymy. Being digital, it expands the explicit. By making two things contiguous it implies sequence.

Thought and act oscillate as the alternation of thinking "what if" and acting "as if" – of imaginative thought and dramatic action. The structural similarity that permits this oscillation is the "gap" between the actual and the dramatic idea, between the two sides of metaphor, and between feelings that differ in degree if only infinitesimally.

Kinds of Seeing

The feeling dynamics of the double process of imagining and dramatic action can be illustrated by using Wittgenstein's notion of "seeing as."[43] This allows us to distinguish the modes of the process: seeing, seeing as, and seeing "as if." This distinction is of necessity an abstraction; in experience, the modes are a unified whole. They are:

- SEEING – *direct experience*
  We perceive (see, hear, smell, taste, touch, and feel) through our direct physical involvement with the environment. This process includes feelings of:
  - Bounded entities. We feel that the Self and the objects we experience are separate and bounded entities.
  - Spatial structure. We feel that our Self and objects have similar orientations to the way we function (up/down, in/out, front/back, etc.). These are "the metaphors we live by."
  - Time. We feel that either: [a] the Self and objects are in motion; or [b] they are static with time in motion – then we learn beginning/middle/end and sequence.

– A Feeling Gestalt. [a] Modes: Perceptual, motor, functional, purpose, etc. [b] Dimensions: Part/whole, continua, highlighting, causation, prototypes, etc. [c] Inherent/interactional effects of objects.[44]

- SEEING AS – *"picturing in the mind's eye"*
For Wittgenstein there is a distinction between "I see this ..." which indicates direct experience, and "I see this as ..." which is "having this image,"[45] or imagination. Ricoeur says, "Half thought, half experience, 'seeing as' is the intuitive relationship that holds sense and image together."[46] Hester calls it "an intuitive experience-act."[47] This is the beginning of similarity: the object and the image are "seen as" having a resemblance. It is not quite metaphor, hypothesis, or verification, but it does include "seeing as not." It is, in actuality, the foundation for subsequent metaphor.

- SEEING *"AS IF"* – *the "double"*
This is to metaphorize existence within the unification of the "as if" idea (imagining + dramatic action). Through similarity (metaphor) and contiguity (metonymy) the mental dynamic oscillates between the actual and the fictional. Direct experience (Seeing) is metaphorized: each mode of feeling ("Seeing – direct experience" above) is given indirect meaning through metaphor.[48]

Internal imaginings become externalized in actions to form productive imagination (in the Kantian sense): "This predicative process 'creates image' and is itself the carrier of semantic analogy."[49] Seeing "as if" implies acting "as if": the expression and feeling of the double in a medium – words (literature), figures (math and science), paint and other materials (visual art), the body (dance), sound (music), the whole Self ("the costumed player" of life and theatre).

SUMMARY

The spontaneous drama of life and improvisation is holistic; feeling as a mental dynamic is an activity and its model is the metaphor. Dramatic play is a living metaphor which feeling generates by oscillating between mental structures. Thus a dramatic act is a signifier of felt-thought (the signified). We can grasp this process through a quaternity model based on the tensions of unity/diversity between two interlinked mental operations: the lateral (the left and right hemispheres) and the vertical (the lower and upper brain). Other useful models include holograms, dialogue, bi-sociation, and synergy. Just as for science energy is not something matter *does* but what matter *is*, so energy is what drama *is*. Within dramatic action:

- consciousness is to be both self-aware and aware of the other as an other in a mutual act;
- dynamics are metaphorical – process is as real as objects, relations are as substantial as substance, and rhythm is inherent in our experience;
- events exist in time (the present) as a process between people, in continual movement not static form; this process creates felt-meaning which functions as energy;
- there is a double relation to time; drama "stops time" like metaphor, and it exists in sequential time like metonymy;
- energy and feelings function between players (and between players and spectators) through oscillations which have many variables; and
- we enact narratives and we ritualize myths that shape our understanding of the world – our "culture."

This leads us to the operations of mind as a whole within dramatic acts in chapter 5.

5 Feeling and Mind

The feeling within dramatic action is a key aspect of the way mind works in the world. I have already considered this in relation to mental structures and dynamics in chapter 4. I can now turn to mind as a whole. I begin with a brief summary of some aspects of my *Drama and Intelligence*; I shall cover some of the same ground as the earlier book, but from another perspective. Then I will examine the whole mind as related to feeling and drama, including in theatrical art.

DRAMA AND KNOWING

Mind is a unified abstraction we create in order to deal with how people make sense of the world. We do so by knowledge processes whereby we can intelligently order the seeming chaos around us.

Two forms of knowledge are discussed by Bertrand Russell, who says that we operate through "knowledge by acquaintance," or direct empirical evidence, and "knowledge by description," or talking about evidence.[1] For Russell, the two are essential for knowing because, like many epistemologists of his time, he was trying to achieve a scientifically objective description of knowledge.

Others, however, say that the scientific is not the only form of knowledge. Thus Michael Polanyi shows that there is a tacit way of knowing[2] that parallels Russell's "knowledge by acquaintance." This has a quasi-independence from discursive knowing, and forms the basis of it. It has also been said that myth, religion, and the arts embody ways of knowing that, although not the same as scientific knowledge, are equally valid. Thus "by following the implicit or explicit injunctions in a musical score, a cake recipe, a mathematical proof, or even when 'getting inside' a poem, re-experiencing is the surest route to understanding, although indirectly, an original experience."[3]

To re-play an experience in the "here and now," as dramatic action does, is a way of knowing that:

- is less differentiated and precise than discursive knowing;
- incorporates the felt-meaning of the event, which discursive knowing is less likely to do;
- is a sign which, on referring to and illustrating other signs, is part of the ongoing flux.

But Russell was right when he said that mind deals with two main kinds of knowing. "Knowledge by description," which only exists in the past tense, arises from mind's capacity to generalize, or abstract. "Knowledge by acquaintance" is embedded in the organism. We, ourselves, *are* knowledge when we dramatize – when we *are* the medium of a "costumed player" – which exercises highly complicated skills apparently "without even thinking."[4] But the mind also possesses *a priori* capabilities for generalization; these enable us to experience particulars from within a structural framework that is created by abstraction. To put this another way, our experience is automatically filtered through a structural grid[5] which *is* knowledge. Information theorists would add that the grid is inherited genetically.[6]

Thus we can say that mind as a whole has the following knowledge characteristics:

- *Tacit knowing is fundamental.*
  Many scholars agree that knowing ultimately rests at some precognitive and unconscious level of experience.[7] From the environment, using actions that create media, we make a hypothesis about the world and try to match experience to it: "If I do it this way, what happens?" Then knowledge
  – is tacit, or implicit,
  – occurs within the experience, and
  – is related to intuition.
  The content of tacit knowledge reflects people's changing needs and does not include absolute truths. Truth is relative to each person's intention, needs, logic, world-view, language, and culture, and is primarily *felt*.
- *Experiential knowledge is prior to discursive knowledge.*
  Knowing IN is prior to Knowing ABOUT. In both life and the dra-

matic "here and now" we gain knowledge that is mostly tacit and unconscious. In reflection we reinterpret it so it becomes discursive. Both knowings can be inherent in how we know, but that of great sportsmen, dancers, or craftsmen can be embodied knowledge which cannot be discussed in words – as is much of our knowing as we experience dramatic action.

- *Tacit knowledge exists mainly in a temporal dimension, but the discursive exists mainly in a spatial dimension.*
  When Derrida says speech is life but writing is death,[8] he metaphorizes talk as a continuous process existing in time – "as if" it is living. When writing developed in the ancient Near East, Ionian scientists found that myths were not objectively "true." Writing "fixed" the myths: it took them "out of of time," put them in the dimension of space (history) and found them wanting. Talk and time are key dimensions of oral cultures. They have not developed the Western objective disciplines – writing, maths, science, deductive logic, or linguistics – although they have the innate capacity to do so. But "speech and writing pertain to complementary modes, although there exist independency and interaction between them."[9]

- *Tacit and discursive knowledge have specific significance in artistic and aesthetic ways of knowing.*
  The aesthetic way of knowing (genus) is based on feeling; our judgment is largely tacit and intuitive. Artistic knowing (species) includes additional factors: while artists use mainly implicit knowledge and audiences mix the implicit and discursive, critics use discursive knowledge. Specific arts vary in their ways of knowing according to form:
  - in temporal forms (theatre, dance, music) artists and audience gain much tacit knowledge;
  - in spatial forms (painting, sculpture, architecture) artists know tacitly, but viewers use both implicit and discursive ways of knowing.

- *There is a knowledge quaternity: tacit/discursive, actual/fictional; the doubles together make a quaternity structure.*
  Both tacit and discursive knowledge can be fictional and actual. In the final analysis, knowing is a whole that can be represented by a quaternity (see figure 11).

SIMILARITY AND TRACE

We have seen that the fundamental structure by which we understand mind today is the gestalt of similarity. Subsequent forms include the double, similarity/difference, whole/part, and metaphor.

The significance of this modern view is obvious when we compare it with the basic model that infused Western thought from the Greeks:

Figure 11
The Knowledge Quaternity

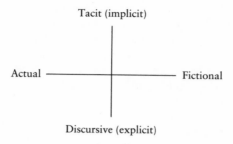

opposition. Warfare was a fundamental metaphor to the Aryans and those tribes, the Dorians, who invaded Greece – to such an extent, in fact, that centuries later when Greek civilization grew, opposition and competition were endemic to the city state. The Olympic Games and the dramatic contests in the Theatre of Dionysos were the most obvious examples. Aristotle said that mind had its different parts engaged in warfare or competition; his thought was dualistic and he created categories that were clearly distinct from one another. Warfare has been so pervasive that Lakoff and Johnson can demonstrate that, of the *Metaphors We Live By*,[10] warfare is the most frequent in the English language today.

Yet since the Einsteinian revolution, more scholars view the fundamental structure of mind as similarity. Thus a contrasting picture to the Greeks is presented; not war but peace is emphasized. Contrasts and contradictions are seen not as oppositions in an Aristotelian manner but as poles on continua – as items more or less similar – while categories often have only hazy borderlines. Derrida is well aware of the distinction between knowing empirical realities that are used as examples, and knowing essences that the examples help us to grasp.[11] Also Barthes shows that all human acts provide double meanings – that Charlie Chaplin demonstrated both blindness and the mirror of blindness by acting both as a man who is blind and as the things he does not see.[12] In this perspective feeling is highly significant because it is inherent in mind as a whole: in tacit and explicit ways of knowing, and in the dynamism and intention that oscillates between wholes and parts of the mind.

Likewise, a dramatic perspective matches this model of mind. Acting "as if" is to be the same only different; a role is an aspect of a person, and a fitting role is much like a hologram – a part of an improvisation that is a replica of the whole.

Derrida, in seeking the relation of speech to writing, found that the concept of difference on which language and thought is founded cannot be primary. There must pre-exist a notion of a "trace," *a simultaneous feeling of sameness and difference*.[13] Indeed, we have known for almost a century that the newborn for some days cannot distinguish one sound from background noise, or a particular light in the visual environment. Moreover, "trace" does not lead to the oppositions of dualism which can be explicit in discursive knowledge. Many years ago, Vygotsky said that when a child learns a language, s/he

Starts from one word, then connects two or three words ... he proceeds from a part to a whole. In regard to meaning, on the other hand, the first word of a child is a whole sentence ... The external and the semantic aspects of speech develop in opposite directions – one from the particular to the whole, from word to sentence, and the other from the whole to the particular, from sentence to word.[14]

As the dynamism and intention of mind lies in the oscillation between part and whole, and vice versa, we may assume that "trace" is –

- the foundation of the part/whole that is inherent in mind;
- the start of the metaphoric relation on the one hand, and of the role (or mask) relation on the other; and
- the basis of the doubles of feeling and drama.

On this view, "trace" operations influence how we perceive and, thus, how we "come to know." Mind resists attending merely to the actual, to the bare manifestation of the sign. *All signs tend to be transparent*; that is, they lead to knowing jointly about the actual and the fictional. In the playhouse or the cinema we exist within the action of the performance through "the willing suspension of disbelief"; yet, at the same time, we are also tacitly aware of the medium of the message. Things are similar when we create art forms; they are mental "substitute signs" for the holistic signification of the human player. This issue is illustrated in figure 12. Finally we should note that the type of knowing involved is both epistemological and ontological.[15]

AESTHETIC-ARTISTIC KNOWING AND FEELING

Aesthetic knowing, which this book and *Drama and Intelligence* have examined in detail, is the genus for the species, artistic knowing: this

Figure 12
Knowing through "Trace"

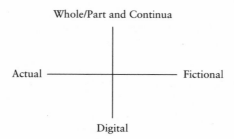

occurs in relation to art works and artistic media, but it still reflects elements of aesthetic knowledge. If the artistic is a species of the aesthetic, what are their differences in knowing? What do we know in spontaneous drama compared with theatre art?

The Prague School of semiotics concentrated upon the study of the type of knowledge that results from the creative use of sign systems in art.[16] Jan Mukařovský, building upon Karl Bühler's analysis of the speech act, says that there are four major knowledge functions of art. These are indicated in figure 13. The three practical functions, says Mukařovský, are subordinated to the aesthetic function in all the arts; but the aesthetic is also *potentially* involved in every human activity, including play and spontaneous drama.[17] This paradox of the fourfold knowledge structure of art descends from the ancient quaternity and is a forerunner of Greimas's semiotic square.

Mukařovský, by relating aesthetic knowledge to the collective unconscious of Jung, says that the work of art is a sign that cannot be identified with the consciousness of the artist, with any state of mind of the perceiver, or with the work of art viewed as an artifact. From Mukařovský's perspective:

The work of art exists as an "aesthetic object" located in the consciousness of an entire community. The perceivable artifact is merely, by relation with this immaterial aesthetic object, its outward signifier; individual states of consciousness induced by the artifact represent the aesthetic object only in terms of what they all have in common.

Every work of art is an autonomous sign composed of: [1] an artifact functioning as perceivable signifier; [2] an "aesthetic object" which is registered in the collective consciousness and which functions as "signification"; [3] a relationship to a thing signified.[18]

Figure 13
Mukařovský's Knowledge Functions of Art

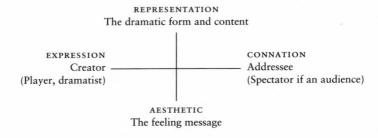

REPRESENTATION
The dramatic form and content

EXPRESSION
Creator
(Player, dramatist)

CONNATION
Addressee
(Spectator if an audience)

AESTHETIC
The feeling message

This view has some parallels with my previously stated position[19] that a work of art, viewed as an aesthetic object, oscillates between the subjectivities of the creator and the perceivers.

The stage, as Petr Bogatyrev showed, transforms all things, giving them a signifying power that they lack in the actual world. Veltruský repeated: All that is on the stage is a sign.[20] But when we know such things artistically, we also know them mundanely, and this applies as much to the actor's presence, movement, and speech as it does to physical objects. This form of artistic knowing is indirect in the naturalistic theatre, but direct in that of Brecht.

Theatre conceived as a sign is complex, but Veltruský's analysis of the pictorial sign[21] (see figure 14) has some interesting implications for all artistic signs. There are differences between:

- a linguistic sign, where the signifier and signified are connected by contiguity (metonymy); and
- the ways whereby the signifier and signified are related within various forms of art.

Like E.H. Gombrich,[22] Veltruský says that art objects do not have one meaning but a whole range of meanings. The knowledge they provide is full of feeling; it is more symbolic than metaphoric. Knowing through ritual or theatrical art is as culture-bound as language; the signifier/signified relationship, however, can be freely changed by the creative artist.

In the arts of performance, artistic and aesthetic knowing parallel each other. A performative sign gives many secondary meanings, including:

- *Selection*
Signs are selected to provide a heightened form of knowing.

Figure 14
Veltruský's Quaternity of Artistic Knowledge

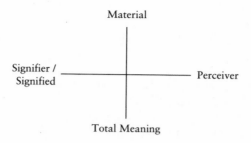

- *Polysemy*
  The signs selected generate a potentially unlimited range of cultural knowledge with a resulting ambiguity of meaning.
- *Self-reference and social reference*
  The sign refers internally to the performance itself (the fiction) and to the society within which it is performed.
- *Subjective/objective variation*
  A dagger can be part of a costume (objective) or it can also signify murder (subjective). This is related to "foregrounding": a sign can be a major part of the audience's attention, or it can be distanced.[23]
- *Aesthetic*
  Performance is aesthetic *sui generis*. It is constituted of and conveys feelings. It results from human choice and judgment and makes a qualitative statement about human life.

Each of these elements affects both artistic knowing and knowing within social interactions.

This is particularly so with deixis – elements of "languages" that point or indicate something. For example, linguistic deixis includes pronouns ("I," "you," "this," "that") and adverbs ("here," "now"). Other examples include pointing with a finger, or the knock on a door which indicates that someone is outside.[24]

Deixis in theatre is an originating sign. For example, "The Vaunt" ("I am ...") tells us that theatre is about to emerge from ritual – as in Greek tragedy with Aeschylus, the English Mummers' Play, or the Japanese *Noh*. Two Vaunts together indicate that the protagonist and antagonist meet. Yet, paradoxically, while deixis is clearly an element of artistic meaning and knowing, it is also a key factor in dramatic social interaction. The notion "I/here/now" is a given in human communication: in life as much as in theatre art it is implied in each person's talk, bodily expressions, gestures, and presence. *Deixis materializes the actor's fictional world*; it emphasizes that his or her utterance, body, and gesture are also part of the actual, mundane world to some degree. Both coexist to the actor and also, if the interaction is successful, to the other in the exchange. In these circumstances, both are aesthetic and feeling-laden.

Different from the Prague School, John Dewey insists that we go from the aesthetic in daily experience to the aesthetic in works of art.[25] He rejects the isolation of art from human experience as a whole, stressing that aesthetic knowledge may appear in all kinds of experience. Thus Arnold Berleant can say that the aesthetic is not a separate kind of experience from others but is rather a mode in which experience may occur – "it is misleading to conceive of art as a form or source of knowledge."[26]

While it is true that art does not provide knowledge in the sense of some absolute "truth," there is clearly a continuity between aesthetic and artistic knowing. Moreover, for those who create or appreciate works of art it *is* "a way of knowing": it creates meaning that changes feeling because the symbols of art, based on similarity and contiguity (metaphor and metonymy), are externalized in the world through meaningful actions.

FEELING AND SEMANTICS

The relation of feeling to meaning raises the issue of semantics. Semantic systems are groups of ideas that

- convey similar meanings to those holding similar beliefs;
- are part of a semantic universe which we create;
- are framed by a certain view and range of feelings, both of the world and of human experience;
- are two kinds – discursive and fundamental semantics – which are activated by all types of dramatic acts in play, improvisation, the use of social roles, ritual, and theatre.

Discursive Semantics

This system works at a purely practical level. It involves a double process (called "actorialization" by Greimas)[27] that distinguishes actors in the network of interpersonal relationships as [1] themes and [2] figures. Practical meaning is conveyed through themes. It is not the abstract theme of "freedom" which is used; rather, it is freedom as a theme that is understood *in specific aspects of human experience* – practical beliefs established by the semiotic system of the believer and/or the authority. Figures ascribe a value to a belief. Themes are manifested in figures, personages, or specific instances, which associate these values with other dimensions of the belief system.

In *Drama and Intelligence* we discussed the parable of the Good Samaritan cognitively. But in semantic terms, what the hearers believe after the parable is told (the discursive semantics) is the integration of two semantic systems that are in sharp conflict with one another. Jesus' semantic system gives positive value to the secular realm but negative value to the religious realm – the reverse of the semantic system held by the original listeners. Jesus' values are exemplified in the thematic roles of the Samaritan (secular) and the Priest and the Levite (religious); and then by figures in the actions that manifest "compassion" (by the Samaritan) and "indifference" (by the Priest and Levite). The first listeners accepted the fiduciary contract with the speaker, and integrated their original semantic system with the semantic system of Jesus.[28]

A similar situation arises in improvisation when fundamental values are challenged. Talk to prepare the play, while initially it may be taken on faith, has to conform to the players' subsequent experience for them to adopt it. It must fit the concrete situations which the player sees as realistic. Then it no longer has merely tacit meaning. It becomes "objective" knowledge *to the player*: knowledge that has been tested.

Contemporary multicultural conurbations provide a further illustration. The initial semantic system of the incoming cultural group meets with that of the receiving culture and (in the same way as with the parable) a new discursive system results, but varying with each person. The implications for improvisation with players from different ethnic groups, separately or together, are obvious.

We have seen elsewhere[29] that aesthetic and artistic programs in schools (such as creative drama) improve students' perception, awareness, concentration, self-concept and confidence, thought style, expression, inventiveness, and motivation. All are personal underpinnings to practical beliefs, and all programs that intend to improve such qualitative changes also aim to produce a new discursive semantic system in relation to artistic knowledge.

In addition, continuous artistic learnings in such programs aim to produce new aesthetic semantic systems.

Fundamental Semantics

Fundamental semantics operate at a deep level; they are more tacit and unconscious than discursive semantics. To put this in Stanislavsky's

Figure 15
The Quaternity of Fundamental Semantic Systems

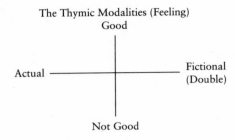

The Thymic Modalities (Feeling)
Good

Actual ———————————— Fictional
(Double)

Not Good

terms, they are the subtext of the dramatic action. That is, they lie beneath discursive semantics. In simple terms, discursive semantic systems relate to practical and surface levels of meaning; e.g., the storyline, themes, characters. In theatrical art these are meanings the audience can discuss later. Fundamental semantic systems relate to unconscious levels of meaning; e.g., meanings that players/audience gain tacitly.

Fundamental semantic systems are based on a continuum of perspectives addressed from two poles: [1] The double is the particular perspective on what is actual/fictional, or the difference between "being" and "seeming" ("the veridictory modalities" for Greimas); and [2] feeling is the particular perspective on what feels "good" and what feels "not good" (pleasure/pain for some Freudians; "the thymic modalities" for Greimas). In other words, doubling and feeling provide "the deep structure" of belief systems, including those revealed by dramatic acts. (See figure 15.)

Transformation

All the quaternities we have been using in this book have been perspectives on Greimas's semiotic square (described in *Drama and Intelligence*): a map of what Greimas takes to be the logical structure of reality, the points of which are fundamental categories of that reality.[30] As a quaternity can be a map of any of the modalities of Being, the square is what Umberto Eco has termed "an ontological structuralism." Thus an interpretation of the square in terms of both metaphor and dramatic action is given in figure 16. On this square, an improvisation can be mapped moment to moment. In a scenario, for example:

Player X and Player Y are both fishermen (similarity) but while X is successful Y is not (differentiation). Y blames X for his lack of success (opposition) but X ignores Y and accepts a prize for his success (contiguity).

Figure 16
The Quaternity of Metaphor and Dramatic Action

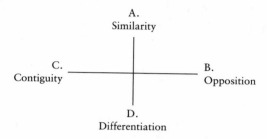

If this is improvised, then figure 16 implies the relations of contrasts, contradictions, and complementarities. (This is a simplistic example given for clarification purposes.)

In practical reality, things are not as easy as this. For example, in applying Greimas's square to literary analyses of Conrad, Balzac, and others, Jameson is frequently able to articulate a concept in only three of the four available positions, the final position [C] remaining an enigma.[31] In such a case, two possibilities arise: either [C] is replaced with concrete content (the direct or constitutional model), or it may take the form of a search for the "negation of a negation" (the transformational model).[32] While both alternatives are important, transformation has particular significance for felt-meaning and dramatic acts.

Transformation takes cultural and, therefore, arbitrary relationships (e.g., blonde vs. brunette) and transforms them into an equipolent relationship; that is, by opposing the negative to the positive (e.g., masculinity *versus* femininity).[33] What is important here is that *it is transformation at the fourth position [C] that is the source of creativity.* Greimas says that this happens by "exploding" the negative term into its complex structure, which is then dissociated "into a disjunctive category"[34] which *generates another semiotic square through synergy.* The result is "neither pure contiguity nor logical implication"[35] but dialogue.

From this we can understand that *transformation makes affirmation into dialogic assertion.* Thus in dramatic acts it is usually contiguity [C] that is transformed and creates a new interrelationship (dialogic and/or dramatic) in a new semantic system.

Actants

A unique quality of Greimas's work is his use of the terms "semes" for units of meaning, and "actants" for their functional equivalents (the two being a parallel to myth/ritual and story/action). This is very revealing of the issues addressed here.

Actants are meaning-units in operational practice: they act in the real world somewhat like actors. There are six actants and they work in the following ways:

subject	*versus*	object
sender	*versus*	receiver
helper	*versus*	opponent

In terms of language, actants are "rightfully anterior to predicates" but they correspond to syntactic categories:

subject	*versus*	direct object
subject	*versus*	indirect object
adverbial modifiers[36]		

Significantly, *the actant processes are essentially dramatic.* That is, they are both the "drama" of the combination of relationships, and the "spectacle" of space and the spectacular. By so describing dramatic acts in time and space, Greimas metaphorically views actants as actors. They can, for example, take on roles: "The distribution of roles to the actants establishes the message as an objectivizing projection, the simulator of a world from which the sender and the receiver of a communication are excluded."[37] In the terms of this book, actors in roles perform dramas of knowledge and power by balancing communication and contest. In Greimas's terms, all discourse has "an essentially bi-isotopic nature."

If we reduce Greimas's six actants to the four points of the semiotic square, the nature of the doubling of dramatic action is clear.[38] Because the fourth position on the semiotic square creates transformation, dialogue and aesthetic choice, "helper *versus* opponent" functions like adverbs. Each is the centre of the drama of transformation.[39] Importantly, *such a dramatic transformation creates a discovery, but a discovery that is culturally bound.*[40] It is a qualitative act that is logically subject to reason rather than quantification.

TALKING ABOUT FEELINGS

Feelings have not been well dealt with in the research literature. It is not just that hard-nosed "number-crunchers" find them difficult; the aesthetic aspect of mind is also complex and not necessarily linguistic; and further, as feeling infuses the whole organism, it does not respond well to most social science research methods. Many, but not all, semioticians usually discuss issues from the perspective of language; almost universally they have ignored feeling, and specifically in dramatic acts. Their discussions take place mostly in a metalanguage, spoken or written, where they regard writing as the prime way of understanding, say, visual representation because it codifies language.

It is in that context that we should start. There are various forms of writing: picture icons for the Aztecs, arbitrary figures for the Egyptians, picture glyphs for the Mayans, cryptographs for the Chinese, and words divided into elementary parts for Western alphabets. These forms of writing are all signifiers, but they show a great range of signification, from the holistic or analogue (picture icons that are concrete, non-arbitrary, and synthetic, like visual art forms) to the digital (the alphabetical languages, which are abstract, arbitrary, and analytic). In other words, written signs have become increasingly abstract over historical time, particularly in Western societies, and less closely related to the whole mind and its mediation with the world.

The scholarly metalanguage about drama, mind, and feeling is normally alphabetic in the West: a digital code combining bits of signs, meaningless in themselves, into a whole that has increased precision and (at least potentially) limitless meaning. Then mental concepts become increasingly explicit and abstract but decreasingly concrete. Wholes, analogues, and world-views tend to be largely unconscious in the West, while the abstract and the precise tend to be more conscious. Thus ideas tend to become condensed and embedded in the mind so that their implicit meanings become increasingly unconscious and abstract.

We can contrast this with Oriental languages and art. Chinese and Japanese societies do not use alphabetical signs. Thus there are cultural differences in the way mental elements are uppermost in people's minds, East and West, and this can lead to many misunderstandings in cross-cultural communication. Those mental elements represented by Oriental art tend to be more whole and their meaning is less precise than those represented by Western art. Indeed, as forms of writing are further removed from mental structures, they are capable of higher metalevels and there is less entropy in the transmission of information.

Talking is more diffuse than writing. People generally do not talk in the way they write. It is not always realized, for example, that many people talk – in both life and improvisation – without completing their sentences. There are also verbal commonplaces, such as clichés, which act as the shorthand of talk. This often has considerable redundancy. In Tasmania, various teachers have found that student talk in improvisation is richer and more developed than in everyday conversation; specifically metaphoric and symbolic levels of language are significantly improved through dramatic activities.

People in all societies have some level of unconscious awareness behind their words. The condensation of mental structures embeds broad analogous images in people's minds: condensed structures become beliefs or expectations that work as tacit knowledge. Where there are differences, they lie in cultural tendencies. Thus in oral cultures conscious and holistic concepts predominate over digital ones. Tacit and unconscious operations are often homologous; their external representations are mostly analogic (e.g., artistic) not digital, and concrete more than abstract. But in literate cultures, conscious digital and holistic mental structures coexist: the digital, when condensed, are tacit and unconscious; the analogic become increasingly tacit and unconscious with maturation; and external representations of thought that are digital (e.g., writing) are more precise and abstract, and capable of more meta-levels, than analogic representations.

Writing fixes the continuous processes of utterance. By making static what is in flux, writing, unlike improvisation and talk, leads to boundaries, categories, distinctions, and classes that breed analysis, objectivity, and scepticism. Spoken and dramatic acts are, by comparison, more whole, more processual, less discrete, and, thereby, more complex. Writing about drama or the arts in a metalanguage can never have the same ambiguous qualities as dramatic or artistic thought expressed in action.

In fact, any representation of mind in any culture is of necessity incomplete. The difference between cultures is one of degree.

DRAMATIC SIGNS AND MEANINGS

Dramatic action is a sign system that conveys the mind's felt-meaning to others. It mediates between inner and outer and, simultaneously, it is a signal from a player (speaker/creator) that stimulates a response from others. Drama as a sign system has the following components:

- The player – sender (in language), creator (in art).
- The responder – receiver (language), percipient (art).
- The "text" – the signal of "utterance," or "work."

Drama as "a text" consists of:

- the medium within which the sign or work is contained (German, say, or "the costumed player," etc.);
- the signifier: the observable sign (e.g., the words we read, the drama we witness) and its implications;
- the signified: the content (implicit and explicit) of the sign (e.g., the "felt-meaning" of a dramatic act).

What the player (sender/creator) understands by the signified may or may not differ from what the receiver/percipient understands. There is often "a gap" between the intended and received meanings.

But as a sign system we must distinguish between dramatic functions and meanings.

Dramatic Functions

Drama as a sign system represents mind in non-discrete way. It has three functions:

- *Expressive*
  The message expresses the user's feelings as:
  – analogical/aesthetic primarily (digital/linguistic occasionally);
  – unconscious and conscious; and
  – paralinguistic (naming, grunts, gestures, etc.).
- *Descriptive*
  The message describes a particular state of affairs as:
  – linguistic;
  – dramatic and/or bodily; and
  – visual and dimensional.
- *Argumentative or explanatory*
  The message presents alternative thoughts, views, or propositions.[41]

Dramatic Meaning

As dramatic signs or messages become more complex, counter-messages arise and confusion is increasingly possible. However, the meanings inherent in dramatic messages are usually distinct. Dramatic and other actions, considered as forms of knowing, generally use a tacit or implicit *showing* rather than an explicit *telling*; thus they are more feeling-laden. From this perspective, the felt-meanings conveyed by such signs are:

- *Expressive meaning*
  These are closed systems of meaning that consist of two kinds of feeling-response: to an inner state; or to an outer object or situation.[42]
- *Descriptive meaning*
  As these presuppose a "philosophy" or world-view, they can both express inner feelings and provoke a response of three kinds: implicit/analogic; implicit/explicit; and explicit (linguistic/scientific models, maps, and diagrams).

- *Argumentative or explanatory meaning*
  These include scientific theories that explain a model, analyse dramas, or explain ideas. They are uniquely human.

These three kinds of felt-meaning are based on intuition, reason, evidence, and the juxtaposition of two or more descriptive messages.

In drama various objects, acts, and events may be juxtaposed in unusual ways: they can be infused with irony, satire, paradox, allegory, and so forth. Likewise, improvisation in the style of Keith Johnstone's "theatresports"[43] contrasts diversity to produce hilarity. Some would say that these examples demonstrate the counterposition of one "text" to another text or texts.

SUMMARY

With theatre we must not confuse the artistic and the aesthetic. The aesthetic includes the artistic. Theatrical art, viewed philosophically as an aesthetic object, oscillates between the subjectivities of the creator and the perceivers, and its knowledge functions are found in the quaternity of representation, aesthetic, expression (of the creator), and connation (of the addressee or spectator).

"All that is on the stage is a sign." The stage transforms all things, giving them a signifying power that they lack in the actual world. The performance is an autonomous sign: it is a signifier of a community's consciousness. Theatre provides a whole range of meanings that are full of feeling, and its knowledge is as culture-bound as language.

Differently, the human drama consists of aesthetic processes: imagining, felt-response to thought or actions, choice, judgment, and "as if" (dramatic) action – the aesthetic signifieds. Artistic meaning is given by theatre art, while aesthetic understanding is conveyed when we gain meaning (the signified) from the actions (signifiers) in play, creative drama, improvisation, and social role play, as well as theatre. Although there is clearly a continuity between aesthetic and artistic knowing, we *are* knowledge when we dramatize. When we *are* the active medium of a "costumed player," we create both knowing and feeling to convey them to others. Units of meaning ("semes") that become functional (as "actants") are the subtext of myth/ritual and story/action. When externalized they perform somewhat like actors; they mediate between inner and outer; and they are a sign from a player that stimulates a response from others.

Dramatic sign systems are excessively complex. They are not only full of feeling but they also continually change. With maturation, successive differentiation gives a progression from relative simplicity to complexity. Viewed structurally, this occurs through substitution: a part is substituted for a whole, and becomes a new whole.

But viewed developmentally, this same progression is formed round "trace": sameness and difference simultaneously – the neonate's first understanding. As the oscillation between part and whole (the dynamism and intention of mind) begins, metaphoric and role relations start. As "trace" evolves to similarity/difference, it becomes the fundamental mental structure.

What the hearers believe after the parable of the Good Samaritan is told (the discursive semantics) is the integration of two meaning systems in conflict. Similarly, improvisation challenges people's fundamental values and meanings. A new system must conform to the players' subsequent experience if they are to adopt it. Then it no longer has merely tacit meaning. It becomes "objective" felt-knowledge *to the player*: knowledge that has been tested.

Deixis materializes the fictional world of the human actor. For those who create or appreciate dramatic activity, it *is* "a way of knowing" whatever form it takes. Dramatic actions, considered as forms of knowing, generally use a tacit or implicit *showing* rather than an explicit *telling*. Thus they are specifically feeling-laden.

Aesthetic processes are indicated in the dramatic doubles of implicit/explicit and actual/fictional – a quaternity structure. From this perspective, feeling is inherent in mind as a whole, in tacit and explicit ways of knowing, in the dynamism and intention that oscillate between wholes/parts of the mind, and in dramatic acts. The transformations of drama change relationships by opposing the negative to the positive. It is transformation at the fourth position on the square that is the source of creativity; it explodes into its complex structure, which generates another square through synergy. That is, drama and dialogue are inherently creative; they bring about a new interrelationship in a new felt-meaning system.

6 Feeling and Emotion

Feeling and emotion are much alike, but so far I have not directly discussed emotion in dramatic action. That is my concern in this chapter.

There is a continuum from feeling to emotion, inclusive of moods, where distinctions are made by innate qualities. Feeling and emotion are dynamics, processes that infuse both our impression and our expression. But the line between them is imprecise; there are times when we are uncertain whether we are talking of one or the other. This may disturb objective thinkers who require precise definitions. But life as we live it is not always as orderly as we may like. *Our task is to deal with reality as it exists, not as we wish it to be.* In reality, the two dynamics overlap.

Some preliminary distinctions, however, can be attempted:

- *Emotions* are affective mental activities, strong internal processes – fear, hate, love, joy, and the like – that are experienced immediately, "in the raw," as it were. When they are extremely powerful, emotions can be unreflective.
- *Feelings* are more discriminating than emotions. They are aesthetic mental activities, internal processes that are linked to cognition and lead to choice and judgment about values and quality. They may be delayed and can vary in strength.
- *Moods* lie between the affective and the aesthetic. They are "emotional feelings," or "felt-emotions," each with a powerful, particular, and implicit atmosphere.

More than in mundane life, dramatic acts can be infused by any one of these mental processes, but only one at a time. They can change gradually or with momentary swiftness.

PERSPECTIVES ON EMOTIONAL THEORY

How does the aesthetic theory of dramatic action, described in this book, relate to theories of emotion? Through most of human history no distinction was made between them; the word "aesthetic" first appeared only in 1750 and then only Kant and Coleridge used it about mental activity. Previously, aesthetic issues were addressed within theories of emotion.

Traditional Theories

Aristotle's theory of catharsis is the most famous statement about emotions and theatre: theatre purges the audience of unwanted emotions through the use of pity and fear. This theory has had isolated adherents, like Sigmund Freud and I.A. Richards. It can be used by some drama therapists, but generally it is avoided by contemporary psychologists.

Our post-Cartesian age is shot through with dualism. It is therefore understandable that an emotion carried by dramatic action has often been treated in two ways:

- as emotional disturbance (and therefore "bad") by Puritans and some behaviourists; or
- as part of our organic nature (and therefore "natural") by romantics like Rousseau and A.S. Neill.

Today the first way is not accepted (although it is implied by default by some behaviourists), but the second way can be.

When the theory of "humours" no longer provided an adequate picture of emotional life, eighteenth- and nineteenth-century mentalists found it difficult to provide a coherent theory of emotions. Herbart's view was that emotion was a mental disturbance resulting from a conflict between representations. The result was that the melodramas of the time presented discordant representations aimed at producing specific emotions in the audience. Should the spectator experience (say) sadness, this would produce tears or, *in extremis*, the organic disorders of suffering. Today we find the emotional life of melodramas almost a caricature of reality.

Other mentalists tried to show that emotion had a physical basis in the visceral nervous system. Human beings were not responsible for their passions any more than they could control circulation, digestion, and secretion. Thus for Charles Dickens people were born with a specific group of emotions; e.g., Bill Sikes is a murderer from the moment he enters *Oliver Twist* and long before he kills Nancy. Even as the twentieth century began, Wundt could say that the "bodily consequences of emotions react in their turn on the workings of the spirit."[1] Human will had little control over emotional life, and theatre audiences were said to be powerless not to respond to "the grand passions" presented in the playhouse. We can understand the Victorians, therefore, when they did not permit spontaneous drama in the classroom, but allowed some bowdlerized stage productions of Shakespeare in schools.

Freud's theory of emotion, however, presents us with a curious paradox. On the one hand, he was revolutionary in showing that the unconscious was the dramatic subtext of our waking life. It is no accident that he continually used terms drawn from drama, like "the Oedipus complex;" or that he and Stanislavsky were theorizing about their different versions of the subtext at the same time. But, on the other hand, Freud found that his subtext revealed emotional disturbance and, because he dealt only with disturbed patients, emotions were often "bad" to him.

Pragmatists and Behaviourists

Modern theories of emotion began with William James's article "What Is Emotion?"[2] He later said: "Our natural way of thinking about these strange emotions is that the mental perception of some fact excites the mental affection called the emotion and that this latter state of mind gives rise to the bodily expression. My theory, on the contrary, is that these physical changes follow directly from perception and that it is our awareness of them as they occur which constitutes the emotion."[3] Using James's terms, we could say that what we improvise as players, and what we perceive in the playhouse, make us aware of the physical changes that result, and this is emotion. Perhaps. Yet, he is right to say that there is a close connection between our inner emotions and our expression, or physical response. This is certainly the case in dramatic acts.

It is difficult to express one emotion "as if" and also experience another without losing the skills of acting. Stanislavsky told us this; all actors know it; it has been shown to be true in normal life under hypnosis;[4] and we should realize that it can affect the emotional range that can be asked of child players. But like that of the mentalists, James's theory has all the problems of introspection; the view that awareness of physical disturbance *constitutes* emotions can neither be proved nor disproved, although many objections to it were made during his life-time.[5]

More commonly today, emotion is related to action. This theory has been held by modern thinkers as influential as John Macmurray, H.J. Blackham, and Sir Karl Popper in Britain, and most pragmatists in the United States. It may be surprising, therefore, to learn that the theory of emotion as a response of an organism to a situation originated with Charles Darwin over a century ago.[6] He considered that many emo-tional responses can be explained either through their usefulness (anger frightens an enemy) or because they are remnants of behaviour found useful at an earlier stage of evolution ("the animal emotions"). This theory was natural to one who began by studying animal behaviour, and it has been followed in many research studies with animals. Yet contemporary psychologists have some sympathy with this theory, it is true, although they mostly consider that Darwin only accounts for some basic emotions. Should we completely accept his ideas, it would reduce the emotions experienced by children in improvisation, or in the playhouse, to simple responses based on their evolutionary heritage. That is clearly not the complete picture.

John Dewey, whose ideas are still fundamental to North American education, avoided dualism through his functional approach which combined the views of James and Darwin: instinct co-ordinates percep-tion and the person's reactions; perception is an active process; and an object or a situation is perceived not only as such but also with its emo-tive value. That is, in Dewey's theory, we perceive a tiger not only as a tiger but also as a dangerous animal; or, when we witness a murder on stage, it is not only a murder but also an act containing for us some emotional content.

What sort of content is that? For Dewey emotion is contextual: "The mode of behaviour is the primary thing and the idea and the emotional excitation occur at one and the same time ... [emotions] represent the tension of stimulus and response in the coordination which determines the behavioural modality."[7] Every act has this double aspect for Dewey. Yet emotion only occurs when instinctive, normal, or voluntary action is thwarted. To fight a tiger or to run away from it, Dewey says, produces no emotion when these acts are normally accomplished (*sic!*). But if conflicts arise ("Will the tiger eat me?") then we experience emo-tion. Dewey says, "The emotion is, psychologically speaking, the adjustment or tension between habits and the ideal, and the organic changes which take place in the body are the literal working out in physical terms of this struggle for adjustment."[8]

This theory of emotion has had a remarkably long history and it underlies the work of many contemporary American aestheticians, like Harry S. Broudy and Eugene F. Kaelin. If they and Dewey are correct, the emotion we experience in an audience arises from dramatic situations which bring about conflicts within ourselves – when the plot and the characters create such turmoil within us that only an emotional response can bring about an adjustment. Then educational theatre becomes a genuinely educative enterprise if it provides children with the opportunity for emotional education without direct experience of disturbing events.

Dewey's theory, however, has much more difficulty in accounting for our emotions as improvisers. If, in spontaneous drama, there is so much turmoil within us that only an emotional response can bring about an adjustment, improvisation becomes therapeutic. But is it, then, viewed as educational? People, particularly teachers, respond differently to this question. This may, perhaps, partly account for why spontaneous drama is more frequent (per head of school population) in Britain and the Commonwealth than in the United States, and why drama therapy practice is more common in America than in the Commonwealth.

Behaviourists went further than Dewey. For John B. Watson, emotion does not matter very much (it did not even warrant a theory!) because it is the reaction of an organism: "A hereditary pattern of responding which involves profound changes of the physical mechanism as a whole and particularly of the visceral and glandular systems."[9] Thus emotions (in life, dramatic life, or in the playhouse) are the simple reactions of the organism. Such a theory has come forward among many behaviourists, particularly B.F. Skinner,[10] whose influence has been considerable. But this theory is simplistic: it is fundamentally physiological, and it cannot account for the differences between emotions felt by individuals within the same improvisation or audience.

Theory of the Unconscious

Freud's theory of the power of unconscious emotions, and his practice of psychoanalysis that resulted, were adapted and changed by others. Pierre Janet, the influential French psychopathologist, for example, considered that emotion arose directly from perception.[11] It was, for him, "bad" – "above all a disorganizing power" that causes loss of memory, disturbance of habits, and a substitution of easy actions for more difficult ones. Yet, despite the pathological content of Janet's work, he clearly showed that emotion was the reaction of the total personality – physiological and psychological – to situations which it finds difficult. This theory was shared by many French social scientists at the beginning of the twentieth century, and, as a result, new theories in French were not forthcoming for nearly fifty years.

It is only recently that research about emotion in dramatic expression has begun in French by Roger Deldime at Brussels, the late Richard Monod at the Sorbonne, and Gisèle Barret at the University of Montreal. For these researchers in *expression dramatique*, the relation of dramatic action and emotion has specific qualities: light/dark and good/bad dynamics based on similarities not oppositions; strong links to the unconscious and creativity; easy adaptability from dramatic media to other media; and a functional relation to the human organism.[12] The emotional theory of *expression dramatique* goes beyond education per se to include theatre, therapy, and other practical areas.

Theories of unconscious emotion are also significant in psychotherapy, particularly among the practices of drama therapists that reveal a theory as a subtext. This has slowly evolved during the twentieth century. It began with Jacob L. Moreno's psychodrama,[13] which had its own rich theory. In Moreno's view, patients in psychotherapy responded more in improvised action than in lying on the analyst's couch and talking. Action was primary (it even included talk) because it was based on the spontaneity of creativity. From the 1920s, first in Vienna and then in New York, Moreno's patients acted out their problems in theatrical style; parts of their own personality, or significant people in their story, were roles taken by Moreno's assistants. His was a socio-interactional theory of emotion: the self is a total of social and private roles that the person plays in his/her interaction with others, and spontaneous performance has a cathartic effect.

However, Moreno developed a whole series of highly structured techniques which others thought too confining. The result was related, but different, theories of emotion which are used dramatically in therapeutic practices:

- *Gestalt therapy*
  "Fritz" Perls, a former Freudian and psychodramatist, adapted Moreno's use of self-presentation from theatrical contexts to life situations.[14] That is, he moved his theory of emotions from theatre to drama. Many of his strategies were based on the alternation of whole/part by the player in the playing; e.g., the patient faced an empty chair where "a significant other" in his/her story was imagined to sit; the patient addressed the imagined person; or was "as if"

the imagined person talking to the self. Such strategies enabled the patient to release "bad" emotions in a fictional context.

- *Existential therapy*

  Here the patient-therapist dyad is a mutality: there are two living human beings, not one confronting a faceless objective scientist. As in Buber's theory of "I and Thou" (not "I and It"), patients are treated as whole human beings, and the patient-therapist relation is dramatic. R.D. Laing assumes that unwanted emotional disturbances are imposed by society, while Rollo May stresses Will to overcome dysfunctions.[15]

- *Drama therapy*

  At the end of the twentieth century there is a whole profession of drama therapists who eclectically use any dramatic technique (psychodrama, improvisation, etc.) if it suits the need of the patient – the kernel of the method.[16] The theoretical assumptions are that all dramatic activity [a] is natural and inherently beneficial to psychological health; [b] can develop an appropriate emotional balance in everyone; and [c] is valuable for

  – medical contexts (diagnosis and cure); and
  – educational contexts (helping others to fulfil their potential).

Developmental Theory

Functionalism was inherent in the theory of the developmental psychologist Susan Isaacs,[17] but in a highly positive way. Her view was that children's growth and development were thoroughly dependent upon early emotional life: there was an appropriate emotional balance in babies and very young children which, rarely achieved, could be compensated for by dramatic play. In other words, *dramatic play was essential for personal and social growth.* London University established the first Institute of Education around her research, which, with her classic works of the early 1930s on the intellectual growth and social development of children, had a great influence on:

- the views of teachers and teacher educators in Britain and the Commonwealth for many years;
- practitioners of "the primary method" and "the play way";
- those who propagated "child-centred education"; and
- specialists in baby care, like Sylvia Brody and Benjamin Spock.

By extension we can say that, for Susan Isaacs, both improvisers and audience members are satisfied or not according to how dramatic action matches their own emotional needs.

Isaacs worked alongside the psychoanalyst Melanie Klein.[18] Klein's theories of the effect of emotion on the development of dramatic play with very young children grew in influence over time. She discovered that, in the first six months of life, the baby achieved two types of emotional identification:

• projective, which provides empathy; and
• introjective, which provides the capacity to "put oneself in another person's shoes" – the earliest form of dramatization and symbolization.

Other psychotherapists who made contributions to emotional theories of dramatic play in mid-century included Anna Freud, Erik Erikson, Eric Berne, and Roberto Assagioli.

Klein's developmental pattern was extended most recently by David Winnicott,[19] who worked out of the Tavistock Clinic, London. He shows that from about six months, the baby plays with "the mediate object" – a soft toy or a piece of cloth ("a cuddle") to which s/he is emotionally attached. The baby puts it in and out of the mouth, relating inner to outer; drops it deliberately so that it can be picked up; and finally gives it to the mother so that she can give it back. The inner and outer are emotionally linked in an act of love. It is from Winnicott's innovation in the developmental theory that we can say that drama provides "mediate knowing": meaning centres in a medium from which subjective and objective meaning emerge.

Elsewhere I have shown[20] that the growth of identification and the use of "the mediate object" come to a climax at about ten months of age with "the primal act." At this stage, the baby performs his/her first act of Being "as if": using identification, empathy, and, now, the self as a mediate object, the baby acts "as if" s/he is the mother. Then dramatic play proper begins; the particular balance of mediate/subjective/objective knowledge becomes unique to each person. This attempt at an emotional balance continues in developmental stages where dramatic acts are the developmental unifier; i.e., they unify personal, social, intellectual, emotional, aesthetic, and psychomotor growths of the total organism.

The major contemporary educational psychologist who addresses the emotional and aesthetic issues of imagining and dramatizing is Otto Weininger,[21] a Canadian. For him, imagination is the "what if" and dramatic play is the "as if." In many research studies about the play of young children, he has followed the Klein-Winnicott tradition and he currently edits the *Journal* of the Melanie Klein association. He has discovered that dramatic play originates at about six months when the baby first attempts to "feed" the mother; that, immediately after "the primal act," the child uses an object for other than the thing it is – which parallels the "projected play" described by Peter Slade;[22] and that dramatic play demonstrates the growth and changes of symbolism, representational thought, social and emotional growth, linguistic development, and so on. Weininger and his graduate students have successfully expanded the basic theory into many new realms so that a significant body of research is now available.

Structuralism and Existentialism

Susan Isaacs's developmental views were countered by Jean Piaget.[23] He was much less interested in emotions but focused upon children's cognition ("scientific thinking"), which suited the educational concerns of our mechanical age. Piaget's developmental psychology is structural, but is disappointing with regard to emotions and dramatic play. This may account for recent adverse reactions to his psychology. Another reason may be the contemporary trend not to accept General Theories of psychology. Freud, James, Dewey, Piaget, and others accounted for emotion within such all-inclusive theories. But Kleinians and other modern psychotherapists are more likely to study particular contexts – to examine emotion in *this* case or *that*, and to limit the generalizabilty of their work.

These limitations did not affect the existential philosopher-playwright Jean-Paul Sartre, who made a unique, extensive, and important contribution to the theories of emotions, feelings, and mind.[24] He says that when we are conscious, we are always conscious of some *thing*. Imagining is based upon perceiving: what I imagine transforms the object I originally perceived. Thus, my imagination functions as a relationship between my inner self and the object or situation – mediately.

Likewise, emotions are always about some *thing*: they are always object-centred, and their purpose is to transform the world so that I can work with it. Sartre says that imaginings and emotions are actions, ways of working on ourselves. Imagination, by relating emotion and knowledge, brings about an *affective-cognitive synthesis*: the imagination of the spectator co-ordinates the knowledge and emotion derived from perceiving some *thing* on the stage and unifies them in a synthetic way. Our imagination enables us to have knowledge, emotion, and feeling about dramatic events, and to unify these in a new species of knowledge. By extension, therefore:

• theatre for children is an educative process – it is a key way in which the young receive epistemological and affective training (in agreement with Dewey); and

- spontaneous dramatic action in improvisation and life roles:
  - expands imaginative potential;
  - synthesizes emotion and cognition in action;
  - provides a unique kind of knowing that is felt.

While Sartre denied the unconscious, his psychological philosophy rests on a background of Freud, Heidegger, and a detailed practical knowledge of dramatic action.

NEURO-PHYSIOLOGY

The research findings of neurophysiology are mainly of little relevance to our immediate concerns here, and will be dealt with briefly. But they do have some implications that are important to the relation of emotion and dramatic action.

We should note, first, that physiologists have observed that certain physical reactions, like respiration, pulse-rate, blood pressure, and so on, increase long before the person consciously experiences emotion. Similarly, psychologists have discovered that pupil dilation signals emotional arousal and interest, and the reverse occurs immediately prior to solving a problem. There are different levels of activation of behaviour, and emotion corresponds to a very strong activation. It is obvious to all drama workers that the more active the improvisers, the greater their emotional involvement in the activity. Many drama teachers, together with theatre directors like Grotowski,[25] use "warm up" activities prior to dramatic activity to prepare for playing.

It is now possible to map the levels of consciousness from deepest sleep to rage or fear through electro-encephalography and other methods. Older theories saw behaviour as dependent on the level of arousal, which may increase progressively from sleep to paroxysms.[26] These studies may be useful to physiologists, but within dramatic action arousal only has significance when related to behaviour in particular events.

For dramatic purposes it is no longer necessary to consider emotion as an isolated phenomenon. Emotion is only one aspect of activity among players and audience members; it should be incorporated within a total holistic perspective. The issue of capturing people's interest hardly applies in drama where the activity itself is inherently interesting.

We have seen (see figure 10) that there are two gross structures to the brain: the upper levels where intelligence and reason are located; and the lower brain common to both human beings and the animals where the major emotions are centred. Research in this field is paradoxical. New studies reverse prior findings, even rendering them useless – and research tends to present fresh evidence day by day. Despite the resulting confusion, data show that the following items are of considerable interest to us:

- *Drama and hemispheric balance*
  Most school activities stress the left hemisphere, but spontaneous drama and the arts emphasize the right. They are thus a welcome difference for students; they motivate them by providing a change. Simultaneously, drama works for hemispherical balance and thus provides a necessary complement to other schoolwork.

  Primary emotions (such as rage) are produced in the cerebral trunk, but emotional reactions depend on the rhinencephalic formations which have both inhibitory and activating roles. Spontaneous drama appears to activate the centres of emotion, which are controlled as a whole by the neoencephalon. This has a double function:
  – it greatly increases the number of stimuli that produce emotions through use of the cortex; and
  – it adapts emotions to the particular situation.
  Properly guided, educational drama activities have built-in controls which allow for the development of both functions.
- *Drama and association*
  Emotional reactions are characteristic of the highly developed association zones. Associative centres are reserves of nervous energy; they are liberated by emotions; and then they affect motor activity.

  The improviser "thinks on the feet," and to achieve well s/he must have continual practice with externalizing associations and controlling the liberated emotions. The child spectator, having many associative centres which can be stimulated to carry emotional significance, is sensitive to the atmosphere of the playhouse and is capable of imagining the present and future consequences of the plot.
- *Adaption of lower emotions to higher brain functions*
  The primitive forms of the primary emotions depend on excitation of the lower brain but become highly complicated by the associative centres of the upper brain. According to Koestler, this indicates a need for education to concentrate upon adapting the lower emotions for specific human purposes. Spontaneous drama and theatre provide highly effective instruments for such intentions.

MOTIVATION

Drama teachers do not, like others, have to design many strategies to motivate students. Players are self-motivated *sui generis*. I have examined the principles of motivation elsewhere,[27] and it remains to consider the effect of emotions on improvisers' motivations.

Mihaly Csikszentmihalyi tells us that motivation

is the ability to find rewards in the events of each moment. If a person learns to enjoy and find meaning in the ongoing stream of experience, in the process of living itself, the burden of social controls automatically falls from one's shoulders. Power returns to the person when rewards are no longer relegated to outside forces.[28]

It is how we look at things that motivates us. As the emperor Marcus Aurelius wrote, "If you are pained by external things, it is not they that disturb you, but your own judgment of them. And it is within your power to wipe out that judgment now." In other words, the alternatives of boredom and motivation are within our own control.

It is a commonplace in educational drama that events that can bore students in real life may often, when dramatized, actively engage the attention of improvisers. Students who are bored in school usually become highly motivated in an improvisation based on school life, and those bored by a text they are studying suddenly come alive when it is dramatized. A teacher's change of strategy from normal methods of instruction to the dramatic method can be highly effective. This accounts for the power of educational drama over the extrinsic learning necessary when students are working in non-drama subject matters.

Motivation is only found when emotions are strong. "E-motion" means to "move" one "out of oneself." Emotion and motivation can stir the organism, and emotion and feeling can stimulate motivation. Motivation at a sufficient level is essential if improvisers are to create their drama well, or if the audience member is to deal with the problems set by the stage action. But what is "a sufficient level"? What is "too much"? and what is "too little"?

If the player is too strongly motivated, he or she is unable to adapt well to these events. When a child overreacts in the playhouse, he or she is over-motivated; there is a maximum degree of motivation above which emotional disturbance appears so the child cannot adjust to dramatic and theatrical situations. One example will serve. In a production for a school of Brian Way's participation play *Mirror Man*, the actor-teachers' control of the audience was faulty and the young children's anger at the witch bubbled over. It became so great that they chased the actress off stage and she had to hide in the women's toilet for safety!

We have known throughout the twentieth century that emotional reactions are inversely proportional to the ability of the higher centres of the brain to meet a given situation.[29] Or as Otto Fenichel phrased it, "an emotional reaction which is abnormally intense is derived from something which had formerly been repressed ... emotional attacks occur when the normal control of the ego has become inadequate through [a] an abnormal influx of excitation; or [b] a previous blocking of the discharge flow."[30] Csikszentmihalyi has recently indicated[31] that this old evolutionary idea, far from being dead, is alive and well at the end of the twentieth century.

Whatever the theoretic explanation, it is quite clear from both experience and research that there are certain contexts where emotion can strongly affect motivation. For example:

- emotion activates motivation when people are in interaction compared with when they are lonely, even if being alone is the person's own choice;[32]
- many talented teenagers fail to develop their skills, not because they have cognitive deficits, but because they react emotionally against being alone; they are not motivated to practise on their own, so they are left behind by their peers who are.[33]

From this we may conclude that:

- interaction with others, as in dramatic activities, assists emotions that positively affect motivation; and
- under negative conditions, interaction with others can so reduce emotion that motivation is lessened.

It is clear that "a sufficient level" of emotion and the particular context are parameters for adequate motivation. Thus workers in educational theatre know that, at any particular moment, there is "a sufficient level" of emotion to motivate the audience; but at another moment there is not. Precisely what this level is, however, is an assessment that the players must make as they act in the "here and now." This underlines the necessity for good training of the players, and supports Brian Way's view that, for Theatre for Young Audiences (TFYA) and Theatre-in-Education (TIE), there is a strong case to be made for expert training of actor-teachers.

An intense level of emotional stimulation harms our efficiency and reduces motivation.[34] Children showing the greatest strain (as measured by dynamographic pressure) are those who give the poorest performance. This indicates that there is an optimum of tension if a child player is to improvise well, and gives support to what has been said above about children who are to adapt well to a performance. It also shows that the quality of an improvisational experience (experience in the aesthetic mode) improves with the players' increased motivation, yet only up to a certain point: when children are excessively motivated their adaptation deteriorates. Malmo has shown[35] that this deterioration is influenced by the nature of the task at hand: a slowing-down where the dramatic pace is fast; confusion when the performance requires thought.

We also have other evidence about the motivation of children when they are members of an audience, as follows:

- Students with weak motivation display little feeling/emotion when confronted by a difficult play.

  This has been observed in a number of situations: among non-European ethnic groups and native peoples when the performance has a strong European theme or content; among less able children and those with mental dysfunctions when the performance has been beyond them, and so forth.
- An easy play requires strong motivation from the audience in order for them to stick with it.

  This is commonly observed when a play is performed before children with a wide age range. This is why many dramatists for TFYA prepare their play for a narrow age range.
- Strong motivation is usually linked to strong feelings of identification and empathy with one or more characters.

  Identification and empathy are the internal keys to dramatic action. Good dramatists in TFYA aim primarily for these emotions.

Emotions of improvisers or an audience may be considered as their form of adaptation to the dramatic or theatrical situation. When a child at home discovers that his/her emotional responses can exert an influence over the family circle, s/he can use these responses as a weapon on those around him/her. A child of five said "I shall go on crying until you give it to me."[36] Similar situations are observable in the improvisations of those who have emotional dysfunctions where similar weapons can be used by the players, or by the roles the players perform. In life, emotion becomes a social form of behaviour.[37] This occurs through dramatization and imitation, which take on the functions of language that have more emotional significance than mere words. Children can also use emotion in a social way when they are members of an audience; for example, by group reactions which can become contagious if their feeling, emotion, or motivation is not captured by the performance.

With children of special populations, drama teachers often come across two forms of emotional disturbance in improvisation: [a] the use of organic upset to influence others (e.g., tears in the hope of pity, signs of fear which are in effect a call for help); and [b] reorganization of behaviour which transforms emotional responses into those relatively adapted to the situation.[38] Drama therapy aims to correct the first but it is the latter at which theatre both by and for children aims: if such behavioural change is achieved then drama and theatre provide an adequate education of the emotions.[39]

If improvisers or audience members are unable to control their emotions, they direct them in such a way as to gain some benefit to themselves. They are increasingly able to control their emotions with maturation. Yet, at any age, lack of control may occur whenever a person is subjected several times to a difficult situation. To begin with, the person has conflicting feelings. In drama therapy, however, the predominant emotions are integrated into the individual's defence system and, in some instances, can be replaced by totally adapted behaviour. This has significance in two ways:

- *Children as performers*
  Children's plays, creative drama and improvisation show increasing degrees of adaptation to difficult emotional situations. Forms of spontaneous drama reflect not only the children's attempts to "try out" possible futures but also to "act out" emotional difficulties in their past. Theatrical performances by adolescents (adding the element of communication to the qualities of purely spontaneous drama) allow them to experience a range of emotional experiences which, as fictions, increase their abilities to face and adapt to difficult emotions.
- *Children as audience*
  TFYA can further this adaptation by providing situations of even greater emotional difficulty which, because they are witnessed and not enacted, can be faced more readily. Yet, at the same time, performing companies must take care to present those emotions which are most suitable to the age range of the audience members. This is not say that TIE teams should or should not confront their audiences; but it is to say that these teams should know what they are doing, and have good reasons for engaging the students' emotions. In such ways, theatrical performances can educate the social use of the emotions.[40]

SUMMARY

For dramatic purposes it is no longer necessary to consider emotion as an isolated phenomenon. Emotion is only one aspect of activity among players and audience members; in practice and theory it should be incorporated within a holistic perspective.

Emotion infuses both our thought and our dramatic expression. As a general rule, both improvisers and audience members are satisfied or not according to how dramatic action matches their own emotional needs.[41] Emotion is part of dramatic action for a plurality of purposes, some of which are:

- to let off steam (catharsis);
- to work as the unconscious subtext of our waking life;
- to activate a response through our actions or expression;
- to adjust our inner conflicts through dramatization (to "act out" emotional difficulties);
- to improve mental health and emotional balance;
- to activate the alternation of whole/part by the player;
- to transform our perceptions of the world so that we can work with it;
- to bring about an affective-cognitive synthesis;
- to unify imagination, knowledge, and feeling into a new species of knowledge through dramatic expression;
- to motivate students by providing a change;
- to work for hemispherical balance through drama activities;
- to promote and control externalized associations;
- to "try out" possible futures through drama;
- to allow "a sufficient level" of emotion in a particular context for adequate motivation;
- to promote adjustments to contexts, including adaptation to the dramatic or theatrical situation;
- to change how we look at things;
- to aid maturation.

The last purpose is an important instance of where emotion should be seen in a holistic context. Dramatic play is essential for personal and social growth, but it is as much aesthetic and cognitive as it is affective:[42]

- in the first six months of life, the baby achieves two types of emotional identification – projective (empathy) and introjective (the earliest form of dramatization and symbolization);
- about six months, the baby plays with "the mediate object" – inner and outer are emotionally linked in an act of love where dramatic play provides "mediate knowing";
- a climax is reached at about ten months of age with "the primal act" – the baby performs his/her first act of Being "as if" and dramatic play proper begins;

- in subsequent developmental stages, dramatic acts are the developmental unifier; e.g., they unify personal, social, intellectual, emotional, aesthetic, and psychomotor growths of the total organism.

In part 1 we have examined aesthetic and affective aspects of the dramatic experience. Our task has been to look at the evidence from the practical perspective of the player.

In developmental drama our task, as described in part 2, is like that of a critic: to draw intellectual conclusions, from the evidence of practice, about the effects of feeling and emotion on dramatic events.

PART TWO

Drama and Inquiry

In part 1 I examined the living drama process: the nature of feeling *within* dramatic action. That is, in the experience itself.

In part 2 I turn to issues of developmental drama: problems that face us when we *study* cognition, feeling, and dramatic action.

What research methods can we use when we address such issues? In chapter 7 I examine a particular method of research for all of the creative arts – a way that has worked in practice. In chapter 8 I project a new research methodology for educational drama based on the hologram. Given these possible solutions to the research problems, in chapter 9 I consider the question: Is social science or another form of science appropriate for our purposes?

7 Practical Research in the Creative Arts

If educational drama is as much of feeling as it is of cognition, what does this mean for research? Most research in the social sciences is both objective and quantitative. This puts us into a quandary: with such a method, how can we study feeling which is such a vague and amorphous entity?

The result is that contemporary inquiries into the arts in general, and educational drama in particular, tend to be qualitative. There appear to be good reasons for this which we will examine here. In doing so, the intention is to improve such inquiries: to increase their value and excellence.[1]

METHOD

In social science, and specifically in education, there is a continual debate as to which research method is "proper," the quantitative or the qualitative. The position taken here, however, is that this is a non-issue. It is the nature of the question that is asked that determines the method to be used.

In the nineteenth century, all research methods were quantitative. Inquiries were based on measurement in answer to the questions, How many? and, To what extent? At that time, this was the method of the physical sciences. In the early twentieth century when human beings became the object of research, social scientists used the only method available to them: the quantitative. Slowly this was found unsatisfactory for many inquiries. Human subjects and social situations had far more variables than atoms and particles; human inquiry was more likely to ask "What is?" than "How many?" And human experience was liable to slip through the categories of quantification.

Many modern social scientists reject mechanical approaches[2] for various reasons. The original models of science followed by social scientists were not faithful imitations of the methods of actual scientists.[3] When contemporary psychology uses the model of the physical sciences it perpetrates various biases. There is no one best method for conducting research; each approach has its own strengths and weaknesses. Furthermore,

The principle of equipotentiality suggests that any good approach may have a number of useful applications... The principle of equifinality suggests that it is possible to start at different beginning points, travel different routes, employ different methods, and still arrive at the same "truth."[4]

Meta-analyses of sets of research studies find virtually no evidence of a relationship between the design of a study and its outcomes.

But those who advocate only qualitative methods fall into the same trap as "hard-nosed number-crunchers." Both assume there is only one adequate way to answer any question. Yet questions differ and require different styles of inquiry. In arts education, for example, to ask, "How many students in this music class attend live concerts?" requires a quantitative method, while, "What aesthetic learnings are obtained by students in this drama program?" will lead to a qualitative inquiry. In other cases, while the major research method may be qualitative, sub-questions may need to use a quantitative approach. All depends upon the nature of the question.

QUALITY AND THE CEQRM

In education, research should be essentially practical. The inquiry, if it is effective, will have effects upon the core of education – teacher and student meeting in a practical situation for the purpose of improving the student's learning. Qualitative research can involve feeling.

This chapter addresses qualitative research and the place of the CEQRM (Comparative-Emergent Qualitative Research Method) within it. Today, many research projects are qualitative and they are both effective and, according to clients, successful. This does not prevent some ardent quantitative researchers, as might be expected, from denying their validity. But the fact remains that clients increasingly ask for qualitative methods when human subjects and social contexts are the focus of the inquiry.

We will begin by examining the nature of qualitative research from a variety of perspectives and then relate these to arts education. Finally the specific methodology of CEQRM will be discussed.

QUALITATIVE RESEARCH

Qualitative research defies simple definition or description. It grew out of a variety of disciplines: anthropology, sociology, psychology. Researchers label their work in diverse ways, as naturalistic, ethnographic, participant observation, etc. They show differences in beliefs and assumptions, in attitudes to research methods, in the criteria to be used, and in ways to assess the research.

Major Characteristics

A qualitative researcher studies (A) qualities in (B) contexts while (C) within the event and (D) uses various methods as the context alters.

[A] *Qualities*
Qualities are characteristics of entities. Thus, "Quality is the essential character or nature of something; quantity is the amount. Quality is the what; quantity is the how much. Qualitative refers to the meaning. .. while quantitative assumes the meaning and refers to a measure of it."[5] Qualities are usually understood comparatively and relatively; e.g., "good" vs "not good"; "better" vs "worse"; etc. The questions addressed are such as:
– Is this performance good?
– What learnings do students secure in this program?

[B] *Contexts*
Qualities must be understood in a specific context, a particular situation or environment which has a considerable influence on the event(s). "What sets qualitative research apart most clearly from other forms of research is the belief that the particular physical, historical, material, and social environment in which people find themselves has a great bearing on what they think and how they act."[6] An act in one context may have a different significance in another context; that is, effectively it may *be* a different act – it may have a different meaning. The qualitative researcher looks primarily for particulars – for qualities in a specific practical setting. Emergents from these may form generalizations.

[C] *The researcher is involved in the event.*
S/he is sited in the setting, working in the living experience of the subject's context – often, but not always, as a participant. The

researcher is not distanced from what s/he studies, as with the experimentalist, so feelings are often involved. More than one perspective is used: even the simplest research project requires the viewpoint/beliefs/ purposes/interests of both the researcher and the subject, often together with their views of each other.

[D] *The researcher varies techniques as the situation changes.*

To capture the qualities of a living moment, the researcher does not allow one standardized method, but chooses one or more to suit the unique event. Many styles of inquiry are used inventively. Thus researchers may describe and justify methods as they proceed.

Use in Applied Fields

These studies are particularly useful in applied fields, such as education, where it is important to affect the practical realities of the human condition. In applied fields, the vital questions are: Will this research make a difference to practice? If not, is it worth doing? But if so, is it worth doing in this way?[7]

Quantitative methods stress internal validity: results are true according to the research design. But applied fields require studies with external validity: they must be true to the practical situations of real life.[8] Nor should we expect too much of any research. Human interactions can rarely be reduced so that we can say, "This is always the case." We grasp what may be true in the particular event. Research results can "inform" practical situations not as "proof" but as a perspective that can be of use.

Kinds of Data

All researchers seek data. In qualitative research this is usually done from observations and/or interviews. But who provides the most accurate picture of what happens, the observer or the participant? This question has occupied qualitative researchers for many years.[9] Observers provide the order of reality from the outside: they describe the phenomenal order of observed events and the acts of the participants. In contrast, participants in the events give an order of reality as elicited by the observer. The actors describe how they organize their experience in their minds, how they interpret new experience, and how they feel about it.

But, in fact, this is to create a needless dichotomy. An observer and a participant both provide a picture of reality that is valid from their perspective. The issue is not whether one is better than another but that they are different. The researcher must recognize that this is the case and use one or the other, depending upon the nature of the research question. If it is possible, both can be used. This is the case with the CEQRM.

Sampling

Data are normally obtained through samples. But what kind of samples? Measures and averages in applied fields can be useless or even counter-productive. In stage architecture, sight-lines were based for many years on the average head height of a person sitting in a seat; in the auditoria, thus, 51 per cent could see the stage clearly but 49 per cent could not![10] In social sciences, group averages not only may fail to describe real people, but also may conceal important differences among them.

Large sample sizes and an experimental design with a $N = 1$ can be useful in a survey. In applied fields this may not be necessary. By using grounded theory it may be sufficient to use a representative pilot sample of, say, ten and then augment it with another twenty. Does the picture change substantially? If not, the sample is large enough. If so, the sample may be augmented by others until the data are consistent.[11] These are contentious issues. The CEQRM has developed a particular method of sampling which will be discussed on pp. 146–7.

Preparing and Treating Data

How are the collected data prepared? The researcher prepares the observation, or what the interviewee says, in *descriptive statements*; e.g., "The teacher, Mr. X., asked the class to divide into groups." It is then subjected to "treatment," analysed in a particular way that depends on the nature of the research question. This is normally done through two kinds of generalization:

- *the empirical generalization:* an inference of the significance of what occurred; e.g., "The class taught by Mr X showed a high level of social cohesion in the art room."
- *the theoretical generalization*, which seeks to explain the former; e.g., "Social cohesion is a means towards good work in the art class."[12]

Thus the normal sequence of analysis is to move from descriptive statements to empirical generalizations, and from there to theoretical generalizations. This procedure is essentially one of logic. In the past, logical reasons were those of either induction or deduction. In contemporary logic there are more reasons than these, as we shall see below.

Inference

In analysing data, the movement from descriptive statement to generalizations is one of inference. All research relies on this. Few facts speak for themselves. They must be interpreted through inference, which needs a sound knowledge of logic, the area being studied, and the audience to receive the report. Inference is a form of "educated guessing." This is the foundation of all knowledge for Popper.[13] As "estimation" it is a basic skill in mathematics. It is the "practical hypothesis" in spontaneous improvisation and underpins the learning of hypothesis proper which, as Piaget[14] indicates, is the ground upon which abstract ("scientific") hypothesis is built. In research, it is important to keep inferences low, answering the criteria of reason and felt-meaning.

Comparison

We can make inferences in a number of ways. One of these is through the use of comparisons. In actual life as we experience it, comparison is used as a common-sense way to obtain information. "This is larger (or smaller) than that" tells us something about this and about that. In human and social situations, however, a comparison cannot provide us with a final answer: "A cat is bigger than a mouse" is true in our experience, but so is "A lion is bigger than a cat."

It is much the same in qualitative research. If the analysis of one set of data provides one set of emergents, it can be compared with the emergents from another set of data. This is liable to produce new emergents that will be of three kinds:

- those shared by both sets of data;
- those only within one set; and
- those only within another set.

The shared emergents may be regarded as "true" in *that* situation in *that* specific time. The second and third sets of emergents above may also be "true" under the same conditions – but we cannot be as certain of them as we are of the shared emergents. This use of comparisons is included in the CEQRM.

EDUCATION

What kinds of qualitative studies are normally used in education? The range of qualitative methods is so great that it is best to examine them through three typologies: research, negotiation, and ethnography.

By Research Type

Most researchers use various types of research according to the problem and the context. However, there is a revealing typology by Smith,[15] who says that there are four types of research:

Interpretive
These researchers believe that mind creates reality; that we gain social knowledge by participating in the felt-meaning that we create with others. They study the personal – the acts of the actors, and the meaning/purpose given to the acts by the actors, which can only be understood from their viewpoint; and the social – the dynamics of the reciprocal acts taken by others within an interaction. Their key question is: How are people in the immediate setting consistently present to each other as environments for one another's meaningful actions?[16]

The data consist of observations, interviews, field notes, maps, tables, and/or figures, while a report contains generalizations and assertions from reviewing the data; narrative/quotes documenting the evidence for the assertions; the frequency of occurrence of the evidence; and an interpretive commentary showing what these mean from the author's point of view.[17]

Artistic
Many studies follow an artistic approach where the primary aim is to explicate meaning rather than to establish "truth."[18] Thus:

The report is an artistic rendering, usually a narrative account, of what the researcher has discovered in the case studied. In research, the investigator seeks to experience directly the qualities inherent in the setting, appreciate the meanings held by the people there, and then represent these discoveries so that the reader can have a vicarious experience of the case.[19]

The researcher has a trained artistic intuition that appreciates, feels, and communicates the qualities of the case, and uses themes to convey to the clients the participants' felt-meaning through storytelling, narration, and dramatic and metaphoric structures. The report can be "the creation of an evocative form whose meaning is embedded in the shape of what is expressed."[20]

Eisner has stressed the artistic view as a model for research methods. Instances are fine art,[21] literary criticism,[22] journalism,[23] theatre,[24] and drama.[25] This model has been adapted to the CEQRM.

Systematic

These researchers wish not only to discover but also to verify. Seeking credibility for their work, they use criteria in two ways:

- *The Logical*
  The work of Best[26] uses the modern logic of Wittgenstein. Best acknowledges not only deductive and inductive reasons but also interpretive and moral reasons, and he uses these in an approach based on "adequate criteria in specific contexts." This methodology is "rationally objective" in comparison with the "empirical objectivity" of quantitative styles. Specifically it can be used to address such questions as: Is this performance good? and Is this arts program working? The approach has been adopted by the CEQRM.
- *The Empirical*
  Researchers may use quantitative techniques in a qualitative framework, for triangulation and replication, or for reliability and validity to assess the research. They believe that "There is a world of reality out there. The way we perceive it is largely up to us, but the world does not tolerate all understandings of it equally."[27] They select evidence from the data carefully (low inference factors, multiple researchers, etc.) to make the study "empirically objective." Their reports are discursive with logical arguments from the data. Unlike others, this method requires checks for both internal and external verification.

Theory-Driven

Those who follow conflict theories (e.g., many critical pedagogues) analyse the meanings of people's acts from a feminist or post-Marxian theory of class and power divisions of society. But those who follow structural-functional theories try to identify how schools function and are structured, and how these relate to the structure and function of society as a whole.[28]

By Types of Negotiation

Starting from the idea that education is "to invite the people to grasp with their mind the truth of their reality,"[29] Andrade[30] describes various historical and theory-driven models of school structure. Each model has specific effects upon research.

Independent Structures

Here, each teacher/student/administrator is seen as working in isolation; school events are singulars. Student problems are seen as psychological; solutions are from accepted norms, not from the values/forces of an individual in a context. Research promotes education as self-sufficient and views teachers as neutral specialists. This model is usually either oppressive, by imposing others' values, or ineffective.

Adaptive Structures

In this model, students/teachers/administrators either adapt to the status quo or help others to conform with it. They view schools and education in business, mechanical, and organizational terms. Their research is pragmatic:[31] it assumes that students "need to learn that they need to improve, and to improve means to accept and adapt to the system as it is, to be incorporated and integrated into it."[32] Teachers, as guardians of the school's status, try to change the socially disruptive behaviour of students; if they cannot, they classify them as having behavioural "problems," referring them to counsellors who make them the subjects of separate research studies.

Dialectical Structures

In this model, adults actively instigate a transformation of the school system and practices "for the benefit of all within the structure."[33] Most critical pedagogues, starting from Freire,[34] view teacher/student in a human relationship; but the teachers also reveal the assumed power relations of the school/society to the students, hoping they will make their own transformation towards a desired end. Research, through dialectic, looks for the expression of human awareness, knowledge, and bias; thus "We prepare ourselves, and others, for real democracy"[35] on the assumption that the world of objects is "really there," in the mode of the naïve realism of Lenin and Freire.

Dialogic Structures

Others use dialogue, not dialectic, as a basis for both schooling and research in an apolitical way. From Buber,[36] they assume that genuine human interaction is based on the "I and Thou." People negotiate with one another; each acknowledges the other as a person like her/himself, with the same humanity and sharing of dialogue; and persons, freely choosing and responsible, create "community" (vs "collectivity") amongst themselves. Education is an emancipatory project of teachers and students mutually;[37] each helps the other experientially in tasks, learning, and instruction.

Dialogic researchers assume that persons:

- have practical knowledge, or "know-how";[38]
- "start from where they are";[39] and
- transform their understanding of the world.

Students may make a political transformation or they may not; students and teachers will transform the world and their understanding of it in their own terms. This process differs between persons and between groups.

Data are collected by an open-ended technique (interviews and observation) with as little bias and as near an approximation to natural human dialogue as possible. The attitude is of the "I and Thou": the researcher puts him/herself "in another person's shoes," and attempts to understand experience "from the other person's point of view" – a dramatic perspective. The analysis is usually emergent, revealing the assumptions of the interviewees and/or the themes within the data.

This is the nearest model in this typology to the CEQRM.

By Types of Ethnography

Increasingly, modern researchers are using ethnographic approaches to education. But many describe the data without using a conceptual framework based on cultural theory[40] necessary to provide coherence. The major cultural theories are:

Evolutionary
Culture evolves in stages but few educational studies are directly evolutionary.[41] However, some do compare education in tribal and industrial societies[42] or cross-culturally.[43]

Functional
Culture functions by satisfying manifest human needs, and through latent functions which only the researcher sees (the origin of "the hidden curriculum" of a school and other functional ideas).[44] Human adaptation to the environment can be studied at the micro-level in single schools (often as case studies) or at the macro-level in national or international education.[45]

Linguistic
Language usage in education reveals a specific cultural reality; e.g., communicative competence,[46] the speech/culture relation,[47] and instruction.[48]

Psychological
There have been a variety of such studies: e.g., in child raising,[49] cross-cultural cognition,[50] cognition,[51] etc.

Structural
All structural approaches say that observed phenomena are instances of a general structure (hidden to the actors, revealed to the researcher) of the mental and social worlds. First thought to be merely binary or dual,[52] this is now extrapolated to a quaternity structure[53] and within aesthetic learning.[54]

Structural functionalists assume that a school's structures contribute to total educational structures.[55] Symbolic interactionists say that culture resides in the media of symbols (verbal and non-verbal) and ritual dramas,[56] leading to studies of adult-child relations,[57] preschool and home settings,[58] a case study of a school[59] and educational innovations.[60]

The conceptual framework of the CEQRM is mainly functional-structural (specifically symbolic interactionist), although it uses elements of the psychological within this framework.

CONTEMPORARY ARTS EDUCATION

As I have dealt with the full parameters of research and inquiry in arts education elsewhere,[61] only the basic issues of qualitative approaches will be discussed here. What makes qualitative research particularly applicable for feeling and educational drama?

Kinds of Program

Nowhere in education are there more misunderstandings than with arts programs. Much of this confusion is because they have changed radically in recent years. Years ago all such programs were based on the model of "the student as artist," which, as few school students became artists, influenced the public to view the arts as "frills" in schools. Such programs seemed of little direct use.

Today, however, there are two kinds of program: those for the few and those for the many. Few students will become professional artists, but those that do require special attention. These young people are the future shapers of our culture and their programs must be firmly based on skills and products. But the second kind of program is equally vital: the arts for the many in the General Program of Studies. This is based on the creative arts. Creativity and spontaneity are encouraged in a variety of art forms; even appreciation with seniors is placed in a creative context. In contrast to arts work with the few, these programs are process-oriented.

Learnings in Creative Arts Programs

The creative arts in the General Program of Studies are processual. The ongoing activity is stressed rather than any art products that result. Researchers study these processes, their goals, and the three kinds of learning they promote – intrinsic, extrinsic, and aesthetic.

Intrinsic learnings are those which improve the essential qualities of human beings; e.g., perception, awareness, concentration, uniqueness of thought style, expression, inventiveness, problem identification and solving, confidence, self-worth, motivation, and negotiation with others.[62] Learnings through the arts provide the necessary foundations for personal and social development and the generic skills required in adult work and leisure.[63]

Extrinsic learnings are those that transfer from arts learnings to those in learning in other subjects, and to life and social learning.[64] For example, intrinsic motivation learned in the arts transfers to many other tasks, say, history. "When you are seven years old and you have acted the role of Christopher Columbus, you never forget that it was *you* who discovered America."[65]

Aesthetic learnings are those that improve the qualities of feeling. Feeling is related to, but not the same as:

- cognition; e.g., the student achieves a form of tacit knowing when dancing or painting; and
- emotion; e.g., there is a feeling difference both when a tiger walks into the room (emotion) and when one contemplates a beautiful sunset (aesthetic feeling), although there are many degrees between them.

Moreover, feeling can be subject-reflexive or object-reflexive and the learnings that result consist of contrasts, semblances, harmonies, and discords in pre-adolescence, and of polarities, identities, syntheses, and dialogics in adolescence.[66] Improvements are made through the experience of choosing, and the discovery of the effect of one's choice, and through making a practical hypothesis and seeing if it works by trial and error,[67] which is the ground for later abstract hypothesis.[68]

The arts, thus, promote learning "across the curriculum" in the form of good human judgment and the ability to foresee the outcome of one's acts. To participate actively in choosing within artistic media, both individually and in groups, is to learn to work with others, to "read" them, to have empathy with them, and to take responsibility for group decisions. In the past, when these processual learnings were ignored in arts programs and products were emphasized, there could be disastrous results, as with the Nazis, or with Nero, who regarded the burning of Rome as an artistic product.

Far from being "frills," therefore, the arts lie at the core of the curriculum; they provide the fundamental qualitative learnings upon which other more conventional learnings are grounded. They are, for example, basic to "the basics." Reading is not possible without prior visual discrimination,[69] and success in two dimensions (as with writing) is not possible without the prior learnings of three dimensions like sculpture, crafts, or creative movement.[70]

Quality in Arts Programs

When we say that arts education programs provide the fundamental qualitative learnings upon which other learnings are based, what does this mean for education? What does it imply for teachers? And what effect does this have on research?

The Basis of Quality

There is a natural affinity between qualitative research and what happens in arts education. Qualitative research attempts to describe the essential character of an event or a program, while arts education works with the essential character of persons, as individuals and social beings. Both start from where people are, and who they are. The creative arts, for example, work primarily with particularities, those of the paint and canvas and those of the person in society. It is said that the arts are expressive. But expressive of what? Painting is expressive of five things:

- the personhood of the painter as an individual; it expresses who s/he is;
- the nature of the painter as a social entity; it expresses who s/he is within his society;
- the culture in which the painter lives; it expresses who s/he is within his or her specific culture;
- the paint and canvas, "the medium" is "the message" because any medium is what relates our inner to the outer, and vice versa; it expresses to others aspects of who s/he is through media; and
- feeling.

Contexts

Quality in arts education is context bound. If the depth of feeling in peoples' response to art is strongly influenced by the conventions of their culture, artistic creativity is even more so. In "the Victoria Project" we compared the play and arts processes of five- to eleven-year-old ethnic British, Chinese, and Amerindians. At five years old, only minor differences were observed. But at eleven years old we found that ethnic British students were superior in linguistic creation; native Indians were superior in movement and dance creation; and ethnic Chinese (from Confucian homes) required more direct assistance but were superior in the care and meticulousness of their work.[71]

Learning

The way students learn in arts education (intrinsically, extrinsically and aesthetically) differs in some ways from learning in other subjects in most schools in Western societies. In other areas, like history, students learn sequentially; they accumulate information in a linear fashion. In arts education, however, they learn in *increasing depth of feeling.* Thus similar materials (what would be "content" in other areas) can appear in arts programs year by year. For example, I have taught "overlapping" in visual arts to a variety of ages and graduates, and I have used "the mirror game" in educational drama from infants to "silver threads."

In arts education the emphasis is more upon the process and feeling of the learning experience than accumulating information or the mastery of skills. What students primarily learn is the quality of felt-meaning carried by the medium. Information and skills are learned less directly. But even the learning of felt-meaning is more indirect than direct, more tacit than explicit. With qualitative learnings "we know more than we can tell," as Polanyi[72] said, and implicit learnings are the ground for those which are explicit. This is somewhat different from learning in other subject areas, and to assess such learnings is far more complex and difficult than to assess those, say, in math or science.

Teaching

Inevitably, therefore, teaching strategies differ. In most Western classrooms, the teacher has the role of "the imparter of knowledge and information," and the learning/teaching act can be metaphorized as the good parent feeding his/her children who are expected to digest the food provided.

In the creative arts this is usually not the case. An appropriate metaphor would be a dynamo that initially charges a series of entities so that they can be self-sufficient in their own energy. Here the teacher has the prime role of the "animateur," activating the students in two ways:

- towards creative actions in various media; and, subsequently,
- by deepening their feelings and experience.

The activity itself lies at the centre of creative arts programs: what the students do, and what they do to improve their doings. To achieve these ends, the teacher takes a variety of animation roles:

- the deliberate opposer of the common view in order to give feedback and aid clarity of thought;
- the narrator who helps to set the mood and register of events;
- the positive withdrawer who "lets them get on with it";
- the suggester of ideas as a group member;
- the supporter of tentative leadership;
- the "dogsbody" who discovers material and (arts) aids;
- the reflector who is used by the children to assess their statements;
- the arbiter in argument;
- the deliberately obtuse person, who requires to be informed; and
- the one who "believes that the children can do it."[73]

Given such differences from normal educational contexts, it is little wonder that researchers in arts education have developed their own methods.[74] But what makes the CEQRM unique is that, although developed for arts education, it has greater applicability.

THE METHODOLOGY OF THE CEQRM

The CEQRM is a research instrument that has been developed over a series of inquiries conducted in Ontario. It grew from the need to tackle specific questions that required qualitative approaches (i.e., a preordinate method would not have satisfied the clients), and what was learned in a prior study was applied to the methodology of the next in a cumulative manner. All the studies involved feeling.

The four studies from which CEQRM emerged addressed specific research questions in arts education, of which three were essentially practical. Two of these three examined particular kinds of arts programs in Ontario: elementary students' learnings (hereinafter cited as LEARNING),[75] and teacher education (hereinafter cited as TEACHER).[76] A third addressed the practical knowledge of elementary arts teachers (hereinafter cited as PRACTICAL).[77] And a fourth was theoretic, addressing the nature of aesthetic learning (hereinafter cited as AESTHETIC).[78]

These research studies were satisfactory to their clients and they also had significant effects on researchers, teachers, administrators, trustees, parents, and government in Ontario.

CEQRM is labour intensive. This did not affect the studies LEARNING and PRACTICAL because they received large-scale funding. TEACHER received little support; thus field workers received minimal training and the physical appearance of the final report left much to be desired. In contrast, AESTHETIC received middle-scale funds, but, as data were not collected in the field, this was a reasonably sufficient level of support. Currently CEQRM is being refined to reduce its labour intensiveness.

Just as AESTHETIC showed that the principles of CEQRM could be extrapolated beyond the practical to the theoretic in arts education, it is to be expected that CEQRM can be successfully adapted to various non-arts areas in education and the social sciences in general. So far, however, this has been attempted only a few times (1994).

In the terms previously used in this chapter, the CEQRM is interpretive, logical, dialogic, and functional-structural.

Basic Research Style

Each of the four studies had to address a question, framed by the client, that might well be reframed as: "What are the essential characteristic (or qualities) of x?" For the different studies, x was:

LEARNING = the intrinsic learnings of students enrolled in the arts in the General Program of Studies in Ontario at the elementary level.
TEACHER = arts teacher education programs in Ontario (specifically in the Toronto area) and areas of necessary improvement.
AESTHETIC = human aesthetic learning.
PRACTICAL = the practical knowledge of elementary arts teachers in Ontario.

All the studies were qualitative. In all cases, there were highly complex variables and so the CEQRM was adapted to grounded theory. Where the variables were less complex and were fairly well defined from the data, the CEQRM was adapted to the case study method (e.g., TEACHER). It is theoretically conceivable that, if the variables are well defined, an objective method might be used.

Basic Issues in the First Study

In the first of the studies (LEARNING), once the elements of the research question had been teased out, the investigators faced a number of major issues. To indicate how the CEQRM evolved, these are described in the order in which they occurred.

1. What are intrinsic learnings?

Opinions in the research literature varied and so it was decided to use summary descriptors (A's) of intrinsic learnings but with no hierarchy. Thus the initial question became several questions: "What are the essential characteristics of A1/A2/A3, etc. of students enrolled in the arts in the General Program of Studies in Ontario at the elementary level?" A literature search and analysis revealed that the A's were the improvement of those items listed above (see top of p. 140).

> 2. How can we discover whether or not each of these A's was learned in the program under scrutiny?

Each of the A's in this arts education program was specifically a quality. Even some A's (e.g., problem-solving) which, in other contexts, might be responsive to mechanical research were not so in this context. Nor could we follow individual students and, with each, observe whether or not each of the A's was improved. This would have required a longitudinal study which was beyond our resources because the inquiry was limited to one year.

> 3. What kind of evidence can we obtain?

A decision was made to rely on the evidence of the opinions of those who ought to know: those who taught the program well. The assumption was that they had good practical knowledge of their students' learning (which was borne out in the later PRACTICAL study). As this evidence was not "hard," it had to be both obtained with rigour and checked against other sources of evidence.

> 4. What kind of criteria can we use, and what kind of checks can we make, so that the evidence obtained is reliable?

A sample of teachers (see below) was selected, the criteria for which were that they were:

- identified as having "highly active" arts programs by at least two persons experienced in arts education;
- reasonably representative of the demography of Ontario;
- reasonably representative of both the integrated arts and the specific arts disciplines recognized in Ontario (music, visual arts, drama, and, in physical education, dance).

The evidence so obtained was checked against:

- interviews with "expert" administrators (e.g., arts consultants, etc.);
- direct observation of the students in the teachers' classes;
- the literature review.

> 5. What kinds of methodology should be used?

Because of the variables, we decided to use grounded theory to elicit responses when interviewing both the teachers and the "expert" administrators. This enabled the interviewer's questions to be open-ended so that the evidence reflected both the explicit and tacit views of the interviewees. It also allowed the sample of interviewees to be limited (see below). Glaser and Straus[79] specifically state that the number in the sample can be minimal before "saturation" is reached in the analysis. To forestall criticism by quantitative researchers, we altered the method and increased the number of interviews to 151 – which was far too large and unnecessary.

Observations were empirical and followed the specific themes of intrinsic learnings. At least one class, and sometimes more, of each teacher was observed, the observers being trained to look for tacit as well as explicit evidence.

Grounded theory was also selected as the method of analysing both sets of data. This enabled the results to be specifically emergent. Each data bank was analysed separately and the emergents of each obtained. Subsequently these emergents were compared, leading to the final results.

Sampling

We have seen how sampling was done in LEARNING. Sampling, however, is a contentious issue and needs to be addressed separately. Measurement uses random sampling. But how large should N be? The subjects needed by qualitative studies may be left out with this method, so, no matter how large the N, bias is inevitable. In contrast, a grounded theory sample includes people who are different from those already within it. It gives rich descriptions and perspectives but not impartial "truth."

When there are complex variables, as so often in arts education, the CEQRM uses rational objectivity. The sample selected is of "experts" who are well informed on the issue in the given context. Thus for "Is this Chinese dance good?" the sample is those who understand Chinese dance well and have good judgment. It would be useless to ask, "How well do grade 10 students learn in an arts program?" of those who do not understand grade 10 arts, or of those who do not teach it well.

From LEARNING and subsequent studies, CEQRM has developed a way of obtaining adequate samples:

- Outside informants, experienced in the issue at hand, identify a list of "experts." For the Chinese dance question, these informants would have good experience of Chinese dance; for learning in the arts, they may be senior arts consultants.
- Any "expert," to remain on the list, must be identified by at least two informants, and preferably more.

• The final informants are selected from the list of "experts" by appropriate criteria. These criteria vary with the research question, but, unless they are applied with rigour, the validity of the study is in doubt. If the dance is of Peking Opera style, one criterion would be that an "expert" should have witnessed it. If an arts program is province- or state-wide, one criterion will be demography.

Comparison

Once a data bank has been analysed by inherent theme, and a list of emergents obtained, this can be compared with another list of emergents. The more the lists of emergents to be compared, the more rationally objective the final emergents will be. Three lists are normally sufficient.

Other factors can be illustrated by a description of the comparisons used in the four projects. In LEARNING, there were four sets of data and four lists of emergents: from the literature search, from interviews with both teachers and administrators, and from observations. It was discovered that the interviews with the administrators revealed virtually nothing that was new, so, in subsequent studies, only three sets of data were collected.

At this stage, an ideal model was constructed with three data banks: A from the literature, B from interviews, and C from observations. Analysis revealed emergents from each bank that were then compared, leading to the final emergents. From the example of LEARNING, bank B was conceived as the core, with bank A leading towards it, and bank C providing checks for it. It was considered theoretically possible that banks A and C might be viewed as core in subsequent studies. In fact, only PRACTICAL followed the ideal model which was refined as a result. The other two studies varied the model.

The TEACHER project had a number of variations. First, there was a dearth of available literature on teacher education in the arts. Data bank A, therefore, became the views of six "experts" who acted as consultants over the life of the project. Three were nationally known arts educators, and three were senior arts consultants in large boards of education. Second, interviews were conducted with respondents who were in different teacher education programs. For data bank B, therefore, there were different sections made up of those in each program; these respondents were treated as a case study as well as being interviewed. Third, limited funds prevented any observations, so there was no data bank C. Comparisons were made between the various sections of banks B and A. This was considered insufficient when contrasted with the ideal model. The results were more tentative than those of LEARNING and PRACTICAL, owing to insufficient support.

For the AESTHETIC project, which was entirely theoretic, the CEQRM, on the surface at least, appeared inappropriate. Addressing the question "What is human aesthetic learning?" was exceptionally complex because the nature of aesthetic thought, action, and learning are so intertwined as to be, in many instances, inseparable. A normal analytic study would have meant taking a specific theoretic perspective, whereas, given the question, what was needed was a research method with as little bias as possible.

In the event, the CEQRM proved most valuable. Data were collected only from the literature and sorted into bank A1 – aesthetic thought; bank A2 – aesthetic acts; and bank A3 – aesthetic learning. Data bank A3 was core: its emergents were compared with those from A1 and A2. Thereafter data were collected and analysed, and emergents were discovered in data bank B (interviews) and data bank C (observation). This procedure had the following effects:

- It was extremely revealing in many instances. Some emergents from the individual data banks provided new knowledge, and some confirmed previous knowledge. When the emergents from the three banks were compared, new light was thrown on the major issues.
- As aesthetic thought-action-learning are experienced as one whole in a feeling context, and can only be separated by abstraction, some of the data had to be reviewed twice or even three times. This put pressure on a one-year study with middle-scale funding and the final results were more rushed than could have been wished.

It is fair to state that the CEQRM was a valuable tool in examining a highly complex theoretical issue. It was, however, very time-consuming, and the conclusion was drawn that it would be better to use normal analytic methods for theoretic studies that are as complex.

Cost

As already indicated, this is the major problem with the CEQRM. It involves more wo/man hours than a straightforward mechanistic study. Of the many refinements in answer to this problem, that of the PRACTICAL study was the only one, so far, to substantially decrease the labour intensiveness. Prior to the establishment of data banks B and C, a provisional set of ideal questions was prepared which the interviewer/observer examined carefully. These questions were specifically not taken into the field. However, the interviewers/observers had the key questions uppermost in their minds, and, as a result, the subsequent data were more focused. As already mentioned, other ways to reduce the labour intensive nature of the CEQRM are now being attempted.

Outline Task Analysis

The following is a simple outline of the tasks involved in the CEQRM:

1. Analyse the research question.
- Refine it so that it is researchable.
- Refine it so that the appropriate criteria are revealed.
- Identify the appropriate context for the question.

2. Establish data bank A.
- Apply the criteria at [1] to a search of the literature.
- Establish the parameters of the study including any amendments to the criteria at [1].
- Create any necessary research instrument.

3. Conduct a pilot study.
- Apply the instrument in a pilot study.
- Make necessary alterations as a result.
- Further refine criteria if necessary.

4. Establish data bank B.
- Select interviewees.
- Apply the research instrument to subjects.
- Collect data fully (preferably recorded and then typed up).

5. Establish data bank C.
- Make observations.
- Record observations.

6. Analysis.
- Analyse data banks, A, B, C according to criteria.
- Make separate lists of emergents from the three data banks.
- Compare the three lists of emergents.
- List the emergents common to the three data banks.

7. Results.
- Write up the results in relation to the research question, the criteria, and the list of common emergents. (See figure 17.)

Figure 17
Major Tasks of the CEQRM

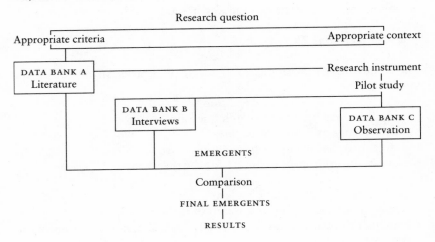

Basic Characteristics of the Method

The above indicates the initial approach and methods of the CEQRM as they evolved over the four projects. These were adapted and refined in the subsequent projects so that we can now say that it has the following basic characteristics:

- It is QUALITATIVE: it examines the qualities, including feeling, in specific instances.
- It is CONTEXTUAL: it examines events in particular contexts.
- It is PARTICIPATORY: the researcher is involved in the event under examination.
- It is ECLECTIC and VARIABLE: it uses a variety of methods (mostly qualitative but quantitative where necessary) and techniques that vary with changing circumstances.
- It is PRACTICAL and has EXTERNAL VALIDITY: it satisfies clients as being a valid picture of reality, and those in the field can work successfully with the results.
- It is INFERENTIAL: it uses inference about various kinds of evidence.
- It is EMERGENT: data are analysed so that major themes emerge.
- It is INTERPRETIVE: it examines both personal and social acts as the creation of reality and social knowledge.
- It is ARTISTIC: it requires that the researcher is sufficiently intuitive and sensitive to the issues addressed.

- It is RATIONALLY OBJECTIVE: it uses adequate criteria in specific contexts and is logical; but simultaneously it acknowledges comparative perspectives and a plurality of realities.
- It is STRUCTURAL: it assumes that media are structural dynamics that convey meaning usually in the frameworks of symbolic interactionism.
- It is mutually DIALOGIC: there is a genuine sharing between the researcher and the subjects who s/he acknowledges start from where they are.
- It is OPEN-ENDED: as far as possible, it does not impose preconceived categories upon the evidence.
- It is COMPARATIVE: it compares emergents from one set of data to the emergents from other data.
- It ACCEPTS THE TACIT: it acknowledges the validity of both explicit and tacit meaning.
- It is progressively and logically ANALYTIC: it moves from descriptive statements, through empirical generalizations, to theoretical generalizations where this is possible.

USE OF THE METHOD

Does the CEQRM provide an accurate picture of reality, or does it not? Single-minded quantitative researchers will say not because it is not based on the rules of mechanical measurement. Those who value both kinds of inquiry, however, understand that when practical issues about human and social situations are addressed, the final question is: Does it work? The four studies using the CEQRM have been highly regarded by their clients, accepted in the field as capturing reality as practitioners know it, and had a number of significant effects upon practice.

Much is due to the reliance of the CEQRM on contemporary logic. By following Best's adage, "adequate criteria in specific contexts," the CEQRM is rationally objective. But an intellectual rigour is required in turning this adage into an effective instrument of inquiry. Commonsense criteria that obey reason within the specific event and the particular circumstance are used for the framework of the research, the sampling and the gathering of data, the forms of analysis and the creation of emergents, and the comparison of different emergents to produce information that is of use.

The fact that the CEQRM has not been finally refined in four studies over seven years should not surprise us. All good qualitative instruments take time to refine. Moreover, they should be capable of continuous change in order to fit the flux of existence.

What is most interesting is the possibility of increasing the range of the CEQRM. It is so structured that, conjecturally at least, it might well address all kinds of questions in the social sciences. It has with success:

- addressed both practical and theoretic issues; and
- used grounded theory and case study as methods.

It is likely to prove an adequate approach in many inquiries where there are complex variables.

Good research tells us that such-and-such is the case in a particular instance. It does not necessarily alter people's views. If that is to occur, research studies have to be *used*. It takes further action to persuade people that, on the basis of one or more research studies, there should be a change in educational theory and practice.

CONCLUSION

The CEQRM specifically captures feeling and other tacit qualities. A response from an interviewee, for example, includes his or her feeling-context. The reporting and analytic stages of the study, therefore, should attempt to include the felt-meaning of the response even though this may be implied rather than explicit.

This inclusion of feeling gives the research the stamp of authority. It demonstrates that the study is based on immediate and direct experience. But to report feelings with some accuracy often means that the researcher must resort to metaphor. This can be in two ways: the use of respondents' own metaphors; and the use of the researcher's metaphors in order to give a holistic description of events.

Having demonstrated a practical method for researching issues of feeling, we can now turn to a projected method.

8 Feeling and the Holistic Method

Dramatic action, based on feeling, is holistic. Holistic approaches to schooling require holistic methods of inquiry. For holism to rely on traditional procedures, empirical or preordinate, is to pour new wine into old bottles. Holists conceive of life as a unity and do not split existence into discrete parts. They do not aim to bifurcate the universe or to descend into the binary world of the either/or. Nor do they oppose the subjective with the objective. They deal not in oppositions but in similarities; differences are seen as contrasts within a whole, or as poles on a continuum.

In scholarly fields where holism is the preferred approach, non-traditional methods of inquiry have already proved successful. Perhaps the most startling is the use of the hologram as the model for inquiry in the field of biblical history, specifically the history of King David by James W. Flanagan.[1] Although preordinate scholars in biblical history have tried to fault this use of the hologram as eclectic, it has been shown to be truly interdisciplinary; it draws together disciplines with balance, restraint, and introspection so that a whole picture of the issue is presented, not merely a part. Flanagan shows that the use of holograms means taking into account partially incongruent information and images from several disciplines, which requires a great deal of trial and error. When the approach is successful, images emerge; when it is unsuccessful, nothing can be seen.

Can a similar success be projected for the hologram as a model for inquiry in educational research, and in educational drama in particular? To discover whether this is the case we will:

- compare the use of the hologram in biblical history with the theoretical possibility of using it in drama education and curriculum;[2] and
- apply the results of this comparison to the feelings found in classroom dramatic activity.

HOLOGRAMS AS MODELS

When the hologram becomes the focus of inquiry it is a model. It is now common in curriculum inquiry to use models "to signify a real or imagined process which behaves similarly to some other thing or process or which is similar in some way other than its behaviour."[3] A model is linked to analogy:

An analogy is a relationship between two entities, processes, or what you will, which allows inferences to be made about one of the things, usually that about which we know least, on the basis of what we know about the other. If two things are alike in some respects we can reasonably expect them to be alike in other respects, though there may be still others in which they are unlike.[4]

The strategy of comparison, and the criteria used in its operation, are basic to such endeavours.

But care must be taken with the use of models. Although a model and its referent are analogous, an analogy may be positive, negative, or neutral. However, in the sciences it may not be possible to identify a negative analogy (i.e., how the things compared are dissimilar). But even where a strong negative analogy coexists with positive and neutral analogies, it is still useful: it expresses a new kind of entity or process different from the one it was modelled on; it is not that analogy is useless or erroneous.[5]

An ideal theory would contain a model that allows for a double analogy – for the modelling of models. In such a two-step model, the second stage aims to describe causes: it is a hypothetical mechanism that is thought to cause the phenomenon under examination. To penetrate both steps requires "disciplined imagination."[6] But a two-step model can be adequate only if it is used to link disciplines into an interdisciplinary matrix. Should a two-step model remain ideal without being practical, it is ineffective. Teaching, learning, and "curricking" (creating programs) are primarily practical activities and, thus, two-step models must remain functional.

Modelling theory has often been applied to ideas of "black boxes" and "translucid (or grey) boxes." In black box theory, an imaginary box conceals its inner workings. Observers can see inputs and outputs, but can only hypothesize about the mental activity that transforms the former into the latter. In behaviourist terms, for example, the position of black box theory is similar to examining behaviours in the experiment. Both deal only with what can be observed and, therefore, are not holistic.

In contrast, grey box theory attempts to explain the nature of systems and to establish links between inputs and outputs.[7] In the investigation of biblical history, according to Flanagan,[8] these are precisely the tasks that Edmund Leach[9] assigns to archaeology (black box) and anthropology (grey box). In the investigation of education, these correspond to "hard" (black box) and "soft" (grey box) methodologies. The appropriate use of one or the other, or both, depends on the nature of the question asked.

In the kind of educational and curriculum inquiry we are discussing, two kinds of models can be used:

• *The holographic*
  Models that assist the investigation (i.e., models of methods), such as holograms, are research designs. They illustrate how a research topic is structured and addressed.
• *The holistic*
  Models that are a society's comprehension of itself can either be the actor's or the observer's mental constructs, or both. People's conceptions, reasons, and explanations of their actions, and the world in which they take place, are seen as holistic and include feelings.

HOLISM AND SOCIAL WORLDS

Holism and modelling are closely related to the theory of social worlds. Of biblical history it has been said:

Social world studies do not offer a single method or theory in the usual sense of the terms. Their dependence [in biblical history] on standard biblical methodologies, archaeology, and comparative sociology make them derivative and eclectic in ways that defy methodological purity. They comprise an approach – in fact, many approaches. These seek to illumine hidden and overlooked information in ancient material and written sources. This means, in effect, that they endeavour to formulate hypotheses and to understand less known ancient societies by illuminating them with comparative information from better known ancient and modern societies.[10]

Likewise, the understanding of educational societies (classes, schools, communities) is also based on the ethnologies and ethnographies of others with similar ecologies investigated by similar approaches. They are specifically holistic because their framework includes the criteria of feeling *and* time (processes, dynamics, transformations, and metamorphoses) *and* space (static phenomena). And each society is regarded as unique.[11]

This approach specifically aims at the liminal: the flow of feeling that exists between static states or statuses, the dynamic between structures.[12] Thus, for example, in initiation rituals (theoretically the prototype of all acts of learning) an initiate both feels and moves from childhood through liminality to adulthood – or, as the once popular song says about the adolescent, "I'm just an in-between." In contemporary investigation, these studies spark imagination, control speculation and intuition, discipline reflection, and the understanding of feeling.[13]

In biblical history, holistic studies rest on the assumption that knowledge of history requires imagination, but disciplined imagination; and that critical thinking is aided and made less arbitrary by integrating archaeology, literatures, and cross-cultural comparisons of the kind Leach, from a non-holistic perspective, finds risky.[14] Holists in education know that neither positive nor negative correlations among samples constitute "proof" that two groups are or are not matched. Holistic and social world studies distinguish between images *of* the past and images *from* the past – in the case of biblical history, between literary and archaeological sources of information, and between ancient sources and interpretations based on modern societies. In the case of education and curriculum, the distinction would be between sources in the literature and data in the current study.

The holistic and social world approaches (including those of drama) depart from earlier inquiries in two closely related ways:

- *They accept homologies and analogues in reasoning.*
  Since Russell and Wittgenstein, Aristotle's logical methods are not the only ones accepted.[15] Hypotheses, for example, are formed on the basis of comparative information, and they are used in efforts to adequately interpret the data.[16] Today, interpretations are seen as hypotheses that offer plausible explanations, guide further reflection, and are subject to constant revision.

  These same offerings occur in the practical hypotheses that underpin our actions in everyday life. In order to act adequately, we think in the "what if" mode (imagination) and act in the "as if" mode (play and dramatic action) in a total operation.[17] We improvise in the role of customer or lawyer, parent or child, by tacit hypothesis. We *try out* our thoughts and actions. If they are ineffective, they are not plausible; if they are effective they are plausible, subject to further reflection, and can be constantly revised.

- *The liminal is implied but can pass unobserved.*

Texts and narratives, testimony to past social worlds, are partial or fragmentary sources of information; yet, entire social worlds produce and are encoded in each. Researchers attempt to reconstitute holistic and felt images of the past on the basis of partial information.

The sources, thus, stand between observers and what was observed. The observers can also include feelings. For example, in biblical history, Wilson understates the issue when he places the sources in the past and speaks of the gap of history that separates readers from the biblical text.[18] Instead, as with educational inquiry, gaps exist that divide investigators from their sources, and stand between the sources and the societies they represent. In this sense, the past sources are, as Binford suggests,[19] modern phenomena. And so are the data of contemporary educational inquiries, including those of feelings, which describe a past perspective but use them in the present tense.

Attitudes to Inquiry

We can theoretically extrapolate the possible agenda for curriculum and educational inquiry as follows:

- Observers' ideas, feelings, viewpoints, and perspectives are distinct from those of the sources they use, which are only a partial source of information.
- Images of events in previous research are hypotheses, and are subject to continual revision. Comparative information affords new openings and controls.[20]
- Modelling, analogy, and metaphor become central concerns, and each is so linked to feelings that they can imply ambiguity. The focus of investigation shifts away from details towards macro-scales and felt-wholes. These examine the relationships that join observers' models, aspirations, and actions on the one hand, and the disciplines that study them on the other. Modelling, analogy, and metaphor are based on a felt-comparison which fits the comparative forms of holism and holograms.
- The social world of educational contexts becomes the object of educational inquiries. Previous studies are re-created; they become the researchers' aesthetic and affective reconstitution of earlier findings from partial information.

In biblical history, social world critics use two related but distinct kinds of sources (material and textual), and each is shaped by factors that are now only partly visible. The social world in which ancient religion resided is not immediately observable; it stands "beyond" the sources. Neither kind of source, individually or jointly, describes or is the exclusive medium through which ancient religion travelled. Religion arose in, was influenced by, and in turn shaped ancient societies. It eludes direct observation; yet it bound ancient domains together and linked disparate peoples. Thus, we tease understandings of it from all available information.

Curriculum inquirers also have two kinds of sources: the literature (the past) and observation(s) of present events. The former is shaped by a combination of factors, including feeling, that are now only partly visible to the inquirer. The social world in which the teaching/learning act was reported in the literature is not immediately observable; it is that about which the source reports (past). Should the source report about educational events in Dar es Salaam or Dakar, Boston or Detroit, it was shaped by a different society from that in which the inquirer exists (say, Toronto in 1994). Thus, today's inquirers tease their understandings out of all available information.

HOLOGRAPHY

To develop a model for the holistic study of spontaneous drama and feeling we must identify a means for sorting information, reintegrating it, and accurately depicting an event; e.g., evaluation of a specific program in Ontario. To this end, we draw upon holograms and the technology of holography, theories and methods used in existing research, together with ritual and developmental drama studies. We do so in the following steps:

- We describe holography and borrow from it the metaphors and models that are used to address the research question.
- We divide information according to ontological categories that are used by anthropologists, but as contrasts not oppositions.
- We devise a holographic model for integrative social world studies based on the technology.

If the research is holistic, the model axiomatically includes feelings.

Holography is a laser-based, vibration-free technology. It encodes visual information on an opaque or transparent plate in a way that allows three-dimensional images to be reconstituted[21] as if the object was there. The image appears to be suspended in space either behind or in

Figure 18
The Surface Components of a Social World

[A] Inner	ideas, opinions, aspirations, and motives	*Personal*
[B] Media	physical and material resources	*Mediate*
[C] Outer	social norms and systems	*Social*

front of the plate. A whole object is holographed, but only partial information is encoded on the plate. From this partial information, the whole object reappears when the hologram is illuminated.[22]

Whole-Part Analogies

Holography depends on part-whole relations and on intelligent thinking in everyday dramatic action.[23] The part-whole relations are generated by feelings. Thus holography has an immediate impact upon this book. Its technology provides analogies useful for holistic research. This is because social worlds are structured as whole-parts:

- The stages in the process of holographic encoding and illuminating, as well as the holographic image, are metaphors and models for several aspects of a social world approach.
- Holography is a metaphor for the processual and feeling relations of a social world. Then the relational theory of metaphor applies. Metaphors involve more than two simple comparisons; the dynamics within any two items are related to each other. The different sets of relationships are drawn out and illuminated by the metaphor.

The components of a social world can be separated theoretically into three groups that are not exclusive, as in figure 18. But these personal, mediate and social factors are, in a sense, only the surface of a social world; they provide information *about* the world. These constituents are not the actual, meaningful "world" that inquirers seek. Discovery of this world is, however, implied in figure 19.[24]

To peel back the surface of figure 18 and peer into the midst of these phenomena in figure 19 exposes the deep felt-meanings sought in the social world:

- The dynamic relations between the constituent elements use feelings to create meanings as part-whole.
- The meanings of feelings (emotional-aesthetic structures) are prior to the cognitive.

Figure 19
The Complex Components of a Social World

[A] Inner –	ideas, opinions, aspirations, and motives ↕ imagination, world view	Personal
[B] Media –	physical/material resources from culture ↕ ideational from the person	Mediate
[C] Outer –	social norms and systems ↕ personal norms	Social

- Processual meanings are prior to consequences and products; the emphasis is upon time within the unity of space-time; i.e., within the "here and now," "now" becomes the focus.

Effects on Past and Present

The gathering of meaning, however, becomes more complex when we make a review of the relevant literature. Past meanings are recoverable in the present, and in a way similar to meaning gained from a current research study.

Previous educational research studies describe events, now seen in the past tense, the full meaning of which existed *then*; it accompanied a particular relation of the components at a moment in time. But *now* part of the significance of the previous moment has been lost. It is knowable only through its effects, and the relations among them. These bear information about the past that can be studied as we attempt to perceive former meanings. Because the past and its meaning cannot be fully regained, however, such perceptions are hypotheses or hypothetical reconstructions.

That is, previous studies have shown findings which educational researchers today use in order to make things happen. But scholars and researchers *now* seek the realities of the processes and the connections among the elements that were at work *then*. They are the content that lurks behind the literature; it is pointed to by questions like, "Who did what?" and "What happened?" To reconstruct the scene, and to understand the social context and norms, are to be in possession of the so-called "facts." But, by themselves, "facts" are the data that researchers must reach beyond in order to gain understanding. In order to penetrate beyond the thoughts and statements of previous inquirers, the links and processes in a social world must be addressed. Each of these is past: they are history, and they are holographic. In Flanagan's terms, history is a hologram.

This also applies to a study that takes place in the present tense. The inquirer may collect data (by observation, etc.) in the present tense of day 1, day 2, day 3, etc. This is transformed into the past tense when s/he treats the data and tries to come to conclusions on day 10, day 11, day 12, etc. On day 11 the inquirer may ask what happened on day 2. Thus, in the terms used here, educational and curricular research is a hologram. A researcher's portrayals of the educational situation are holograms in that they reconstitute past meanings. They are more than attempts to recover the "facts." Settings, scenes, feelings, and statements are important for two reasons: they carry information; and at a specific moment they have a particular relation to each other.

Reconstructions of the relations and what they stood for – more than knowledge about effects and products – comprise the focus of a holist's view. Holists seek the holograms that existed in the past, and they offer holograms of the past – yet as they create them their holograms exist in the present tense.

It is the technical processes of holography that are a model for a holistic research design. In the field of biblical history, for example, this includes the use of:

- literary and archaeological disciplines to examine the information in ancient artifacts, and
- information drawn from comparative sociology to illumine the ancient information and the relations among individual sources of information.

In a similar way, the field of curriculum uses both itself and other educational fields (psychology, sociology, etc.) to illumine the data and the relations between individual sources of information.[25]

The procedural sequence becomes: *metaphor – model – metaphor.* Thus biblical historians move from an ancient social world to a study of the social world, and from there to an image of a social world of antiquity. Curriculum researchers move from earlier studies (distant past) to a study of their social world (present), to an image of their social world as it existed *then* (immediate past). In both cases, the past is a hologram, the research design is modelled on holography, and the image of the past is a hologram; and the sequence is from content (and metaphor) to discipline (and model) to content (and metaphor).

Relations and Technology

Four technical aspects of holograms are important for understanding the sequence of, and the relations among, the items in the metaphors and model. Each is connected to the whole-part-whole phenomenon that links an object that is holographed, a holographic plate, and a hologram image:

- *Holograms encode entire objects in partial information so that images of the whole object may be reconstituted.* Thus:
  - entire social worlds are "remembered" in fragmented sources, and by means of comparisons; and
  - a world's multi-dimensional images are reconstituted from partial information.

  The pattern of information makes reconstructions of past sources possible and necessary.[26] When the information pattern that unites and divides the sources is illuminated, lifelike and holistic "images" are created. These, like holograms, are reconstituted from partial information out of sources that are only partly coherent with each other.

- *Holograms provide entire images reconstituted from each part of a holographic plate.*[27] The effect is like looking through a window partly obscured by a shutter. Viewers standing away from the window see only part of the scene framed by the window. By moving closer, they widen their view and see the entire scene as if the window shutter was open. The closer they are, the more perspectives they see. With holograms, the entire original image is within each portion and can be reconstituted from each piece. Perspectives are lost when the plate is divided, not access to the total scene.

  Biblical historians who employ this technology gain holistic images reconstituted from partial information. When more information is available, rarely does it cause them to discard an entire framework of a study. Mostly it clarifies the image or adds perspectives that were missing, as in education. It figuratively expands the size of the window onto the past.[28]

  The third and fourth aspects of the relationships pertain to the quality of the image.

- *In holograms, the image is both real and elusive.* Viewers do not see an image in the holographic plate as a photo is imaged on photographic paper. With holograms, viewers do not actually see the plate or anything on its surface.[29] They see the "original" light rather than an image of the object (as would be the case in a photograph).[30] Rather, viewers see "as if" the object itself was there. The object is not present but, in a three-dimensional way, it *seems* to be. The image is simultaneously rich and powerful, distant and elusive. It causes ambivalent feelings of *the actual and the fictional.*[31]

- *This spreading of information and the dimensionality gives rise to another analogy with biblical history.* The information about the ancient social world that is encoded in the sources is spread holistically across the entire "plane" of the sources. Leach argues as much for texts.[32] The same is true of archaeological remains because each artifact, typology, or site, in a sense, represents with varying degrees of clarity an entire social world.

  In educational research, partial sources of information come from a variety of fields and, while each contains holistic data, it gives only a limited perspective on the whole, despite the force of feeling.

Images of past educational research are "not there" until illumined. In holism, the light beam consists of comparative models from various disciplines; these contain relationships similar to those encoded both in and between the information sources. The "gaps" between verbal claims and research information tell stories of their own; they have parallels in other contexts and they can be used to illumine the patterns left in past sources. The reconstituted image seems to be the image viewers would have seen in the past; however, their view depended on their ability to recognize relations that, without the comparisons, would have gone unnoticed. It is the relationship as much as the information that is illumined. Data from past studies can be interpreted as a hologram.

INTERDISCIPLINARY MODEL

When we wish to find a holographic model for interdisciplinary research, we must return to black boxes, grey boxes, and two-stage modelling which above we have briefly discussed.

Examples from Biblical History

Robert Wilson's analysis of genealogies can be interpreted as an example of stratified black and grey box modelling.[33] He shows the patterns, contradictions, and inconsistencies within the biblical genealogies; alongside these, he places genealogies from other archaic societies and shows the patterns in them. In this model, Wilson claims the patterns to be analogous to each other: he establishes that the social organizations and processes in the extra-biblical model groups caused their patterns; and he hypothesizes that similar social processes caused the patterns in the biblical genealogies. Wilson shows how the distinction of form and process allows investigators to move towards causal explanations. But there are drawbacks: Wilson uses relatively uncomplicated biblical materials; he draws information from only two disciplines rather than three or more; and he does not address the problems of the relations among material and textual sources, or the epistemological issues confronting the social sciences.

A second example from biblical history is a study by G.E. Wright.[34] He posited literary analysis as a first step, and established the ancient ecology via archaeology as a second. By mixing stable (ecological) and highly variable (notional) information he left himself open to criticism that he used archaeology to interpret the text. Flanagan has said that if Wright had reversed the order of inquiry, he might have used literary information as a grey box; then he could have offered plausible interpretations for the black boxes established by archaeology. Had he applied grey box theory to a given historical case, any number of interpretations from ancient literature or archaic societies could have been tried until a case was built. The order of presentation in most archaeological reports – literary and documentary information first, material information second – implies a similar reversal.

Education

The implications of these two examples for educational and curriculum inquiries are that:

- grey box theory can be applied to a given anthropological study;
- this can offer plausible interpretations for the black boxes formed by other studies;
- a case can be built, either based on a combination of models or, with negative analogies, constructed anew from them and from the subjects' differences.[35]

Education and curricular studies that are truly interdisciplinary require a two-stage model:

Stage 1: For gathering and interpreting data in each discipline used.

Composite holographic images are made from multiple exposures of a single master hologram, or from several masters exposed simultaneously.

Stage 2: For integrating stage 1 information.

To make composite holograms, several first-stage master holograms are illuminated simultaneously or serially; three (or at least two) object beams project images of master holograms which, interfered with by the reference beam, produce a second generation, or double exposure, hologram.[36]

Possible examples in holistic inquiries can be projected. In the case of reading, for example, empirical studies of six-year-old children learning to read, and statistical information about words known in society at that age, present contrasting images of reading capabilities. Both are firmly rooted in valid but separate sources. Yet, together, they create a composite image in which the two elements depend on viewers' perspectives. But when viewers stand where they can "see" both images, a third image of reading appears. Adjusting either image in order for it to cohere exactly with the other distorts the data, limits the perspectives on reading, and obscures the "real" composite image that appears beyond the sources. Thus, the relation between the images when illuminated makes the reading hologram interesting and true to life.

In this example, empirical, statistical, and other sources formulate images separately. Holistic studies draw eclectically on a number of disciplines whose studies can be conceived holographically; e.g., the psychology of reading. These arise from independent fields or sub-fields: Their conclusions are separately valid without being integrated by comparative methods. Yet these studies can also be understood as the first phase in making curricular holograms. Individual disciplinary "master templates" are created first and then used in making second-level composite interdisciplinary holograms.

Comparisons can also be made at the first level, the disciplinary stage. Indeed, disciplines often seek to become interdisciplinary; yet in practice they are often cross-disciplinary more than interdisciplinary. Disciplines collect information according to their own specific models, interpreting the models systemically, and hypothesizing about social processes. Research that combines disciplines adequately is concerned more directly with integration, illumination, and interpretation than with the accumulation of new information. Interdisciplinary (holographic) models aim to integrate disciplinary hypotheses and information in order to create holistic hypotheses (holograms) about, say, reading. Rightly, interdisciplinary models are dependent upon the disciplines they use.

When we project truly interdisciplinary studies in education in a two-stage model (for information in each discipline and for integrating that information), individual disciplines become heuristic. By placing images beyond the sources, literalism is avoided, and information is distinguished from interpretation. Partial or incomplete sources can be used because their images are recognized for what they are; they are not confused with definitive reconstructions. Further, multiple "stories" or "histories" occur because images depend on the perspectives of the investigators.

MOBILE HOLOGRAMS

Holograms are essentially static images while "stories," "histories," and educational events are processual. To compensate for the difference, it is helpful to envisage a model as a sort of mobile hologram. Dramatic acts and rituals serve this purpose.

David Bohm

Some of David Bohm's theoretical proposals, including his hypothetical holomovements that connect structures and dynamics, address the static vs the process components of reality.[37] Bohm, one of the leaders in holographic studies, takes aim directly at the space-time Cartesian-grid problem that for generations has plagued both biblical history and education. Bohm says:

Scientific laws and theories are abstractions and idealizations that hold true only to a certain degree of approximation within limited domains. Scientific progress is not identified with convergence toward some absolute truth, but consists in the proposal of new theories, often based on radically new conceptual frameworks, which reveal the limitations of older theories, suggest new kinds of experiment and establish new criteria of relevance.[38]

Bohm believes that the same kind of order pervades the universe. When an implied order evolves into a form (as with dye injected into an organism), a tacit order becomes explicit.

Tacit and manifest orders are different expressions of the same thing: the order exists, but it may or may not be "seen." An implicit order is the ground for an explicit order we see and identify. Tacit orders are not made up of parts; *what we call "parts" are orders in which things "enfold" one another.* This concept underpins many holistic ideas; e.g., in epistemology, implicit knowledge is the ground for explicit knowledge.[39]

Bohm borrows a second analogy from holography. Photographic analogies for science wrongly emphasize part-to-part relations; to see science as "photographing" is to exaggerate the accumulating of detailed "facts." This leads others (falsely) to seek more powerful figurative lenses in order to observe ever smaller parts; to believe that they can gain ever greater knowledge of the wholeness of a phenomenon. Theoretically this results from the Cartesian view that the universe and people are machines.

Bohm shows that holograms retain whole images *within* their parts; they model the dynamic relations between tacit and explicit orders, i.e., the dynamics between the process and its manifestations. He calls dynamics "movements," and expands imagery by speaking of holomovements, holofluxes, and photographs of movements.[40] Educational researchers who follow Bohm seek dynamics more than structures, knowledge, etc.

Bohm also uses wave theory. Waves carry the various orders tacitly enfolded in themselves; they are unfolded in the explicit order. The whole movement of the universe (process) carries the tacit order that becomes explicit in the world we see (form). History and events are merely ripples whose meaning depends on what lies behind them.[41]

Bohm extends the part/whole analogy to the unconscious/conscious relation: the latter is an explicit manifestation of the former's tacit order.[42] Perception is comparable to the way relatively constant features in an environment are abstracted to create memories and maps; these select and store invariables until they are used to affect later perceptions. Thus, cartographers record curves in roads but not variables (e.g., a crack in the concrete) because these are apt to change; they will be of no use for further perceptions of a similar kind.

If we fail to recognize a person we know, Bohm argues, it is not because the individual is an illusion, or on account of some other thing "out there." It is because of problems with the relations between the old map stored in memory and the present appearance of the person. The relationship to the wholeness, not just to individual parts, has been lost.

Ritual

In a significant parallel, Flanagan suggests that a society's rituals incorporate many of the relations that Bohm describes within scientific perceptions of physical realities. In this, Flanagan uses the findings of contemporary social anthropologists, like Victor W. Turner,[43] who shows that rituals are:

- primary social acts,
- metaphors and feelings for fundamental social change, and
- regulators of human relations.

They contain and manifest underlying social representations, feelings, structures, and processes which unfold and become visible in social actions – specifically in primary acts like rituals. This is also assumed by ritologists in many disciplines; e.g., McLaren in education.[44]

Ritual is a focus in any society. This is obvious in traditional cultures (e.g., birth, initiation, marriage, and death rituals); or it can be less obvious, as in the innumerable fragmented rituals in contemporary post-industrial cities (e.g., opening a bridge, or a degree ceremony). Rituals are sited at, encode, reveal, and affect the relations of social indicators as:

- canonical (traditional) and indexical (current) signifiers;
- status reversals and elevations (synchronic relations) and social change (diachronic relations);
- felt beliefs and actions.

Rituals operate as holograms: they are parts that carry the meaning of wholes. They are a "controllable, unambiguous, orderly pattern of action" that effectively reorders "the uncontrollable, ambiguous, or otherwise dangerous aspects of a situation."[45] Rituals are microcosms of macrocosmic processes of change. They are both tacit forms of explicit orders and explicit forms of tacit orders; that is, they *encapsulate* as well as expose structures and processes in societies. In our model, holomovements and rituals belong to the illuminating phases of holography.

Spontaneous Dramatic Action

Rituals are one kind of dramatic act (see figure 1). Like rituals, *dramatic acts are parts that carry the meaning of wholes.* This is so *within* all dramatic acts.

In contrast, developmental drama is *about* the personal, social, and cultural developments of spontaneous dramatic action. Its studies include role playing and improvised actions in everyday life, festivity, children's play, and educational drama.[46] These activities can also be crystallized as a functional performance within a society: as ritual, as theatre, and as "social dramas" involving the whole of a community (e.g., a national election or a revolution; a local ceremony, or a strike). One way of looking at this difference is through the contrast of process and form. Spontaneous dramatic action is a process activity, while ritual and theatre are forms. *Spontaneous dramatic acts have the same holistic function in practical life that holograms have in all types of research and inquiry.*

Victor W. Turner demonstrates that the rituals within social dramas are the settings in which texts are produced. These texts encode the tensions, liminalities, and dramas present in the social world. At the same time, as Roy A. Rappaport shows,[47] rituals expose previously tacit processes embedded in the static information encoded in texts and recovered during research. James W. Flanagan says that rituals are microcosms of life, and are holomovements where the ritualizer is the hologram.

While studies in developmental drama agree with this in general, they indicate that not merely the ritualizer but *all human performers are holograms of the meanings they convey.* The differences between the meanings they carry depend on the degree to which a role is assumed, from that of a casual shopper in a supermarket to that of someone in a trance state.[48] It is basic to this field that all human action is *dramatic*, either overtly or covertly, and that the actions of a human being in social life are symbolized by "the costumed player."[49] As "costumed players" in all our life actions, we encapsulate (as microcosm) the meanings of existence (macrocosm). That is to say, all that we *do* functions as a hologram.

We can summarize this issue not merely in ritual but also in a number of other ways:

- In educational drama
  - improvising students represent grey boxes;
  - the content (story) represents the black boxes of disciplines (say, history for an improvisation based on Columbus); and
  - the two-stage model uses grey and black boxes as above.
- In improvised theatre
  - improvising actors represent grey boxes;
  - the content and themes represent the black boxes of disciplines (say, the story of Macbeth and the theme of greed for power); and
  - the two-stage model uses grey and black boxes as above.
- In curriculum development
  - those who engage in curriculum practice ("currickers") improvise everyday actions represented by grey boxes;
  - the content (from disciplines) represent the black boxes (say, curriculum theory, applied psychology, educational sociology, etc.); and
  - the two-stage model uses grey and black boxes as above.

In other words, human spontaneous dramatic action operates in practice in much the same way as a hologram operates in research and inquiry.[50]

CONCLUSION

We began this chapter by asking: What research method do we use when we address questions of feeling and spontaneous drama? Quite obviously, in any practical research situation we require a methodology that adequately reflects the essential meanings in the dramatic context that is being investigated. In this chapter we have considered holism and the hologram as such a research method.

The player's world exists in the flux of the "here and now." It is always distinguished from the impressions of it in the minds of investigators. Players "know" and feel IN the present tense. Researchers "know" and feel ABOUT the same events in the past tense. The latters' images of the former are holograms and holomovements, i.e., reasonable images of the life investigators would see if they were within the event. In their different ways, however, what both the players and the investigators "know" and feel are wholes, and the parts of wholes.

In the models used here, studies of texts are primarily responsible for past information from the domain of notions; conversely, the living drama process is responsible for the domain of actions. Comparative relations illuminate the meeting of domains and the worlds behind them. The work of the holistic inquirer reflects feelings and ideas: what people in the past were thinking, feeling, and saying, or what others claimed they were thinking, feeling, and saying.

In education and curricular inquiries, the first-stage model sorts the phenomena of events *for comparative purposes:* they are not separated into dualistic opposites but into contrasts existing in a totality. Any analysis, therefore, is not normally between entirely discrete categories; groups of phenomena are often found to overlap with other groups. A discipline's priorities can be identified according to the *emergence* of the phenomena, subject matter, and themes that the data focus on most directly. By recognizing this, investigators begin to realign many important issues.

The disciplinary and the subsequent interdisciplinary stages that are structured in the holographic model enable one discipline to respect the other. Each discipline interprets its own information and offers a plausible explanation of the data as seen from its own perspective. Later such "master templates" (disciplinary images) can be integrated and reinterpreted when they are compared and combined in the second-level interdisciplinary stage. There, not the actors' but the investigators' models will be reordered and reshaped to make a plausible hologram of the models and the world of the actors.

In curricular terms, the first and second stage divisions are practical. They allow researchers to proceed without forcing their views into a common mould, but by including information about feelings. The player *is* a hologram, and studies of human players (developmental drama) are holographic. By identifying inquiry as the integration of two or more disciplines, researchers do not have to make all data "match" in an artificial and mechanistic way. But, although an inter-disciplinary approach does not impose disciplinary straitjackets, it re-quires special disciplinary integrity – part of which is of feeling. Thus, for example, the research question, "Does educational drama improve the reading capabilities of grade 3 students?" might require disciplin-ary evidence from learning theory, reading, and educational drama. The approach to each requires integrity, but all data from the three dis-ciplines do not have to "match."

It has been shown that, theoretically, holograms can be very useful to holists studying education. The method is truly interdisciplinary: it pre-sents a whole picture of the focus of the inquiry, and it draws together disciplines with restraint, balance, and introspection. The use of holo-grams means taking into account partially incongruent information and images from several disciplines. Unlike many other research styles, it incorporates data on feelings. Making holograms, therefore, can be projected as a successful strategy for holistic inquiry in educational re-search, specifically in curriculum inquiry.

9 Drama as a Human Science

A dramatic act is a form of inquiry. The human player operates in a scientific mode because an act is an hypothesis: it resembles the opening of the syllogism in that it uses fiction to test actuality. But to the player it also has inductive power: the more a role is successful, the more it is likely to be played.

The player's inquiry in the present tense, however, goes further than merely deduction and induction. In Wittgenstein's sense, it is not merely an objective inquiry. It is mainly rational; it can also subject data to interpretative and moral reasons. If so, just what kind of science is this?

Since Kant, reason has been understood to be, to put it crudely, of two kinds: experimental reasoning about nature, which proceeds from doubt towards certainty; and intuitive reasoning about moral culture, which operates between ideas of indeterminancy and constraint. This is the origin of C.P. Snow's famous two-cultures thesis and the popular view that there is a bifurcation of knowledge: truth/possibility, body/ mind, nature/culture, objective facts/social values, and so forth. The social sciences were created at the beginning of the twentieth century on the basis of natural science and for many years proceeded quantitatively and experimentally. More recently, however, ethnological and ethnographic methods have been used by social scientists in qualitative studies. For many years, the battle of quantitative vs qualitative has raged.

The real issue, of course, is whether or not science can properly investigate the universe as a whole, natural as well as cultural. Can the common view, that the objective and the subjective are mutually exclusive, be broken? The case presented here, albeit briefly, is that if it can, then it is the discipline of drama which can bridge Snow's duality. Dramatic action embodies a practical, indeed a technological, method of inquiry. As we have seen, drama gives the player mediate knowledge, but for the researcher the drama of players is a "domain" which can be explored by means of a method that is very like normal science in that it is experimental, but unlike it in that it is also experiential. Drama affirms the integrity of the subjective experience but can use objective methods within that context. It has the value system of being aggressively committed to the active defence of consciousness, but assumes that there are both subjective and objective ways of knowing. It acknowledges, with Heisenberg, that indeterminacy elevates perspectives to a genuine way of examining data and it denies the Faustian quest for absolute knowledge.

Drama is not then, in *strictu sensu*, a science. It is not solidly objective or only concerned with number-crunching. But it is certainly scientific and may, possibly, indicate future ways in which science can once more address the totality of human experience and the universe.

DRAMA AND THE HUMAN CONDITION

University drama programs are condemned, in Gilbert Ryle's words, to "an intellectual no-man's land" while they depend on other disciplines for their legitimacy. To get these programs started, the scholars responsible were, indeed, answerable to those in other disciplines; their arguments and rationales, as a result, were made in terms other than their own. But those days are long past. Drama is now well established in colleges and universities, and it is time it came out of the closet and declared itself for what it is.

The focus of drama as a discipline is the human condition: the human being in dramatic action, a unity of "what if" thought (imagination) and "as if" action (drama) that is felt and meaning-giving in its transformative power. First it provides experiential knowledge in the present tense: Knowledge IN the experience that we live through in the "here and now." "Dramatic knowing" is contiguous to, analogous with, and transformative of everyday and mundane knowing, from which it differs in its heightened significance. It is, *sui generis*, fictional. Secondarily, we obtain Knowledge ABOUT the dramatic experience in the past tense: we engage in discourse, talking or writing about what occurred in the "there and then." The essence of the drama method is that the second form of knowledge is dependent upon the first: *experience has primacy over discourse.*

On this view, virtually all current programs require recasting. They implicitly rely on the intellectual categories of Aristotelians: Theatre history and dramatic criticism have primacy over the students' experience, which, in many instances, is regarded as non-examinable; and the traditional "academic paper" tries to make the discipline "respectable." There is no bravery here, merely a political expedient. This does not acknowledge drama in its own right; it is, simply, an attempt to gain credibility in a world that died before Einstein and Wittgenstein. For drama does not rely on a body of abstract information, nor are its experiments entirely with physical objects. It is a temporal process common to all humanity, the forms of which are the play of children, the roles we play in life, improvisation, and (the tip of the iceberg) scripts and theatre as an art form.

In our felt-world, drama is a science. As we experience drama *hic et nunc*, it rests on the empiricism of "going and seeing" – its data are perceived phenomena. It is a genuine explanatory mode, obeying the three conditions that make a discipline scientific:[1] an explanatory corpus that explains phenomena within performance (e.g., a production of *Hamlet* displays statements about the human condition); highly philosophic theories from Aristotle and Kalidasa to Bertolt Brecht and Bernard Beckerman; and a mythology, or drama's suppressed premises that provide insights into its usefulness in coping with existence.

Like the "objective" sciences it hinges on hypothesis, estimation, and other forms of "guessing" that Popper says are the foundation of all knowledge. When a protagonist hypothesizes his role as A, his action becomes Y. But if he hypothesizes his role as B, his action becomes Z. The difference between drama and other sciences, however, is that hypothesis is elevated to the same level as objective knowing: each is a double of the other – a living metaphor in the world of action that, at best, is symbolic of human life. It is not just the simple parallelism of "All the world's a stage," but the metaphoric, analogic, and parabolic meanings of "We are such stuff / As dreams are made on."

From this perspective, *drama as a discipline is developmental.*[2] Transformation ensures that it is in continual change: personal, sociocultural, aesthetic, and artistic (theatrical) change become the subject of study once drama enters academe. No dramatic action is ever subject to replication. *This* dramatic act is always different from *that*, but it is always, to one degree or another, spontaneous.[3] A classic example from the theatre was Michael Redgrave's Hamlet, where his interpretation was in constant flux from night to night.

Not that all change is immediately observable by a researcher. Dramatization is most obviously overt in external action which is observable. But it can be covert ("in our heads"), which a witness must infer. With very young children, an action is mostly overt, but, with maturation and increased differentiation, it becomes more covert. Covert or not, as Piaget tells us, an action is still an action. Adults may assume they have grown out of it until they inadvertently catch themselves talking to a mirror, or rehearsing for a job interview.

DRAMA AND THE DOUBLE

Thus far we have been concerned with laying the groundwork for conceiving drama as a university discipline in a new way. It is usually thought of in two styles. First, it can be object-centred. There are "facts" that the student should know; e.g., the Greek influence on August Strindberg, or the historical data of the career of Madame Vestris. This is to emphasize dramatic criticism or theatre history and is common in Britain and Europe. Second, it can be vocationally centred. There are vocational skills the student should acquire; e.g., directing in the manner of Alexander Dean, or acting for summer stock. These programs are not part of genuine professional schools (such as the National Theatre School, Montreal). They are meant to produce drama/theatre professors who can continue the vocational tradition. These programs are common in the United States, usually based on the models of Yale or Carnegie.

Here we are considering a program with a very different focus: the human being performing in life (drama) or art (theatre). This is to conceive of drama as a human science, related to if different from the natural or social sciences. Drama is a medium: it carries felt-meaning from one human being to another, from one protagonist to another, each of whom is symbolically "a costumed player," whether in life or art. Drama, like language to Bakhtin, lies on the borderline between oneself and another.

This is to conceive of drama as a metaphoric and dialogic operation. It is metaphoric in the sense that the first player sees the second as "a person like myself." In the linguistic metaphor "The roses in her cheeks," the second subject (the roses) is seen in terms of the first (her cheeks) to create a new double meaning. Oedipus sees Creon in such a way, just as we see a member of our family in everyday life. This is also a dialogic situation. The actions of "a costumed player" are a particular point of view on the world: they represent a particular world view that interacts with another. The actions of each are characterized by their own objects, felt-meanings, and values. They may be juxtaposed to one another, mutually supplement one another, and be interrelated dialogically.

Drama lives, as it were, beyond itself, projected towards another person. The two dramas in an interaction do not exclude each other: each is inclusive of the other in a whole dialogic relation which, as a processual medium, conveys a new meaning between the two world views. Our two dramas encounter one another and coexist in our joint consciousness.

It is almost that our drama is half someone else's. It only becomes my own when I populate it with my own intentions, my own speech and gesture. Prior to this moment, our drama does not exist in a neutral context but in other people's acts, in their intentions, speech and gesture. From their drama I must take these actions and, through reinterpretation, I must make them my own. The drama which I appropriate – our cultural life – is full of the intentions of others, part of which is the stratification of society which includes social roles. Each role has its own drama that, compared with that of our consciousness which conveys personal and social meanings, conveys mostly social meanings.

These elements of human life are signified in the dramatic script. A dramatist has the difficult task of representing people's acts only through their talk. But it is made doubly difficult because a playwright must use a personage's acts of two kinds, those of consciousness and those of roles. Indeed, the dramatist intensifies the diversity of acts and creates his or her own style. These personages and their acts are at a greater or lesser distance from the dramatist and his or her intended felt-meaning; e.g., Brecht's vs Stanislavsky's interpretation of Chekhov. The dramatist does not express him or herself in these simulated acts; rather, he or she presents them as unique, significant acts elevated almost to the level of ritual. Just as ritual collapses past and present into a unified, sacred time, so the dramatist unifies dramatic time into the significant and reified present. It is not the dramatist who acts, speaks, and gestures but representations of human persons who, within the script and reinterpreted by players, establish a special order, a unique artistic re-creation, that dramatizes the theme of the dramatist. In other words, *the dramatist acts through acts,* and the history of dramatic scripts is a function of the deepening of the essence of metaphor and dialogue. Contemporary scripts demonstrate the increasing scope of theatrical acts that move into deeper and deeper meanings in smaller and smaller units – from Shaw to Beckett, or from Grillparzer to Hochwalder. Yet the written drama subtly echoes the tiniest shifts of the social atmosphere and re-creates, in the historic time of the dramatist, the most significant elements of human existence: "birth, copulation and death."

But the significations of human life within the script are carefully wrought so that two further levels of dramatic acts can interpret them in human terms: the players and the audience. Both, as Derrida might say, "fill in" the ultimate human meanings within the theatrical medium. Theatre may be "two boards and a passion," for, after all, it can exist without the dramatist's script, but the passion is its focus. The playhouse is human life *in extremis:* the ultimate death we must all face, as in tragedy, and all those little social deaths we suffer day to day, as in comedy.

We are, indeed, "costumed players" whatever the form of our dramatic acts. The possessed and masked ritualist, the child at the dressing-up box, the adult as "the severe father" or "a humble servant," the actor-as-President or the performer as professional – all are signifiers, within a specific milieu, of human Being and Becoming. And it is this which is the essence of drama as a discipline.

DRAMA AND EDUCATION

We create culture through dramatization. By acting "as if," we create the great cultural structures upon which society is built: politics, law, medicine and therapy, education, the arts, communications, and so on. Our concern here is education. The purpose of education is learning, and all activities centre on the learner. The focus of drama departments and educational drama is learning through dramatic action.

Curriculum

When personal, sociocultural, aesthetic, and artistic (theatrical) change is seen as the foundation of drama curricula in universities and colleges, educational drama becomes highly significant. It infuses all other aspects of a drama program – e.g., how actors learned their trade from Burbage to Irving, how a genuine Canadian drama emerged in the 1960s and 1970s, how students learn within a drama program, and so on. Although the increased use of spontaneous drama in Western schools is one of the best kept secrets of the twentieth century,[4] educational drama goes beyond schooling: dramatic transformation is inherent in parenting, social learning, learning to learn, increased differentiation, maturation and re-creation.

While educational drama in a university program is fundamentally experiential, its purpose includes, but is more than, the education of drama teachers. It is the study of dramatic transformation as a total educative process. Drama is holistic in its educative effect. As a unity of imaginative thought and dramatic action, it produces positive changes that transform the way we think, the way we learn and feel, and our moral and ethical attitudes, and it can result in a change of consciousness.

This is a large claim and it needs some explanation. Dramatic action returns us to fundamental mental structures of our early life. As we have seen in *Drama and Intelligence*, the baby, from an initial consciousness of similarity, develops the first forms of differentiation – similar/different and part/whole – which become complicated to continua and comparison. In all forms of later development, these structures remain tacitly constant. These are precisely the same structures as those of dramatic thought and action; as a result, drama refurbishes such structures with and through the dynamics of identification, transformation, and substitution.[5]

These dramatic structures and dynamics operate through the fiduciary contract. By "putting ourselves in someone else's shoes," and "seeing things from another's point of view," one actor comes to trust both the second actor and also the action they mutually create. With juncture rather than disjuncture, dramatic acts re-emphasize a primal mutuality; by encouraging us to see ourselves as similar to others and vice versa, they promote co-operation and de-emphasize stereotypical thinking. This is specifically not to operate in the dominant Western ethos of conflict and competition, but, through the tensions of the contrasts, contradictions, and complementarities of metaphoric thought, it can lead to working well with others, and a moral stance of being a midwife to others.[6] When students function in such a way, we begin to understand the remarkable social cohesion and personal bonding, as well as the changes to our inner life, that can occur under best conditions.

When much educational drama at the university level is based on spontaneous and experiential workshops, it is intended for the developmental learnings of the participants. The specifics of these learnings show a broadening of drama's scientific attitude through a practical human experiment, a "working laboratory of life."[7] Then we holistically and simultaneously explore and improve:

- *intrinsic learnings:* perception, awareness, concentration, different thought-styles, expression, creative problem-solving, inventiveness, confidence and self-worth, motivation, and transfer;[8]
- *extrinsic learnings:* learnings not about the activity itself but its content, or subject matter; e.g., the life of Galileo if that is the subject of the improvisation;
- *aesthetic learnings:* our felt-responses to inner and outer stimuli, our discrimination, choices, and judgments;[9]

- *emotional learnings:* where the literature claims catharsis,[10] our research shows that raw emotion can be gradually displaced on to discrete feelings;[11]
- *artistic learnings:* elements of theatre introduced by the instructor to suit the expressive and developmental needs of the active participants; and
- *social learnings:* through mutuality and the fiduciary contract so that the dramatic experience is a living exemplar of Buber's *I and Thou.*[12]

As these learnings occur when we live through experience in the "here and now," many of them are tacit. Participants quickly learn that if they put them into words afterwards, their meanings alter, and that there is tacit value in the dramatic experience which allows teachers better to infer the intuitive value of their own students' work. Our research also shows that arts and drama teachers place the highest value on the intuitive aspects of learning,[13] perhaps because it reveals aspects of human existence that the Western educational system usually avoids.

Howard Gardner has put forward a theory of multiple intelligences.[14] Instead of seeing intelligence as a general function of mind, Gardner shows that there are linguistic, personal, logico-mathematical, spatial, bodily-kinesthetic, and musical intelligences. On this view, a major claim can be made that there is also a dramatic intelligence. It differs from Gardner's other intelligences in that:

- it provides the fictional experience we live through in the "here and now" with a way of knowing; it combines "as if" thought and action as a fictional double of what is actual;
- as the dynamic context for cognitive, affective, aesthetic and psychomotor learnings, it provides metaphoric meaning and understanding of the human condition;
- it ensures, as Marshall McLuhan has said, that "re-play is re-cognition";[15]
- it teaches generic skills – those skills required in adult work and leisure, such as human negotiation.

Educational Drama

There is a common belief among university teachers that someone who has a BA in, say, math or history does not really require preparation as a teacher. In this fallacy, the content of *what* is taught is all that matters: if a teacher knows differential calculus, say, he or she can teach it. This assumes that school students are miniature adults and can be taught in the same way as university students: by giving them information to regurgitate back to the professor. (The belief accounts for some bad university teaching!) This method began with Locke and reached its apogee with Mr Squeers. It is totally unsuitable for our "global village," where students must learn not so much "the facts" as how to obtain information and how to use it. Contemporary teachers cannot "play God" but must be facilitators for students to learn how to act productively in the world.

Educational drama has a place in liberal arts and fine arts programs, as well as the B ED, for two reasons. First, each program also produces drama teachers and must provide them with a basic core of practical skills, but with varying emphases: all teaching skills in the B ED; skills for high schools in the BFA; and skills to use drama extrinsically in the BA.

But second, educational drama is part of a total ethos. The discipline of developmental drama assumes, as previously outlined here, that dramatization and transformation are the nub of human understanding. Performance centres on the workings of the processual activity of the players, as great improvisational teachers like Viola Spolin and Keith Johnstone have been saying for years.[16] What matters is "the way of working" – dramatic action itself.

This affects traditional aspects of a university drama program, such as theatre history. Glynne Wickham led the way, some thirty years ago, when he staged replicas of performances in history and, as a form of dramatization, discovered previously unknown information, such as the precise use of the "great cloths" in Elizabethan stagecraft.[17] In 1968 in the Faculty of Fine Arts at the University of Victoria, I taught Elizabethan theatre history to undergraduates who, individually but with their class peers as performers, directed scenes that were difficult to stage, and they literally discovered ways to stage them. I acted not as a normal instructor but as a facilitator. Their dramatizations of history were so successful that one student "re-played" the notorious bower scene from Kyd's *The Spanish Tragedy* and published his findings in a paper that probably is still the best solution to the problems.[18]

Production

When we turn from curriculum concerns to the specific issues of stage production, examples best illustrate the issues. Two will serve, one with school students and one with university students. In the 1950s, I specialized in drama with socially deprived youth. The Borough of Smethwick in England had nearly one million people in one mile square (with back-to-back row houses, many with no running water). We established two evening youth clubs working entirely in drama … then residential weekends in large buildings outside the borough … and, finally, a ten-day drama course in a large facility on the hills above Stratford-upon-Avon. All activities were based on improvisation, but the ten-day course finished with an improvised production, back in a Smethwick school before the teenagers' parents, local teachers, and administrators. These productions grew entirely out of the young people's improvisations. They created and made all the scenery and costumes, with adults as facilitators. Only the lighting was in the hands of adults, two youth leaders who set up the equipment back in Smethwick, all ready for the busloads of teenagers who arrived for their dress rehearsal one afternoon, and the single performance in the evening.

By the third year of the residential course, among the fifty young people who arrived were about twelve who had a lot of improvisation experience with us – and they decided to create a medieval Mystery Cycle! Their creative and spontaneous decisions were extraordinary and were exemplars of how to deal with historical material in a contemporary way. The medieval "houses" were small platforms around the four walls of the hall to which actors walked in procession. They created items like a three-sided screen representing the Ark which Noah brought in under his arm; and a fantastic Hell Mouth, based on *The Book of Kells*, on huge sheets of paper which they pinned to the wall, with the mouth itself as the doorway through which the audience entered. But perhaps their most startling decision was to seat the audience in the middle on swivel chairs so that they could turn themselves towards the action. My most vivid memory is of the Three Shepherds (three illiterate boys) as they wandered through the audience, counting them as the sheep – slowly, on their fingers. The face of the Director of Education, when he discovered he was Sheep No. 4, was a study.

The university example is my production of Goldoni's *The Liar* at Calgary in 1971 as part of a pre-professional program. It is the transition play of "the Great Season" of 1750 where Goldoni combined three views of personality: *commedia* masked figures, elegant lovers, and small realistic vignettes. To stress the point, the protagonist, Lelio, is a pathological liar who changes his personality to suit any situation. I used two directoral techniques that are of relevance here. First, early rehearsals were built around each "discovering" his or her personality, and its relation to others, through improvisation in the dramatic process and self-presentation. Second, before each rehearsal and performance, Keith Johnstone worked with Lelio and the *commedia* actors in an hour's improvisation. Thus they arrived "high," with the incredible energy that Johnstone's "Impro" brings,[19] providing a revealing difference with the other performers' levels of personality. These characters, placed against a formal *scène Italienne*, in gorgeous period costumes and executing very formal group movements amongst the comic frenzy, well captured the pathology of multiple personality.

Figure 20
Types of Canadian Drama Programs

PROGRAM	SCHOOL	COLLEGE	UNIVERSITY	DEGREE
Liberal Arts		Arts	Arts and Science	BA
Education			Education	B ED
Technical		Technical		
Pre-professional			Fine arts	BFA
Professional	Professional			

Given the high level of many theatre arts skills required to "pull it off," I would not have attempted the Goldoni production with students in a liberal arts or education program. Too often, in such programs, second-rate conservatory productions are passed off as "educational." Much is due to institutional pressure for the "showcase." But Brian Way[20] has provided us with a basic principle – "Start from where they are" – which must infuse not only public productions but all aspects of a drama curriculum. When dramatization and transformation are viewed as the nub of human understanding, they must be placed in the context of the learners.

PROGRAMS

What is the place of educational drama in universities, colleges, and professional schools in Canada?

Types of Drama Programs

Drama programs as a whole must be designed according to student and social needs. The most common styles of undergraduate programs in Canada are given in figure 20. Examples are: BA in liberal arts (McGill University); B ED in education (University of Toronto); technical (Humber College); BFA (University of Calgary); and professional (The National Theatre School).

These categories are not necessarily exclusive. Some existing liberal arts programs are nearer to degrees in English literature than to drama; others, such as at Calgary, overlap with the BFA. Canada's fine arts programs in drama vary widely as between Victoria, Calgary, Concordia, and York; some regard themselves as professional, yet the National Theatre School expects that their entrants should normally have a bachelor's degree. Some of this confusion is understandable

Figure 21
Relative Balance of Drama Programs

PROGRAM	CONTENT	METHOD	PERFORMANCE SKILLS
Liberal Arts	D* S* L* E* H*	P T	I* X* Z* R* A C
Education	D* S* L E* H*	P* T	I* X* Z* R A C*
Fine Arts	D* S* L E H	P* T	I* X* Z R A* C
Professional	D* S* L H	P* T	I* X* Z A

LEGEND

CONTENT	METHOD	PERFORMANCE SKILLS
D = Dramatic process	P = Experiential	I = Intrinsic
S = Self-presentation	T = Traditional	X = Extrinsic
L = Lit/criticism		Z = Theatre education
E = Educational drama		R = Research (workshop)
H = Theatre history		A = Theatre arts
	* = Emphasis	C = Practice teaching

because, when these programs began, they had to fit the existing structures of their institutions. But that circumstance no longer applies.

What is now required is a rigorous examination of each program in terms of curriculum design. This is to ask: What should be the

- principles (the criteria of program and context)?
- intentions, aims and objectives?
- content?
- methods?
- style(s) of evaluation of programs and assessment of students?
- purpose in staging productions?
- place of educational drama within the program?

Space precludes an exhaustive discussion of these matters here. We can, however, examine some of the key issues.

Outline of Model Programs

Figure 21 provides an overview of four model programs. These are ideal frameworks which will be altered by institutional and regional considerations. It will be noticed that there are considerable overlaps between programs, but that each has its own unique emphasis.

Liberal arts programs provide a general education through a broad program of studies that includes the human dramatic process, self-presentation, world dramatic/theatrical literature/history/criticism, and educational drama. Both experiential and formal instruction methods are used. Performance emphasizes intrinsic skills (personal/social development and self-presentation), extrinsic skills (in text, interpretation, and history), the skills of theatre education, and the skills of drama and theatre as a research methodology, together with the basic skills of theatre as an art. The intention of the program is to produce graduates who will have a skilled critical appreciation as audiences, be good community leaders in all aspects of drama and theatre, and, perhaps, be good teachers. It aims to enliven the spirit of inquiry, thinking at metalevels, and practical human exploration.

Educational programs provide teacher education with an emphasis on the dramatic process and self-presentation, educational drama, and a sound liberal arts background including dramatic literature/criticism/history. Experiential methods are most commonly used. There is a strong emphasis on pre- and in-service drama practice teaching; more than other teachers, those in drama take great risks and their drop-out rate is high; thus extra care must be taken in their preparation, which, in pre-service, should be spread out over three years or more. Other performance activities stressed are specific skills: intrinsic, extrinsic, theatre education, and the use of inference to assess dramatic activity. Basic skills of theatre arts and of drama as a research methodology are also provided. Future high school teachers, in addition, should have the performance skills to understand script. The major intention of the program is to produce teachers who are highly proficient. They should also be able to teach well; design and implement programs for, and adapt flexibly to the needs of, their students; adequately assess students and evaluate programs; deliberate the key issues with their peers; and act as advocates with the general public.

Fine arts programs provide a pre-professional education that emphasizes the dramatic process, self-presentation, and specific skills: intrinsic, extrinsic (to understand text), theatre education, and theatre arts – improvisation, acting, practical interpretation, playwriting, directing, design/technical, and business administration. A basis is provided in dramatic literature/criticism/history, regular experience in educational drama, and drama as a research methodology. The program intention is to produce graduates who will either take a further professional course, or become drama teachers at the senior high or college levels.

Professional schools provide a professional theatre education so that their graduates are employable. Their programs have the same emphases as those in fine arts, but to a higher level. Considering the high proportion of the Canadian theatrical profession employed in Theatre for Young Audiences, performance should also provide skills necessary to be employed in this form.

CONCLUSION

University and college education must focus on the learning of students, and drama is no exception. Our prime aim is for students to experience dramatic action in the "here and now" for the purposes of learning – about the human condition, how we cope with life and death and the trials of existence, and how we work with others to move the action progressively onwards. It is this which provides drama its fundamental legitimacy in institutions of higher learning. How we focus on students's learning will depend upon the particular emphases of the program.

But the task is not easy. It requires a particular kind of teacher, one who can live with process, who is in the ever-present "now" and does not know, in Ortega's words, "what happens next." These abilities hinge on the education of feeling – the aesthetic quality that enables each player to choose well and make appropriate judgments in the present tense. As that great acting teacher, the late Powys Thomas, once said, "A teacher of players lives like an acrobat on a high wire." Similarly, Dorothy Heathcote talks of school drama teachers as "risk takers."[21]

Such teaching requires, on the surface, great self-confidence. It is my experience that the best drama teachers may appear brave, but their constant existence in the uncertainty of spontaneous drama leads them to doubt their abilities. It is no wonder that good drama teachers in schools are subject to quick burn-out. It is easier to duck and run. Yet the same alternative faces us in life: there are some of us who do not want to put ourselves on the line every minute of the day, and who retire into the protection of the known. But there are others who face the existential reality, who live in constant process, and take constant risks with "what happens next." It is among such people that we will find the next generation of good drama teachers.

Will they be the human scientists of the future? That question has been the kernel of this discussion. No doubt readers with a traditional bent will shake their heads. But we should recall that purely objective science has led us, in this century, to divorce basic human concerns from nature. And do we really want to continue that tradition?

Conclusion:
Future Thinking

You can never step into the same river twice.

Heraclitus

Change has become so rapid that it is now a whirligig. Earlier in the twentieth century we have been through the revolutions of space-time, the telephone, flight, radio, television, the atom, the global village, space travel, the shrinking heavens, the computer and the microchip. We must now adjust to bio-engineering and the ecology of the universe. We have responded by continually changing our time-calibrations. Now, in the last decade, we face a new change symbolized by the collapse of the Berlin Wall, and the questions arise: Have we abolished global war? Have we, after "desert storm," established "a new world order"?

THE MENTAL REVOLUTION

To workers in spontaneous drama, these changes have been no surprise. Indeed, we can expect far more as the human mind itself alters. From the end of the nineteenth century, mind has been going through as great a transformation as happened with the wheel, or writing, or Plato's world of forms that created abstraction. Aristotle invented classical logic, began objective science, and chopped existence up into categories. Only slowly did this mental revolution trickle down the centuries so that the printing press mechanized speech and Descartes created the machine metaphor. As human beings were thought of as machines, Newton mechanized the universe. The effect was radical. Two-dimensional melodrama had its parallel in Dickens: his people were fixed in their categories, were incapable of change, and had to obey "the rules" like clockwork.

My grandfather, a teacher who inherited such traditions, thought that spelling was either right or wrong. There was only one way to spell a word, so he thought Shakespeare was not the writer of his plays – how could he be when he was so ignorant as to write his name with different spellings? Yet simultaneously the editors of the great Oxford Dictionary discovered that spelling was in constant change.

My other grandfather was a businessman who in the week got as much work out of his workers for as little pay as possible, but, on Sunday, went to church to love his neighbour. In the reign of Queen Victoria there were clear rules in all of life – things were black or white, right or wrong, good or evil in a world of machines like the railway engine, of empires with their hierarchies, and of the objective scientist, dispassionate and distanced from feeling.

But once Einstein said that $E = mc^2$, it was inevitable for Heisenberg to show in the uncertainty principle that the observer was part of the experiment – a fundamental modern notion that Pirandello had already explored in his theatre. We have lived throughout the century in the wake of Einstein's revolution where spelling, language, and rules alter with usage, where truth is relative to the person and the criteria used, and where life can be seen in either the perspective of time or that of space. As more and more people become aware of this mental development, we are beginning to change our environment like all species that survive. But the mental revolution is not complete and we can expect further changes.

Inherent in the new mental revolution is the dramatic perspective. When the observer is part of the experiment, human beings dramatize existence. As the century began, and Einstein and Pirandello were bringing the revolution to science and art, Caldwell Cook said, "The natural means of study in youth is play."[1] Dramatic activity is the way we learn. Like all revolutionary changes, this began slowly, but it has rapidly increased. Before World War I, Caldwell Cook and Harriet Finlay-Johnson[2] were the only teachers using improvisation in schools anywhere in the world. By 1988, in Ontario alone, there were nearly sixty thousand high school students registered in regular spontaneous drama classes, over two thousand drama teachers (many with graduate degrees), and about one hundred drama consultants. Part of this educational revolution has been that spontaneous drama accepts feeling and emotion as part of the activity because it begins where people are.

A PERPLEXING CASE

Parallel with the use of spontaneous drama in schools, theatre performances for audiences of children, once called Children's Theatre and now known as Theatre for Young Audiences (TFYA), also began early in the twentieth century. Despite its early promise, it is today in crisis. After a resurgence in the 1960s and 1970s, good companies have not increased as we might have expected, and their budgets are cut. In North America it is common for a company to arise one year, develop good work for a while, and then slip into oblivion. Nor can we say that modern plays for TFYA indicate a renaissance.

On the other hand, paradoxically, for nearly twenty years as many Canadian actors have been employed in TFYA as in theatre for adults! So it is not that TFYA is marginally relevant in contemporary culture. Everyone in the field assumes it is highly significant. But the majority show, by their lack of support, that they do not agree. There is a clash of fundamental beliefs and assumptions today, and the arts are the innocent victim of the battle.

Nor did it help that in the 1960s educational theatre groups in Britain and Australia introduced left-wing confrontational politics to young audiences. Then in the 1970s and 1980s there was a conservative reaction to these groups and, thus, also to the mental revolution in which we exist. Politicians like Ronald Reagan and Margaret Thatcher, with a low level of cultural aspiration, wanted to return to "the good old days." Those who controlled funds for the arts became increasingly mechanist. They measured success in two ways: by quantity and by matching. The successful entrepeneur was the ideal model. He put men on the moon or made better mousetraps, built housing estates and made a fortune, or tested children so they were categorized, labelled, and told they were failing. People bought the same mediocre furniture or fashions. Like the Victorian entrepeneur, these people thought the perfect consumer was machine-made. That these ideas were out of date, and that contemporary capitalism was far in advance of them, made little difference, it seems, to those who held the public pursestrings for the arts. And as theatre groups had not changed with the times, things became very difficult for many of them.

ADJUSTING TO CONTEMPORARY THOUGHT

What place can educational drama and theatre have when such values are paramount? To mechanists they appear irrelevant. You cannot measure their importance; it is a matter of *quality*. When specific outcomes must match behavioural objectives, or there is only one right way, or problems are solved by routine, then mechanists control budgets and the arts are the first things to go.

We are in an age when two conflicting metaphors are paramount:

• *The old paradigm*
  Quantity and rigid rules are praised. Each person is a machine with

its input and output, and whose parts must match the parts of others; and decisions are made without reference to feeling.

• *The new paradigm*
Quality, flexibility, and adaptability are praised. The whole person processes information in a unique way, and what s/he makes is personally and socially creative, and has felt-significance.

The greatest danger is to argue for the arts in mechanist terms. That battle is always lost.

But all is *not* lost. Despite the surface success of mechanism, it is doomed. Time is on the side of the holistic metaphor, and drama and theatre education. Throughout this century, the new mental revolution has regularly taken two steps forward and one step back. Year by year more people learn to think and act "as if;" and business is coming to realize that it requires people who are flexible and adaptable. In all probability drama and theatre education may achieve a remarkable rejuvenation in the years to come. Three examples show that mechanism is doomed:

• *Economics*
Many advocates of "fiscal responsibility" are economically incompetent. They try to balance the budget, cut education, social services, and the arts – and end up with a bigger deficit than ever!

• *Education*
Despite the billions of dollars spent this century on educational research (almost all of it mechanical), can we say that education has improved as a result? President John F. Kennedy asked the same question of his new director of Health, Education and Welfare, Francis Keppel; but after Kennedy's assassination, similar studies continued.

• *War*
The incapability of mechanism is best seen from the global war machines. The military leaders both in Vietnam and Afghanistan tried to conclude these wars by matching and quantity; at times, both the United States and the Soviet Union appointed new commanders in the field and each one "did the same only more so." The failure of mechanism in Vietnam was repeated in Afghanistan. Somehow mechanists cannot learn from their previous mistakes. But that is because, to them, there is either a right or wrong way of doing things. And if they were "right" the first time, even if it didn't work, they are right the second, surely? Unfortunately military mechanists cannot see the irony of their situation.

Yet contemporary research in all fields has steadily moved away from mechanism. If drama and theatre education is to have a genuine future, it must reject worn-out assumptions and think in a contemporary fashion. Beginnings have been made. Twenty years ago, TFYA performances were like peas out of a pod: each matched the other. I saw virtually the same show in Seattle, Los Angeles, and New York – but by different companies. Now they can be formal, informal, rehearsed, spontaneous, improvised, or musical, conservative revivals or forms of participation. The field has begun to develop a plurality of frameworks, a complexity of forms, a variety of perspectives on theatre and learning that are as modern as Heisenberg's theory of indeterminacy or Shannon's theory of communication.[3]

As we have seen in this book, Being "as if" is the prime way to operate in Einstein's universe. We think imaginatively by comparing the actual and fictional in a specific context, and this is relative to a similar comparison in another specific context. In the "here and now" human beings operate in space-time: all things are both processual and felt. And we understand them through a gestalt that is continually in flux – an important form of which is "putting oneself in someone else's shoes," or thinking and acting dramatically.

Yet this change is still resisted. Some of us, particularly theatre artists who are caught up in the dominance of old liberal, humanist, and romantic notions, find it difficult to face the variety of intellectual perspectives required by contemporary thought. Life is no longer explicable in the either/or terms of the nineteenth century. It is complex, fragmented, dynamic, ambiguous, and even paradoxical. This is the world of our children who watch more hours of television in their first sixteen years than they have hours of schooling. Today's children no longer learn to think primarily in beginnings/middles/ends. Ask a four-year-old to tell you the story he has just seen on TV, and he will say: "Fred Flintstone threw a stone and it hit Barney, and the man drove the Chevy down the road, and another man told us about the sale, and then a man ate a chocolate bar, and then Barney threw a stone at Fred, and then ... and then ..." Wise teachers today tell stories in fragments so that the TV generation can understand them. We can regret the change and wish it had never happened, but we cannot put the clock back. Teachers who rely on old structures are increasingly taking an early retirement.

In other words, drama and theatre education must alter with the change in human mental structures and dynamics that has occurred in the last generation. If it is to survive, it must be grounded on the fact that today's children, whose minds are strongly influenced by TV (the most successful babysitter of all time), will be the adults of the next century.

It can be both terrifying and exciting to live when human mental structures are changing. This must have happened when the Neolithic revolution brought the change from hunting to farming, or when the ancient Mesopotamians invented the wheel. Previous beliefs were overturned and new ways of thinking brought a massive uncertainty. Einstein destroyed the machine metaphor, Bertrand Russell destroyed classical logic, and today more and more people realize that

- truth depends upon the observer;
- beauty is in the eye of the beholder;
- life is a drama we create;
- the name does not create the fact;
- maps are not territories, and
- rigid categories dissolve in the space-time continuum.

Even knowledge is not the same. Years ago, it was absolute. Today, as Sir Karl Popper has said, it is the result of "informed guessing": mathematics, for instance, relies on estimation and probability. Or, as Michael Polanyi indicates, the explicit knowledge that we talk about hinges upon the knowledge that is tacit, intuitive, and based on feeling. As a result, we understand that drama and theatre are the enactments of possibilities, the testing of hypotheses, while contemporary educational researchers examine "practical knowledge," a mix of the tacit and explicit, otherwise known as "know-how."

FUTURE QUESTIONS

TFYA is theatre directed towards young people and, increasingly, their ways of thinking are the result of the contemporary revolution. If we present a performance with fixed values, absolute morality, and rational ideals, they may applaud. After all, children are easy to fool, for a while at least. But if we do not start from where they are, the effect upon them will be minimal and the company may not be engaged again. If we do not look to *their* future we are wearing blinkers.

What sort of future will they have? As we all know, the major societal change in the West is from heavy industry to communications, and people will require new skills. Modern research in "generic skills" tries to discover the skills learned in school that can transfer to adult life; skills that will be necessary in both work and leisure tomorrow. This is not the old mechanist notion of "vocational" skills, how to write a letter for future secretaries or how to hammer a nail for the budding carpenter. The modern notion of generic skills is different and is advocated by leaders of business and industry who are future thinkers.

What are "generic skills"? In a society where more and more people will change jobs, or even be out of work between jobs, and will have increased leisure, things are different from what they were even a generation ago. Generic skills make up the "practical knowledge" that everyone will need: flexibility and adaptability, positive response to change, strong motivation and devotion to a task, enthusiastic problem identification and solution, and the fundamental abilities of human interaction and communication – the skills of negotiation. Generic skills, like mental structures, are activities with no necessary content. The skills needed by a bank teller are similar in structure to those of, say, a lawyer, but the content varies widely.

But, you may ask, surely these are the human skills taught by improvisation and contemporary TFYA? Precisely! If we can fully realize the modern revolution in human thinking, educational drama and theatre will become the fundamental tools of all education in the future.

When the president of a major Canadian company says that the most important generic skill for his employees is that of human negotiation, he is addressing virtually the same issues as we are. Yet self-presentation and negotiation were also ancient concerns: they were the domain of the Egyptian god Thoth, Socrates lived by them, Pythagoras advocated them, and Augustus Caesar's last thoughts were of them. When mechanists could not cope with self-presentation and negotiation, they became the domain of artists: Shakespeare, Cervantes, Sterne, and Pirandello. Today scholars in many fields use them, together with the use of paradigms and models in both science and social science: Kenneth Burke in criticism, Erving Goffman in sociology, Victor W. Turner in anthropology. Dramatization occurs in advanced business studies and the space program. And performance reality is a major concern of modern philosophers as diverse as Vaihinger, Heidegger, Gadamer, Sartre, and Fink.

It is no wonder, then, that human dramatic performance and self-presentation are increasingly infiltrating school classrooms. Many educators have come to accept that spontaneous drama provides the human, social, and aesthetic grounding for both generic and artistic skills. They accept that varieties of theatricality provide artistic experience for the players, and models of generic skills provide it for the audience. When TFYA supplements classroom drama, it is a powerful medium for the learning of generic skills. Audiences identify with theatrical personages who are more or less successful in life. But the nature of that success differs with time. In the mass media today, success is materialist and mechanist. In TFYA in the past, it was romantic and idealist. Increasingly, however, a few TFYA companies are holist and interpersonal and, therefore, their work is directly related to the actual feelings of young audiences and their concerns for the future.

Audiences bring to the theatre certain patterns or codes whereby they understand meaning: performance codes (what the actors do) and fictional codes (what the play is about). Both codes are based on general assumptions about human existence and conventional rules. But today both codes are in continual change, and among contemporary young audiences these changes are radical.

Take Barrie's *Peter Pan*, for example. This classic mixture of theatricality and sentimental whimsy belongs to the world of Edward VII and the final glories of the British Empire. Yet it has altered its appeal over time. As a child, I had a fictional code that allowed me to identify somewhat with Wendy and the children of the Darling family; but responses indicate that modern audiences rarely do so. I brought to the play a performance code that accepted a woman acting as Peter who flew on a wire. Contemporary urban children, however, acknowledge "reverse drag" on stage for what it is, and they think that Peter's flying is but a pale imitation of the filmic pyrotechnics of Steven Spielberg. On the other hand, Captain Hook, Smee, and the crocodile continue to be hugely enjoyed. Why is that?

Such changes are even more obvious in modern performances of the English Mummers' Play. With the horrors of modern cinema behind them, contemporary children are liable to cheer as much for the Dragon or the Turkish Knight as they are for St George. Fifty years ago, the performance and fictional codes of young people could never have made James Reaney's *Colours in the Dark* the important play for children that it is today. Why is that?

Human feelings of space are changing. The fixed grandeur of the proscenium stage with the audience as voyeurs has less appeal to young audiences than it did fifty years ago. In contrast, flexible and intimate spaces allow them to participate more in the created meaning. Scenery of three-dimensional realism leaves less feeling to be created by the audience than a minimal setting on a bare platform; this interpersonal space of actor and audience allows young people to create maximum feeling and meaning. Space not only varies between groups in our multicultural society, but also most modern audiences demonstrate a need to decrease distance and increase closeness. Why is that?

Theatrical time, as we know, provides six kinds of temporal meaning: the perpetual present, segmental time, plot time, inner chronological time, historical time, and performance time. Today young audiences are far less demanding about the accuracy of segmental plot, inner, and historical time than their peers thirty years ago. They will even, on occasion, suspend the "here and now" for story theatre. Why is that?

But perhaps the greatest change is that young people accept performance as metadrama at an earlier and earlier age. Thirty years ago it was still common for young adolescents to confuse theatrical fiction with actuality. As the hero approached the place where the villain was hiding, they would call out: "Look out! He's round the corner!" Today it is rare for an eight-year-old to suffer the same confusion. Recently a nine-year-old, watching *Death of a Salesman* on TV, said of Willy Loman, "That's Dustin Hoffman, isn't it?" From this age, young people in Western cities share with adults the conventions that the fictional world is distinct from the real world but it is treated as if it is actual; the actor is distinguishable from the role and from the audience; and the performance operates in both real and virtual space and time. Why is that?

These questions reflect a significant trait throughout the Western world, namely *an increasing consciousness of the dramatic medium as a feeling- and meaning-giving operation in life as a whole.* As McLuhan was wont to say, with many variations: the medium is the message (the medium is the mass age ... the medium is the massage ...). This concept indicates the future.

Young people of the electric generation increasingly envisage other realities, temporarily dwell within them, and even treat them as real. Yet, as they do so, they know that they are fictions – that they are not literally taking place at all. They know that they themselves are the play-within-the-play. Provided theatre starts from where they are, it has an immediate appeal. Young people can acknowledge both the characters and the actors performing them, and can accept that this double reality is both fictional and actual.

Young people feel increasingly that the whole of life is liminal. Drama and theatre to them, therefore, are liminoid: they are a microcosm of the macrocosm of human existence. They allow them to re-create reality in novel ways. They transform them and their feelings. They are a means whereby they can communicate with the ultimate reality. They represent the reality behind the role-playing masks. Young people use such masks in order to reveal the possibility of the true face. Thus drama and theatre contain the seed of a fundamental critique of all social structures.

Under these circumstances, it is not too much to claim that drama and theatre are basic and necessary experiences for adults of the future.

Notes

Introduction

1 Richard Courtney, *Drama and Intelligence: A Cognitive Theory* (Montreal: McGill-Queen's University Press, 1990), passim.

2 G. Wilson Knight, Preface to Richard Courtney, *The School Play* (London: Cassell, 1966).

3 Richard Courtney, *A Study of Drama Teachers*, Research Report (Toronto: Ontario Institute for Studies in Education, 1978).

4 Brian Way, *Development through Drama* (London: Longman, 1968).

5 *Dorothy Heathcote: Collected Writings on Education and Drama*, ed. Liz Johnson and Cecily O'Neill (London: Hutchinson, 1984).

6 *Dorothy Heathcote*, 63–9.

7 Richard Courtney, *Re-Play: Studies of Human Drama in Education* (Toronto: Ontario Institute for Studies in Education Press, 1982).

8 Michael Polanyi, *Personal Knowledge* (New York: Harper and Row, 1962), 6.

9 "Turning the world upside down" is an ancient concept; by reversing roles human beings had the power to reverse the cosmos (e.g., the transformation of shamans, the Feast of Fools). This became inherent in Western comedy.

10 Keith Johnstone, *Impro* (London: Faber and Faber, 1979).

11 Jean-Paul Sartre, *Being and Nothingness*, trans. H.E. Barnes (New York: Washington Square, 1968).

12 For the "Vaunt" and the proposition, see Courtney, *Drama and Intelligence*, 32–3, 151.

CHAPTER ONE

1 The word "aestheics" was first used objectively by Baumgarten in 1750. In contrast, Kant used it for a style of thought.

2 Robert W. Witkin, *The Intelligence of Feeling* (London: Heinemann, 1974), 5.

3 Witkin, *The Intelligence of Feeling*, 12.

4 Alfred Korzybski, *Science and Sanity* (Lakefield, Conn.: Beacon Press, 1954), passim.

5 Richard Courtney, *Drama and Intelligence: A Cognitive Theory* (Montreal: McGill-Queen's University Press, 1990), 54–6.

6 Paul Ricouer, *Rule of Metaphor: Multidisciplinary Studies of the Creation of Meaning in Language*, trans. Robert Czerny with Kathleen McLaughlin and John Costello, sj (Toronto: University of Toronto Press, 1977), 214.

7 Floyd Merrell, *Semiotic Foundations: Steps toward an Epistemology of Written Texts* (Bloomington: Indiana University Press, 1982), 64.

8 Thomas S. Kuhn, *The Structure of Scientific Revolutions* (Chicago: University of Chicago Press, 1962); Steven C. Pepper, *World Hypotheses* (Berkeley: University of California Press, 1942); Max Black, "Models and Archetypes," in *Philosophy of Education Research*, ed. Harry S. Broudy (New York: Wiley, 1973), 483–501; Gregory Bateson, *Steps to an Ecology of Mind* (New York: Chandler, 1972).

9 René Descartes, cited in Colin Murray Turbayne, *The Myth of Metaphor* (New Haven, Conn.: Yale University Press, 1962), 39.

10 See Turbayne, *The Myth of Metaphor*; Karl H. Pribram, *Languages of the Brain* (Englewood Cliffs, NJ.: Prentice Hall, 1981).

11 Anthony Wilden, "Semiotics as Praxis: Strategy and Tactics," *Semiotic Inquiry*, 1 (1980): 11.

12 Victor W. Turner, *The Ritual Process: Structure and Anti-Structure* (Harmondsworth: Penguin, 1974), 29.

13 C.A. Bowers, "Curriculum as Cultural Production: An Examination of Metaphor as a Carrier of Ideology," *Teachers College Record*, 82 (1980): 125.

14 Richard H. Brown, *A Poetics for Sociology* (New York: Cambridge University Press, 1978), 78.

15 Peter L. McLaren, *Schooling as a Ritual Performance* (London: Routledge and Kegan Paul, 1983), 562.

16 Bowers, "Curriculum as Cultural Production," 287.

17 Nancy Munn, "Symbolism in a Ritual Context: Aspects of Symbolic Action," in *Handbook of Social and Cultural Anthropology*, ed. John J. Honigmann (Chicago: Rand-McNally, 1973), 973.

18 McLaren, *Schooling as a Ritual Performance*.

19 I.M. Lewis, *Social Anthropology in Perspective* (Harmondsworth: Penguin, 1976).

20 Gilbert Lewis, *Day of Shining Red: An Essay on Understanding Ritual* (Cambridge: Cambridge University Press, 1977), 57.

21 Lewis, *Day of Shining Red*, 58.

22 Vladimir Lenin, *Collected Works* (Moscow, 1931).

23 G.H. Mead, *Mind, Self and Society* (Chicago: University of Chicago Press, 1934).

24 Howard Gardner, *Frames of Mind* (New York: Basic Books, 1984).

25 David R. Olsen, "The Arts as Basic Skills," in *The Arts, Cognition and Basic Skills*, ed. Stanley S. Madeja St Louis, Mo.: CEMREL, 1978), 59–81.

26 Nels Johnson, "Palestinian Refugee Ideology: An Inquiry into Key Metaphors," *Journal of Anthropology Research*, 34 (1978): 524–39.

27 Johnson, "Palestine Refugee Ideology."

28 Sherry Ortner, "On Key Symbols," *American Anthropologist*, 75:5 (October 1973): 1338–46.

29 Abner Cohen, *Symbolic Action and the Structure of the Self* (London: Academic Press, 1977), 123.

30 R.K. Merton, "Bureaucratic Structure and Personality," in *Social Theory and Social Structure*, ed. R.K. Merton (New York: Free Press, 1957), 195–205.

31 Louis Althusser, *Lenin and Philosophy, and Other Essays*, trans. B. Brewster (London/New York: New Left Books/Monthly Review Press, 1971).

32 Jacques Lacan, "The Function of Language in Psychoanalysis," in *The Language of the Self*, ed. A. Wilden (Baltimore: Johns Hopkins University Press, 1968).

33 J. Laplance and J.B. Pontalis, *The Language of Psychoanalysis* (London: Hogarth Press, 1973), 251.

34 Kenneth Burke, *Language as Symbolic Action* (Berkeley: University of California Press, 1965).

35 Anthony Wilden, *System and Structure* (London: Tavistock, 1972).

36 Bateson, *Steps to an Ecology of Mind*.

37 Gregory Baum, *Religion and Alienation: A Theological Reading of Sociology* (New York: Paulist Press, 1973).

38 Rollo May, "The Significance of Symbols," in May, ed., *Symbolism in Religion and Literature* (New York: George Braziller, 1961).

CHAPTER TWO

1 Victor W. Turner, *From Ritual to Theatre: The Human Seriousness of Play* (New York: Performing Arts Journal Publications, 1982), 91.

2 R.S. Perinbanayagam, "The Definition of the Situation: An Analysis of the Ethnomethodological and Dramaturgical View," *Sociological Quarterly*, 15 (Fall 1974): 534.

3 Miles Richardson, "Putting Death in Its Place in Spanish America and the American South: Application of the Dramaturgical Model to Religious Behaviour," paper presented at the Wenner-Gren Foundation for Anthropological Research Symposium no. 89, "Theatre and Ritual." The Asia Society, New York (Summer, 1982).

4 Mary Douglas, *Natural Symbols: Explorations in Cosmology* (New York: Random House, 1973), 72–3.

5 Robert Harrison, "Where Have All the Rituals Gone?" in *The Imagination of Reality: Essay in Southeast Asian Coherence Systems*, ed. A.L. Becker and Aram A. Yengoyan, (Norwood, NJ.: Ablex Publishing, 1980), 55.

6 David A. Frank, "'Shalom Achshav' – Rituals of the Israeli Peace Movement," *Communication Monographs*, 48 (September 1981).

7 Michel Foucault, *Discipline and Punish: The Birth of the Prison* (New York: Pantheon Books, 1973).

8 See *Myth, Symbol and Culture*, ed. Clifford Geertz, (New York: Norton, 1971); Sherry Ortner, "On Key Symbols," *American Anthropologist*, 75:5 (October 1973): 1338–46; David M. Schneider, *American Kinship* (Englewood Cliffs, NJ: Prentice Hall, 1968); Victor W. Turner, *The Ritual Process: Structure and Anti-Structure* (Harmondsworth: Penguin, 1974), 29.

9 Nancy Munn, "Symbolism in a Ritual Context: Aspects of Symbolic Action," in *Handbook of Social and Cultural Anthropology*, ed. John J. Honigmann (Chicago: Rand-McNally, 1973) 973.

10 Ronald L. Grimes, cited in Peter L. McLaren, *Schooling as a Ritual Performance* (London: Routledge and Kegan Paul, 1983), 29.

11 Roy A. Rappaport, "Concluding Remarks on Ritual and Reflexivity," *Semiotica*, 30: 1/2 (1980): 181–93.

12 Roland A. Delattre, "Ritual Resourcefulness and Cultural Pluralism," *Soundings*, 61 (1978): 283–301.

13 McLaren, *Schooling as a Ritual Performance*, 562.

14 Barbara Meyerhoff, "We Don't Wrap Herring in a Printed Page: Fusion, Fictions and Continuity in Secular Ritual," in *Secular Ritual* (Amsterdam: Royal Van Gorcum, 1977).

15 McLaren, *Schooling as a Ritual Performance*.

16 Urban T. Holmes, "Liminality and Liturgy," *Worship*, 47:7 (August 1977): 58–75.

17 Rollo May, "The Significance of Symbols," in *Symbolism in Religion and Literature*, ed. May (New York: George Braziller, 1961).

18 Abner Cohen, *Symbolic Action and the Structure of the Self* (London: Academic Press, 1977), 123.

19 Umberto Eco, *A Theory of Semiotics* (Bloomington: Indiana University Press, 1976); I.M. Lewis, *Social Anthropology in Perspective* (Harmondsworth: Penguin, 1976).

20 Munn, "Symbolism in a Ritual Context"; Grimes, *Beginnings in Ritual Studies*.

21 Mircea Eliade, *The Sacred and the Profane* (New York: Harcourt, Brace, 1959), 130.

22 T.G.H. Strehlow, *Aranada Traditions* (Melbourne, Australia, 1947), 56–7.

23 Arnold Van Gennep, *Rites of Passage* (Chicago: University of Chicago Press, 1960); Victor W. Turner, *The Drums of Affliction* (Oxford: Clarendon Press, 1968).

24 The function of ritual, says Ernst Cassirer, in *The Philosophy of Symbolic Forms*, 3 vols., trans. Ralph Manheim (New Haven, Conn.: Yale University Press, 1957), is to unite the Self and the external world symbolically. For Suzanne K. Langer (*Feeling and Form* [New York: Scribner's, 1953]), ritual is like art: both are transformations of experience into symbolic truths.

25 Meyerhoff, "We Don't Wrap Herring."

26 McLaren, *Schooling as a Ritual Performance*, 41.

27 Victor W. Turner, "Process, System and Symbol: A New Anthropological Synthesis," *Daedalus*, 106: 3 (Summer 1977): 73.

28 P.G. Clancy, "The Place of Ritual in Schools: Some Observations," *Unicorn*, 3 (March 1977).

29 Ronald L. Grimes, *Symbol and Conquest: Public Ritual and Drama in Santa Fe, New Mexico* (Ithaca, NY: Cornell University Press, 1976).

30 Victor W. Turner, *Process, Performance and Pilgrimage: A Study in Comparative Symbology* (New Delhi: Concept Publishing, 1979).

31 Hans Georg Gadamer, *Truth and Method* (London: Sheed and Ward, 1976).

32 Clifford Geertz, "Religion as a Cultural System," in *Reader in Comparative Religion, An Anthropological Approach*, 2nd ed. (New York: Harper and Row, 1965).

33 Johan Huizinga, *Homo Ludens* (Boston: Beacon Press, 1955).

34 Turner, "Process, System and Symbol."

35 Douglas, *Natural Symbols*.

36 Delattre, "Ritual Resourcefulness."

37 It was held as such by the evolutionary workers early in this century as it is by contemporary thinkers; e.g., Ernest Theodore Kirby, *Ur-Drama: The Origins of Theatre* (New York: New York University Press, 1975); James L. Peacock, *Rites of Modernization: Symbolic and Social Aspects of Indonesian Proletarian Drama* (Chicago: University of Chicago Press, 1968). For E.J. Burton (paper privately circulated, 1985), the same dramatic impulse infuses all types of ritual – in life, in education, in society, and in theatre.

38 Richard Schechner and Mady Schuman, *Ritual, Play and Performance: Readings in the Social Sciences/Theatre* (New York: Seabury Press, 1976).

39 Turner, *From Ritual to Theatre*.

40 Jerzy Grotowski, *Towards a Poor Theatre* (New York: Simon and Schuster, 1968).

41 Grimes, *Beginnings in Ritual Studies*.

42 McLaren, *Schooling as a Ritual Performance*, appendix B.

43 Erik H. Erikson, *Childhood and Society* (New York: Norton, 1966).
44 This is supported by findings in child psychology; e.g., Melanie Klein, *Narrative of Child Analysis* (London: Hogarth Press, 1932); David W. Winnicott, *Playing and Reality* (Harmondsworth: Penguin, 1974); Otto Weininger, *Play and Education: The Basic Tool for Early Childhood Learning* (Springfield, Ill.: Charles C. Thomas, 1979, 1982).
45 Aidan Kavanagh, "The Role of Ritual in Personal Development," in *The Roots of Ritual*, ed. James Shaughnessy (Grand Rapids: W.B. Eerdmans Publishing, 1973).
46 Rappaport, "Concluding Remarks."
47 Roy A. Rappaport, *Ecology, Meaning and Religion* (Richmond, Calif.: Atlantic Books, 1979), 84.
48 Barbara Meyerhoff, "Rites of Passage: Process and Paradox," in *Celebration Studies in Festivity and Ritual*, ed. Victor Turner (Washington, DC: Smithsonian Institute Press, 1982), 28.
49 Ortner, cited in Meyerhoff, "Rites of Passage," 129.
50 Contemporary scholars have discussed these issues in a variety of ways: as "performative utterances" (John Langshaw Austin, *How to Do Things with Words* [Oxford: Oxford University Press, 1962]), "speech acts" (John R. Searle, *Speech Acts: An Essay and the Philosophy of Language* [Cambridge: Cambridge University Press, 1969]), "operative acts" (John Skorupski, *Symbol and Theory: A Philosophical Study of Theories of Religion in Social Anthropology* [Cambridge: Cambridge University Press, 1976]), and "factive acts" (Doherty, cited in James L. Richmond, *Race and Education* [1973]).
51 Rappaport, *Ecology, Meaning and Religion*, 190.
52 David R. Olsen, Jeremy Anglin, et al., eds., *The Social Foundations of Language and Thought: Essays in Honour of Jerome S. Bruner* (New York: Norton, 1980).
53 Jacques Derrida, *Dissemination*, trans. Barbara Johnson (Chicago: University of Chicago Press, 1981), 91.
54 Theodore Jennings, "On Ritual Knowledge," *Journal of Religion*, 62:2 (April 1982): 111–27.
55 Jacob L. Moreno, "The Creativity of Personality," *New York University Bulletin, Arts and Sciences*, 46:4 (January 1966): 19–24.
56 Jean-Paul Sartre, *Being and Nothingness*, trans. H.E. Barnes (New York: Washington Square, 1953).
57 A.F.C. Wallace, *Religion: An Anthropological View* (New York: Random House, 1966). A number of contemporary studies have examined the importance of the body in learning. Thus, for example, we learn proxemic relations – spatial codes which provide us with a semiotically loaded choice subject to powerful cultural rules (Edward T. Hall, *The Hidden Dimension* [New York: Doubleday, 1966]); each culture selects from an immense po-

tential a strictly limited number of units of human movement (Ray L. Bird-whistell, *Kinesics and Context: Essays on Body Motion Communication* [Philadelphia: University of Pennsylvania Press, 1971]), but indication is prior to signification in the "language" of gesture (Julia Kristeva, "Prob-lemes de la Structuration du Texte," *Nouvelle Critique*, 5:10 [1968]: 55–64). Elam puts it that "A major role of gesture – particularly on stage – is to indicate the intentionality of a given utterance. Simultaneous movement will serve to emphasize, or even define, the kind of speech act being per-formed by the speaker (and thus the character) in uttering a given sequence of words, be it a question, a command, a demand, an affirmation, etc." (Keir Elam, *The Semiotics of Theatre and Drama* [London: Methuen, 1980]).

58 Evan M. Zuesse, "Meditation on Ritual," *Journal of the American Acad-emy of Religion*, 44:33 (1975): 518.

59 Grimes, *Beginnings in Ritual Studies*.

60 Rappaport, "Concluding Remarks."

61 Claude Lévi-Strauss, *The Scope of Anthropology*, trans. S.D. Paul and R.A. Paul (London: Cape, 1967).

62 Anthony Wilden, "Semiotics as Praxis: Strategy and Tactics," *Semiotic Inquiry*, 1 (1980).

CHAPTER THREE

1 Roland Barthes, *Système de la Mode* (Paris: Seuil, 1967), 12.

2 A.-J. Greimas, *Structural Semantics* (Lincoln: Nebraska University Press, 1983), 121.

3 H. Marshall McLuhan, *Understanding Media: The Extensions of Man* (London: Routledge and Kegan Paul, 1964).

4 Floyd Merrell, *Semiotic Foundations: Steps toward an Epistemology of Written Texts* (Bloomington: Indiana University Press, 1982), 15.

5 Ernest Becker, *The Denial of Death* (New York: Free Press, 1973).

6 Ludwig Wittgenstein, *Philosophical Investigations*, trans. G.E.M. Anscombe (New York: Macmillan, 1953), 200E.

7 This is the view of both contemporary information theory (Jeremy Camp-bell, *Grammatical Man: Information, Entropy, Language and Life* [New York: Simon and Schuster, 1982]) and epistemology (Karl R. Popper, *Ob-jective Knowledge* [London: Oxford University Press, 1972]).

8 Umberto Eco, *A Theory of Semiotics* (Bloomington: Indiana University Press, 1976); Umberto Eco, *Semiotics and the Philosophy of Language* (Bloomington, Indiana University Press, 1984).

9 Merrell, *Semiotic Foundations*, 24.

10 Charles Sanders Peirce, *Collected Papers*, ed. C. Hartshorne and P. Weiss, vols. 1–6 (Cambridge: Harvard University Press, 1931), 5.220.

11 To measure the length of a wall is really a comparison or a ratio – the ratio of the length of a wall to that of the standard metre. A measurement of length involves both the cardinal and ordinal aspects of numbers: whereas cardinal numbers designate size or amount, and ordinal numbers express rank or sequential order, a measurement implies both. See Roger S. Jones, *Physics as Metaphor* (New York: New American Library, 1982).

12 Duality is, for example, assumed by some structuralists (Jonathan Culler, *Structuralist Poetics* [Ithaca, NY: Cornell University Press, 1975]; Claude Lévi-Strauss, *Totemism*, trans. R. Needham [Boston: Beacon Press, 1968]), but not all, and it is the basis for some semiotic inquiries (Peirce, *Collected Papers*; Ferdinand de Saussure, *Course in General Linguistics* [New York: McGraw-Hill, 1966]). George Kelly (*The Psychology of Personal Constructs*, 2 vols. [New York: Norton, 1955]), said that each individual creates "a personal construct" with a bi-polar pattern that he or she tries to fit to reality. There are many instances of contemporary theories of thought that have dualistic elements, including the play and imitation of Piaget, the intuition and intellect of Jerome Bruner (*On Knowing: Essays for the Left Hand* [Cambridge: Harvard University Press, 1962]), the innovative and fixed rules of Michael Polanyi (*Personal Knowledge* [New York: Harper and Row, 1962]), and the two hemispheres of the brain delineated by contemporary neurology (see pp. 119–20). Duality was the basis of computer science and the development of artificial intelligence (Norbert Weiner, *The Human Use of Human Beings* [New York: Doubleday, 1950]).

13 Stephen C. Pepper, *World Hypotheses* (Berkeley: University of California Press, 1942), 142.

14 Cited by Carl Gustav Jung, "A Psychological Approach to the Trinity," in *Psychology and Religion* (London: Routledge and Kegan Paul, 1958), 123–7.

15 Mircea Eliade, *The Sacred and the Profane* (New York: Harcourt, Brace, 1959).

16 Eliade, *The Sacred and the Profane*, 47.

17 Carlos Casteneda, *The Teachings of Don Juan: A Yaqui Way of Knowledge* (New York: Ballantine, 1968), and other volumes.

18 Jones, *Physics as Metaphor*, 148–9.

19 Alfonso Ortiz, *New Perspectives on the Pueblos* (Albuquerque: University of New Mexico Press, 1972), 143.

20 Richard Courtney, "The Dramatic Metaphor and Learning," in *Creative Drama in a Developmental Context*, ed. Judith Kase-Polisini (Lanham, Md.: University Press of America, 1985), 39–64.

21 Colin Murray Turbayne, *The Myth of Metaphor* (New Haven: Yale University Press, 1962), 22.

22 Jones, *Physics as Metaphor*, 4.

23 Historically this was the origin of the later concept of Heaven and Hell.

Today, a devout Christian believes in two spiritual worlds: the righteous dead go to Heaven yet he places flowers on their graves.

24 Joseph Campbell, *The Masks of God*, 4 vols. (New York: Viking, 1968), 1:210–15.

25 Hyemeyohsts Storm, *Seven Arrows* (New York: Ballantine, 1972), 6.

26 Wallis Budge, *Gods of the Egyptians* (repr. New York: Dover, 1969), 1:210.

27 E.J. Burton, paper privately circulated (1985).

28 Wallis Budge, *The Literature of the Ancient Egyptians* (London: Dent, 1914), 21.

29 Juan Eduardo Cirlot, *A Dictionary of Symbols*, trans. Jack Sage (New York: Philosophical Library, 1962).

30 These concepts were echoed in Celtic and Greek myths.

31 Ann Rosalie David, *Religious Ritual at Abydos* (Warminster, UK: Aris and Phillips, 1973).

32 There are two actable versions of this ritual drama: H.W. Fairman, *The Triumph of Horus* (London: Batsford, 1974); Richard Courtney, *Lord of the Sky* (Jackson's Point, Ont.: Bison Books, 1989).

33 C.J. Bleeker, *Hathor and Thoth, Two Key Figures of the Ancient Egyptian Religion* (Leiden: Brill, 1973).

34 Peter Gorman, *Pythagoras – A Life* (London: Routledge and Kegan Paul, 1979).

35 Gorman, *Pythagoras – A Life*.

36 Herman Diels, *The Older Sophists* (New York: Columbia University Press, 1972), 282.

37 Daniel 7:2.

38 Revelation 7:1.

39 Carl Gustav Jung, "Archetypes and the Collective Unconscious," trans. R.F.C. Hull, in *Collected Works of C. G. Jung*, vol. 9 (Princeton: Princeton University Press, 1959).

40 Jung, *Psychology and Religion*.

41 Ralph Metzner, *Maps of Consciousness* (New York: Collier, 1971), passim.

42 Cirlot, *A Dictionary of Symbols*, 256–7.

43 Malcolm Crick, *Explorations in Language and Meaning* (New York: Wiley, 1976), 148.

44 Heinrich Zimmer, in *Myths and Symbols in Indian Art and Civilization*, ed. Joseph Campbell (Princeton: Princeton University Press, 1946), 52.

45 Cirlot, *A Dictionary of Symbols*.

46 Common Hindu sayings.

47 Four as a sign plays a large part in Chinese thinking. For example, in the Han Dynasty of the second century BC, coffins were made out of four boards from four different trees; coloured drapery was hung over the coffin according to the four points of heaven while the sides were adorned with animals signifying the four quarters; on the top, drapery was drawn to-

gether in a pyramid to signify the North Pole; and the seven stars of the
Great Bear were distributed over the whole. This constellation was known
as the Great Dragon, the chariot in which the sun journeyed over the heav-
enly sea at night; as the setting sun was the metaphor of death, death was
known as "the Night Sea Journey" – which has similarities with Egypt and
Greece. What the quaternity signified was the ultimate meaning of life/
death, the seasons, and the cosmos.

48 Yolande Jacobi, *Complex/Archetype/Symbol in the Psychology of C.G.
Jung* (Princeton: Princeton University Press, 1959), 184.

49 Lama Anagarika Govinda, *Foundations of Tibetan Mysticism* (New York:
Samuel Weiser, 1969).

50 Giuseppe Tucci, *The Theory and Practice of the Mandala* (New York:
Samuel Weiser, 1969).

51 *The World Is as Sharp as a Knife: An Anthology in Honour of Wilson Duff*
(Vancouver: British Columbia Provincial Museum, 1981).

52 Tucci, *The Theory and Practice of the Mandala*.

53 José and Miriam Arguelles, *Mandala* (Berkeley: Shambhala Press, 1972),
92.

54 Eco, *A Theory of Semiotics* and *Semiotics and the Philosophy of Language*.

55 Audrey Selincourt, ed. *Herodotus* (Harmondsworth: Penguin, 1955), 160.

56 Strabo (XVII) 1:37.

57 Paul Edwards, cited in *An Exploration in Religious Education* (Indepen-
dence, Mo.: Harold, 1967), 174.

58 Hans Georg Wunderlich, *The Secret of Crete*, trans. Richard Winston (New
York: Macmillan, 1974), 314.

59 Sir Arthur Evans, *The Palace of Minos*, 4 vols. (London: Macmillan, 1921–
35).

60 Wunderlich, *The Secret of Crete*.

61 W.H. Matthews, *Mazes and Labyrinths* (New York: Dover [1922] 1970),
70.

62 The Greek myth of the Cretan Minotaur and Theseus was of a much later
date than the time when the Cretan labyrinth was an active religious site.
How true a picture it provides of the necropolis is difficult to tell, but, compared even with the existing ruins, it appears somewhat simplistic. Indeed,
the picture of Knossos given by Wunderlich (*The Secret of Crete*) is of a
structure so complex as to resemble the polydimensional network of meaning of Eco's "Model Q." What is clear, however, is that the Cretan labyrinth
was a sign, or model, that conveyed the meaning of life, the cosmos, and the
way in which the human mind comprehended existence.

63 Evans, *The Palace of Minos*.

64 The tapered or conical pillars are found on coins where they were named
after Agyieus, who first established shrines at Delos and Delphi; they both
were phallic signifiers and signified life after death. The "petasus" from

which bells were suspended by chains, making a tinkling sound "as was done in bygone times at Dodona," may well indicate a connection with the necropolis of Crete, where this also happened.

65 Illustrated in several nineteenth-century volumes.

66 Labyrinthine motifs are found in Roman mosaics dating from the first century AD, from all over Europe (Matthews, *Mazes and Labyrinths*). One has survived intact at Salzburg, Austria, the central feature of which has Theseus about to kill the Minotaur.

67 Matthews, *Mazes and Labyrinths*.

68 Nigel Pennick, *The Ancient Science of Geomancy: Man in Harmony with the Earth* (London: Thames and Hudson, 1979), 64.

69 Pennick, *The Ancient Science of Geomancy*, 65.

70 *Drychy Prit Oesoedd* (1740), cited in Matthews, *Mazes and Labyrinths*.

71 John Aubrey, ed. *Remaines of Gentilisme and Judaisme*, ed. J. Britten (W. Satchell, Peyton and Co., 1686). See also W. Treves, *Highways and Byways in Dorset* (London: Macmillan, 1952), 325.

72 Lady Alice Gomme, *Traditional Games in England and Wales*, 2 vols. (repr. New York: Doubleday, 1974), 1:223.

73 1 Samuel 13:32–3.

74 Pliny indicates that "we must not compare the Egyptian and other labyrinths with what we see on our mosaic pavements, or to the mazes formed in the fields for the entertainment of children" (Pliny xxxvi, 19, 4).

75 Jackson Knight, *Elysion: Ancient Greek and Roman Beliefs concerning Life after Death* (London: Rider, 1970).

CHAPTER FOUR

1 Gilbert Ryle, *The Concept of Mind* (New York: Harper and Row, 1949).

2 J.B. Watson, cited in Floyd Matson, *Image and Affection in Behaviour* (Matson Publishing, 1913).

3 Clark L. Hull, *Principles of Behavior* (New York: Appleton, 1943).

4 B.F. Skinner, *Science and Human Behavior* (New York: Macmillan, 1953).

5 Jung also distinguished the personal unconscious, of dimmed memories and repressed materials, from the collective unconscious that was shared by all human beings: "the inherited possibility of psychical functioning ... the brain structure" (Carl Gustav Jung, *Aion: Researches into the Phenomenology of the Self*, trans. R.F.C. Hull [London: Routledge and Kegan Paul, 1959]). Jung shared the concept of the collective unconscious as a major form of signification with de Saussure, members of the Prague School, and various other semioticians.

6 Others shared the view that mind was dynamic through the oscillation between diverse parts like the alternating current of electricity. Erich Fromm (*The Heart of Man* [New York: Harper and Row, 1966]) said that we men-

tally create the choices between two poles on a continuum: decay and growth. Otto Rank (*The Myth of the Birth of the Hero and Other Writings* [New York: Vintage Books, 1914]) and Ernest Becker (*The Denial of Death* [New York: Free Press, 1973]) proposed an oscillation between life and death: mind denies death to rid itself of the painful paradox of life-in-death. For Becker, we create ideologies to deny death, whereas Silvan Tomkins ("Left and Right: A Basic Dimension of Ideology," in *The Study of Lives: Essays on Personality in Honor of Henry A. Murray*, ed. Robert W. White [New York: Atherton, 1963]) says that ideology is the prime characteristic of mind: it provides the oscillating hypotheses by which we work in the world.

7 Soren Kierkegaard, *Sickness unto Death* (New York: Anchor, 1954).

8 Rollo May, *The Meaning of Anxiety* (New York: Norton, 1977).

9 Paul Tillich, *The Courage to Be* (London: Collins, 1952).

10 Jean-Paul Sartre, *Being and Nothingness*, trans. H.E. Barnes (New York: Washington Square, 1953).

11 R.D. Laing, *The Divided Self* (Harmondsworth: Penguin, 1965).

12 P.D. MacLean, "Psychosomatic Disease and the 'Visceral Brain': Recent Developments Bearing on the Papez Theory of Emotion," *Psychosomatic Medicine*, 11 (1949).

13 Julian Jaynes, *The Origins of Consciousness and the Breakdown of the Bicameral Mind* (Boston: Houghton, Mifflin, 1976).

14 Karl H. Pribram, *Languages of the Brain* (Englewood Cliffs, NJ: Prentice Hall, 1981).

15 Martin Buber, *I and Thou* (New York: Scribner's, 1958).

16 Maurice S. Friedman, *Martin Buber: The Life of Dialogue* (New York: Harper, 1969).

17 Arthur Koestler, *The Act of Creation* (New York: Macmillan, 1964).

18 Frank Barron, *Creativity and Personal Freedom* (Princeton: Princeton University Press, 1968).

19 R. Buckminster Fuller, *Synergetics* (New York: Macmillan, 1975).

20 Abraham H. Maslow, *Motivation and Personality* (New York: Harper and Row, 1954).

21 Ludwig Von Bertalanffy, *Robots, Men and Minds* (New York: George Braziller, 1967).

22 Jonas Salk, *Man Unfolding* (New York: Harper and Row, 1972); Jonas Salk, *Survival of the Wisest* (New York: Harper and Row, 1973).

23 Gregory Bateson, *Steps to an Ecology of mind* (New York: Chandler, 1972).

24 Jeremy Campbell, *Grammatical Man: Information, Entropy, Language and Life* (New York: Simon and Schuster, 1982).

25 James J. Gibson, *The Senses Considered as Perceptual Systems* (Boston: Houghton, Mifflin, 1966).

26 John W. Dixon, Jr, "The Metaphoric Transformation: An Essay on the Physiology of the Imagination," *Sociological Analysis*, 34:1 (1973): 61–2.

27 Dixon, "The Metaphoric Transformation," 63.

28 Dixon, "The Metaphoric Transformation," 64.

29 Victor W. Turner, *The Ritual Process: Structure and Anti-Structure* (Harmondsworth: Penguin, 1974).

30 Floyd Merrell, *Semiotic Foundations: Steps toward an Epistemology of Written Texts* (Bloomington: Indiana University Press, 1982), 41–2.

31 Keith Johnstone, *Impro* (London: Faber and Faber, 1979).

32 Ricoeur, in dealing with Jakobsen's famous article on metaphor and metonymy, indicates that there is a richness in the distinction: "Poetic forms show a predominance sometimes of metonymy, as in realism, and sometimes of metaphor, as with romanticism and symbolism ... In painting, one can speak of metonymy in connection with cubism, of metaphor with surrealism. In film, the synecdochic close-ups and the metonymic montage of D.W. Griffith contrast with the metaphoric montage of Charlie Chaplin" (*The Philosophy of Paul Ricoeur*, ed. Charles Reagan and David Stewart [Boston: Beacon Press, 1978], 177–8). But Ricoeur warns that, should the distinction be extended into discrete categories, it would be of much less value.

33 Yet, despite Aristotle, we do learn metaphor. Primarily, we learn to create when we learn to think and act efficiently within "the double." Two understandings are basic to such learning: "that tension, contradiction, and controversion are nothing but the opposite side of the reconciliation in which metaphor 'makes sense'"; and "that resemblance is itself a fact of predication, which operates between the same terms that contradiction sets in tension" (Ricoeur, *Philosophy*, 195). This learning has its basis in play.

34 Another perspective on this process is to see a metaphor as a kind of "category mistake": "The presentation of facts belonging to one category in the idioms appropriate to another" (Ryle, *The Concept of Mind*, 10). The metaphor in a poem, novel, or a song is a speaking of one thing in terms of another that resembles it (Ricoeur, *Philosophy*, 197). The metaphor in a drawing, a painting, or a sculpture is something which is perceived to be other than how it is ordinarily perceived, although there is a resemblance to the ordinary perception. In the same way, children playing at "mothers and fathers" are involved in a "category mistake": they engage in a mental "flip" between the two sides of the "double" (the actual and the imagined), although there is a resemblance between the two.

35 Selma Jeanne Cohen, ed., *The Modern Dance* (Middleton, Conn.: Wesleyan University Press, 1966).

36 Ricoeur, *Philosophy*, 196.

37 Herrschberges (1943), 434, cited in Ricoeur, *Philosophy*.

38 Merrell, *Semiotic Foundations*, 57.

39 Norbert Weiner, *The Human Use of Human Beings* (New York: Doubleday, 1948), 199.

40 See David Bohm, "Quantum Theory as an Indication of a New Order in

Physics," in *Foundations of Physics I* (Toronto: University of Toronto Press, 1971, 1979); Albrecht and Thorell de Valois, "Cortical Cells: Bar and Edge Detectors or Spatial Frequency Filters?" in *Frontiers in Visual Science*, ed. S. Cool and E. L. Smith (New York: Springer-Verlag, 1978), 544–556; Pribram, *Languages of the Brain*.

41 Merrell, *Semiotic Foundations*, 57.
42 Merrell, *Semiotic Foundations*, 61.
43 Ludwig Wittgenstein, *Philosophical Investigations*, trans. G.E.M. Anscombe (New York: Macmillan, 1953)
44 George Lakoff and Mark Johnson, *Metaphors We Live By* (Chicago: University of Chicago Press, 1980), 176–7.
45 Wittgenstein, *Philosophical Investigations*, 2: ix.
46 Paul Ricoeur, "The Function of Fiction in Shaping Reality," paper delivered at the Pennsylvania State University (February 1977), 213.
47 Marcus B. Hester, *The Meaning of Poetic Metaphor: An Analysis in Light of Wittgenstein's Claim That Meaning Is Use* (The Hague: Mouton, 1967), 180.
48 Lakoff and Johnson, *Metaphors We Live By*, 178–9.
49 Ricoeur, "The Function of Fiction in Shaping Reality," 200.

CHAPTER FIVE

1 Bertrand Russell, *Human Knowledge* (London: Allen and Unwin, 1948).
2 Michael Polanyi, *Science, Faith and Society* (Chicago: University of Chicago Press, 1964).
3 Floyd Merrell, *Semiotic Foundations: Steps toward an Epistemology of Written Texts* (Bloomington: Indiana University Press, 1982), ix–x.
4 Adriaan D. Groot, "Perception and Memory Versus Thought: Some Old Ideas and Recent Findings," in *Problem Solving*, ed. B. Klienmuntz (New York: Wiley, 1966), 19–50.
5 Merrell, *Semiotic Foundations*, 2.
6 Jeremy Campbell, *Grammatical Man: Information, Entropy, Language and Life* (New York: Simon and Schuster, 1982).
7 See Rudolf Arnheim, *Visual Thinking* (Berkeley: University of California Press, 1969); Peter Berger and Thomas Luckmann, *The Social Construction of Reality* (New York: Doubleday, 1966); Jerome S. Bruner, *Contemporary Approaches to Cognition: A Symposium Held at the University of Colorado* (Cambridge: Harvard University Press, 1957); E.H. Gombrich, *Art and Illusion* (London: Phaidon, 1960); Ulrich Neisser, *Cognitive Psychology* (Englewood Cliffs, NJ: Prentice Hall, 1967); A. Paivio, *Imagery and Verbal Processes* (New York: Holt, Rinehart and Winston, 1971); Jean Piaget and Barbel Inhelder, with H. Sinclair-deZwart, *Memory and Intelligence* (London: Routledge and Kegan Paul, 1973); Michael Polanyi, *Personal Knowl-*

edge (New York: Harper and Row, 1962); Karl R. Popper, *Objective Knowledge* (London: Oxford University Press, 1972), as well as many semioticians.

8 Jacques Derrida, *Dissemination* (Chicago: University of Chicago Press, 1981), 143.

9 Merrell, *Semiotic Foundations*, 5.

10 George Lakoff and Mark Johnson, *Metaphors We Live By* (Chicago: University of Chicago Press, 1980)

11 Jacques Derrida, *Margins of Philosophy*, trans. A. Bass (Chicago: University of Chicago Press, 1982).

12 Roland Barthes, *Le Plaisir du Texte* (Paris: Seuil, 1973), 40.

13 Anette Lavers, *Roland Barthes: Structuralism and After* (Cambridge, Mass.: Harvard University Press, 1982), 170.

14 L.S. Vygotsky, *Thought and Language*, trans. Eugenia Haniman and Gertrude Vakar (Cambridge. Mass.: MIT Press, 1962), 126.

15 When we look at the words of a novel, or the colours and shapes of a painting, we always do so from a particular perspective, or frame of reference. We "see" what we knew we would "see." Thus, "it can in a certain way be said that 'seeing' is a form of knowing, knowing is cognition, and re-cognition is knowing again" (Merrell, *Semiotic Foundations*, 72). Re-play is re-cognition, as McLuhan said. Our original thought and action have affected our mental structures by both condensing the structures and increasing their tacit knowledge; when we re-think them and re-act with them, we recreate their meaning in a new context.

16 Ladislav Matejka and Irwin R. Titunik, *Semiotics of Art* (Cambridge, Mass.: MIT Press, 1976).

17 Matejka and Titunik, *Semiotics of Art*, 275–6.

18 Matejka and Titunik, *Semiotics of Art*, 8–9.

19 Richard Courtney, *Play, Drama and Thought: The Intellectual Background to Dramatic Education* (4th rev. ed. Toronto: Simon and Pierre, [1968], 1989).

20 Matejka and Titunik, *Semiotics of Art*, ch. 8.

21 Matejka and Titunik, *Semiotics of Art*, 245–64.

22 E.H. Gombrich, J. Hochberg, and Max Black, *Art, Perception and Reality* (Baltimore: John Hopkins University Press, 1972).

23 Keir Elam, *The Semiotics of Theatre and Drama* (London: Methuen, 1980), 5–18.

24 Elam, *The Semiotics of Theatre and Drama*, 22.

25 John Dewey, *Art as Experience* (New York: Capricorn Books, 1934).

26 Arnold Berleant, *Aesthetic Field: A Phenomenology of Aesthetic Experience* (Springfield, Ill.: Charles C. Thomas, 1970), 124.

27 A.-J. Greimas and M. Courtes, *Semiotics and Language: An Analytical Dictionary*, trans. D. Palk et al. (Bloomington: Indiana University Press, 1982).

28 Daniel Patte, "Greimas' Model for the Generative Trajectory of Meaning in American Discourses," *Journal of Semiotics* 1:3 (1982).

29 Richard Courtney and Paul Park, *Learning through the Arts*, research report, 4 vols. (Toronto: Ministry of Education, 1980).

30 Fredric Jameson, *The Prison House of Language: A Critical Account of Structuralism and Russian Formalism* (Princeton: Princeton University Press, 1972), 46–7.

31 Jameson, *The Prison House*, 166.

32 A.-J. Greimas, *Structural Semantics* (Lincoln: Nebraska University Press, 1983), XII, 5.e.

33 Greimas, *Structural Semantics*, II, 7.

34 Greimas, *Structural Semantics*, XI, 3.

35 Greimas, *Structural Semantics*, XI, 2ff.

36 Greimas, *Structural Semantics*, XI, ii.

37 Greimas, *Structural Semantics*, VII, 3.d.

38 At this point of his discussion, Greimas draws near to the views of Claude Lévi-Strauss, *Structural Anthropology*, trans. M. Lagton (New York: Harper and Row, 1976).

39 "The contest appears first as the confrontation of the helper and the opponent, that is to say, the manifestation, at the same time functional, dynamic, and anthropomorphic, of what could be considered as the two terms – positive and negative – of the complex structure of signification. The confrontation is immediately followed by the function "success," which signifies the victory of the helper over the opponent, that is to say, the destruction of the negative term to the profit of a single positive term. The contest, thus interpreted, could well be the mythical representation of the exploding of the complex structure, that is to say, of that metalinguistic operation where the denial of the negative term lets only the positive term of the elementary structure stand" (Greimas, *Structural Semantics*, XI, 2.f). This reminds Greimas of "the essential traits of the functional model: the possibility which it offers to transfer onto the actants the dynamism which is contained in the functions and to manifest it in the form 'power of acting'" (Greimas, *Structural Semantics*, XII, 4.a).

40 That is to say, "It is a discovery, not of something out there, but of the freely ('arbitrarily') chosen isotopy of discourse, chosen in time – at a particular time" (Greimas, *Structural Semantics*, 1). It is "non-recurrent and for that very reason cannot, like natural phenomena, be subject to exact and generalizing treatment" (Hjelmslev, "Some Reflections on Practice and Theory in Structural Semantics," *Language and Society* [Copenhagen, 1971], 8.)

41 Karl R. Popper, *Conjectures and Refutations* (New York: Harper and Row, 1963, 1972).

42 Robert W. Witkin, *The Intelligence of Feeling* (London: Heinemann, 1974).

43 Keith Johnstone, *Impro* (London: Faber and Faber, 1979).

CHAPTER SIX

1 W. Wundt, *Elements of Physiological Psychology*, 2 vols. (London: Swan and Sonnerschein, 1904).

2 William James, "What Is Emotion?" *Mind*, 9 (1884): 188–205.

3 William James, *Psychology, Briefer Course* (New York: Holt, 1892), 499.

4 N. Bull, "The Attitude Theory of Emotion," *Nervous and Mental Disease Monographs* (1951).

5 W.B. Cannon, "The James-Lange Theory of Emotions: A Critical Examination and an Alternative Theory," *American Journal of Psychology*, 39 (1927): 106–24.

6 Charles Darwin, *The Expression of the Emotions in Man and Animals* (London: Murray, 1872).

7 John Dewey, "The Theory of Emotion: II. The Significance of Emotions," *Psychological Review* (1895): 19.

8 Dewey, "The Theory of Emotion," 30.

9 John B. Watson, "A Schematic Outline of the Emotions," *Psychological Review*, 26 (1910): 165.

10 B.F. Skinner, *Science and Human Behavior* (New York: Macmillan, 1953).

11 Pierre Janet, *De l'angoisse á l'extase*, 2 vols. (Paris: Alcan, 1928).

12 Gisèle Barret, "Arts-expressions en pédagogie: Pour une pédagogie de l'expression," in *Repères*, 7 (1986): 1–4; Roger Deldime, *Le quatrième mur* (Brussels, 1990).

13 Jacob L. Moreno, "The Creativity of Personality," *New York University Bulletin, Arts and Sciences*, 46:4 (January 1966).

14 F.S. Perls, *Gestalt Therapy Verbatim* (Lafayette, Calif.: Real People Press, 1969).

15 R.D. Laing, *The Divided Self* (Harmondsworth: Penguin, 1965); Rollo May, *The Meaning of Anxiety* (New York: Norton, 1977).

16 Gertrud Schattner and Richard Courtney, eds., *Drama in Therapy*, 2 vols. (New York: Drama Book Specialists, 1981).

17 Susan Isaacs, *Intellectual Growth in Young Children* (London: Routledge, 1933).

18 Melanie Klein, *Narrative of Child Analysis* (London: Hogarth Press, 1932).

19 David W. Winnicott, *Playing and Reality* (Harmondsworth: Penguin, 1974); Richard Courtney, *Play, Drama and Thought: The Intellectual Background to Dramatic Education* (4th rev. ed. Toronto: Simon and Pierre, [1968], 1989), 90–4.

20 Richard Courtney, *The Dramatic Curriculum* (London, Ont.: University of Western Ontario, Faculty of Education; New York: Drama Book Specialists; London: Heinemann, 1980).

21 Otto Weininger, *Play and Education: The Basic Tool for Early Childhood Learning* (Springfield, Ill.: Charles C. Thomas, [1979], 1982).

22 Peter Slade, *Child Drama* (London: London University Press, 1954).
23 Jean Piaget, *The Child's Conception of Time* (London: Routledge and Kegan Paul, 1969).
24 Jean-Paul Sartre, *The Transcendence of the Ego* (New York: Noonday Press, 1957); Jean-Paul Sartre, *Being and Nothingness*, trans. H.E. Barnes (New York: Washington Square, 1953).
25 Jerzy Grotowski, *Towards a Poor Theatre* (New York: Simon and Schuster, 1968).
26 D.B. Lindsley. "Emotions and the Electroencephalogram," in *Feelings and Emotions: The Mooseheart Symposium,* ed. M.L. Reynert (New York: McGraw-Hill, 1950); D.B. Lindsley, "Emotion," in *Handbook of Experimental Psychology,* ed. S.S. Steves (New York: Wiley, 1951).
27 Richard Courtney, *Re-Play: Studies of Human Drama in Education* (Toronto: Ontario Institute for Studies in Education Press, 1982), chap. 3.
28 Mihaly Csikszentmihalyi, *Flow: The Psychology of Optimal Experience* (New York: Harper and Row, 1990), 260.
29 Courtney, *Play, Drama and Thought*, part 2; F.A. Hodge, "The Emotions in a New Role," *Psychological Review*, 42 (1935): 555–65.
30 Otto Fenichel, *The Psychoanalytic Theory of Neurosis* (London: Paul Kegan, [1946], 1953).
31 Csikszentmihalyi, *Flow,* 270.
32 Csikszentmihalyi, *Flow,* 272.
33 Csikszentmihalyi, *Flow,* 272; D.B. Lindsley, "Psychophysiology and Motivation," in *Nebraska Symposium on Motivation,* ed. M.R. Jones (Lincoln: University of Nebraska Press, 1957), 44–104.
34 Csikszentmihalyi, *Flow,* 272; E. Duffy, "The Relationship between Muscular Tension and Quality of Performance," *American Journal of Psychology,* 44 (1932): 535–46.
35 R.B. Malmo, "Activation: A Neuro-psychological Dimension," *Psychological Review,* 66 (1959): 367–86.
36 Janet, *De l'angoisse,* 135.
37 H. Wallon, *Les origines du caractére chez l'enfant* (2nd ed. Paris: PUF, 1949).
38 P. Fraisse, "The Emotions," in *Experimental Psychology. Its Scope and Method: V. Motivation, Emotion and Personality,* ed. P. Fraisse and Jean Piaget (London: Routledge and Kegan Paul, 1968).
39 Courtney, *Play, Drama and Thought,* 176–7.
40 Csikszentmihalyi, *Flow,* 272; F.L. Goodenough, *Anger in Young Children* (Minneapolis: Minneapolis University Press, 1931).
41 Courtney, *The Dramatic Curriculum.*
42 Courtney, *Drama and Intelligence,* 54–6.

CHAPTER SEVEN

1 This chapter is based on my *Practical Research* (Jackson's Point, Ont.: Bison Books, 1988). This was published in a limited edition with the assistance of the Forum for Arts and Media Education, a co-operative enterprise of faculty members at the Ontario Institute for Studies in Education and the Faculty of Education, University of Toronto. The chapter has been much altered for publication in this book.

2 Lloyd W. West, "Improving Research in Counselling Psychology: A Point of View," in *Natcon 9*, ed. R.V. Peavey (Ottawa: Canada Employment and Immigration, 1985), 193–200.

3 Karl Popper, *Objective Knowledge* (Oxford: Oxford University Press, 1972).

4 West, "Improving Research," 195.

5 J.M. Dabbs, Jr, "Making Things Visible," in *Varieties of Qualitative Research*, ed. J. Van Manen, J.M. Dabbs, Jr, and R.F. Faulkner (Beverley Hills: Sage, 1982), 32.

6 Mary Lee Smith, "Publishing Qualitative Research," *American Educational Research Journal*, 24:2 (Summer 1987): 175.

7 West, "Improving Research," 196.

8 West, "Improving Research," 198.

9 W.H. Goodenough, *Explorations in Cultural Anthropology* (New York: McGraw Hill, 1964).

10 Richard Courtney, *The Drama Studio* (London: Pitman, 1966).

11 Marlene B. Anderson, "The Development and Evaluation of a Study of Thanatology at the Tertiary Level of Education", ED D dissertation (University of Toronto, 1981); R.A. Clark, "Aesthetic Self-Disclosure in Visual Arts", ED D dissertation (University of Toronto, 1987).

12 D. Kaplan and R.A. Manners, *Culture Theory* (Englewood Cliffs, NJ: Prentice-Hall, 1972).

13 David Miller, ed., *Popper Selections* (Princeton: Princeton University Press, 1985).

14 Jean Piaget, *Play, Dreams and Imitation in Childhood* (New York: Norton, 1964).

15 Smith, "Publishing Qualitative Research."

16 F. Erickson, "Qualitative Methods in Research on Teaching," in, *Handbook of Research on Teaching*, ed. M. Wittrock (New York: Macmillan, 1986), 121.

17 Erickson, "Qualitative Methods," 140–9.

18 R. Donmoyer, "The Rescue from Relativism: Two Failed Attempts and an Alternate Strategy," *Educational Researcher*, 14: 10 (1985): 13–20.

19 Smith, "Publishing Qualitative Research," 178.

20 Elliot W. Eisner, "On the Differences between Scientific and Artistic Approaches to Qualitative Research," *Educational Researcher* 10, 4: 6.

21 Elizabeth Vallance, "The Application of Aesthetic Criticism to Curriculum Materials: Arguments and Issues," unpublished paper presented at AERA Conference, 1976.

22 E.F. Kelly, "Curriculum Evaluation and Literary Criticism: Comments on the Analogy," *Curriculum Inquiry*, 5 (1975): 87–106.

23 B. MacDonald, "The Portrayal of Persons as Evaluation Data," unpublished paper presented at AERA Conference, 1976.

24 M.R. Grumet, "Curriculum as Theater: Merely Players," *Curriculum Inquiry*, 8 (1978): 37–64.

25 Richard Courtney, *The Dramatic Curriculum* (London, Ont.: University of Western Ontario, Faculty of Education; New York: Drama Book Specialists; London: Heinemann, 1980); Geoffrey Milburn, "Derivation and Application of a Dramatic Metaphor for the Assessment of Teaching", ED D dissertation (University of Toronto, 1982).

26 David Best, *Expression in Movement and the Arts* (London: Lepus, 1974) section E; David Best, *Philosophy and Human Movement* (London: George Allen and Unwin, 1978); David Best, *Feeling and Reason in the Arts* (London: George Allen and Unwin, 1985).

27 J. Kirk and M.L. Miller, *Reliability and Validity in Qualitative Research* (Beverley Hills: Sage, 1986).

28 Peter L. McLaren, *Schooling as a Ritual Performance* (London: Routledge and Kegan Paul, 1983); P. Willis, *Learning to Labor: How Working Class Kids Get Working Class Jobs* (New York: Columbia University Press, 1981); H.F. Wolcott, *Teachers versus Technocrats* (Eugene: Center for Educational Management, University of Oregon, 1977).

29 Paolo Freire, *Pedagogy in Process* (New York: Seabury Press, 1978).

30 M.G. Yaga de Andrade, "School Settings and Functions of Counsellors," in *Natcon 9*, ed. Peavey, 259–68.

31 F.A. Nugent, *Professional Counselling: An Overview* (Monterey: Brooks/ Cole Publishing Co., 1981).

32 Andrade, "School Settings and Functions of Counsellors," 262.

33 Andrade, "School Settings and Functions of Counsellors," 263.

34 Paolo Freire, *The Pedagogy of the Oppressed* (New York: Herder and Herder, 1970); Paolo Freire, *Education for Critical Consciousness* (New York: Seabury Press, 1973).

35 Andrade, "School Settings and Functions of Counsellors," 264.

36 Martin Buber, *I and Thou* (New York: Scribner's, 1958).

37 R.V. Peavey, S. Robertson, and M. Westwood, "Guidelines for Counsellor Education in Canada," *Canadian Counsellor*, 16 (1982): 135–43.

38 Michael Polanyi, *Personal Knowledge* (New York: Harper and Row, 1962).

39 Brian Way, *Development through Drama* (London: Longman, 1968).

40 John H. Chilcott, "Where Are You Coming From and Where Are You Going? The Reporting of Ethnographic Research," *American Educational Research Journal*, 24: 2 (1987): 209.

41 H.D. Fishbein, *Evolution Development, Children's Learning* (Pacific Palisades, Calif.: Goodyear, 1976).

42 Margaret Mead, *Coming of Age in Samoa* (New York: Mentor, 1963).

43 Jules Henry, "A Cross-Cultural Outline of Education," *Current Anthropology*, 1: 4 (1960): 267–306.

44 B.B. Khlief, "The School as a Small Society," in *School and Society*, ed. M. Wax, S. Diamond, and F. Gearing, (New York: Basic Books, 1971), 144–55.

45 B. Grindal, *Growing Up in Two Worlds: Education and Transition among the Sisala of Northern Ghana* (New York: Holt, Rinehart and Winston, 1972); J.W.M. Whiting, "Effects of Climate on Certain Cultural Practices," in *Explorations in Cultural Anthropology*, ed. W.H. Goodenough, (New York: McGraw Hill, 1964), 511–44; H.F. Wolcott, *A Kwakitul Village and School* (New York: Holt, Rinehart and Winston, 1967).

46 S.B. Heath, *Ways with Words* (Cambridge: Cambridge University Press, 1983).

47 B.B. Bernstein, "A Sociolinguistic Approach to Socialization: With Some Reference to Educability," in *Directions in Sociolinguistics*, ed. J.J. Gumperz and D. Hymes (London: Routledge and Kegan Paul, 1972), 465–97.

48 K. Au, "Participation Structures in a Reading Lesson with Hawaiian Children: Analysis of a Culturally Appropriate Instructional Event," *Anthropology and Education Quarterly*, 11: 2 (1980), 91–115.

49 Margaret Mead, *Coming of Age in Samoa*; J.W.M. Whiting, "A Model for Psychological Research on Culture and Infancy," in *Variations in Human Experience*, ed. P. Liederman, S. R. Tolkin, and A. Rosenfeld (New York: Academic Press, 1977), 29–48; J.W.M. Whiting and I. Child, *Child Training and Personality* (New Haven: Yale University Press, 1953).

50 J.W.D. Dougherty, ed., *Directions in Cognitive Anthropology* (Urbana: University of Illinois Press, 1985).

51 John H. Chilcott, "Yaqui World View and the School: Conflict and Accommodation," *Journal of American Indian Education*, 24: 3 (1985): 21–32.

52 Claude Lévi-Strauss, *The Savage Mind* (Chicago: University of Chicago Press, 1962).

53 A.J. Greimas, *Structural Semantics* (Lincoln: Nebraska University Press, 1983).

54 Richard Courtney, *Aesthetic Learning*, research report (Ottawa: Social Sciences and Humanities Research Council of Canada, 1985).

55 N.B. Johnson, "The Material Culture of Public School Classrooms: The Symbolic Integration of Local Schools and National Culture," *Anthropology and Education Quarterly*, 7: 3 (1980), 173–90.

56 Hugh Dalziel Duncan, *Symbols in Society* (New York: Oxford University Press, 1968); Victor W. Turner, *The Ritual Process: Structure and Anti-Structure* (Harmondsworth: Penguin, 1974); Victor W. Turner, *From Ritual to Theatre: The Human Seriousness of Play* (New York: Performing Arts Journal Publications, 1982).

57 A.V. Cicourel, "Basic and Normal Rules in the Negotiation of Status and Role," in *Studies in Social Interaction*, ed. D. Sudnow (New York: Free Press, 1972), 229–58.

58 N.K. Denzon, *Childhood Socialization* (San Francisco: Jossey-Bass, 1977).

59 Peter L. McLaren, *Schooling as a Ritual Performance* (London: Routledge and Kegan Paul, 1983).

60 R.B. Everhart and W.J. Doyle, "The Symbolic Aspects of Educational Innovation," *Anthropology and Education Quarterly*, 11: 2 (1980): 67–90.

61 Richard Courtney, *The Quest: Research and Inquiry in Arts Education* (Lanham, Md.: University Press of America, 1986).

62 Richard Courtney and Paul Park, *Learning through the Arts*, research report, 4 vols. (Toronto: Ministry of Education, 1980).

63 Richard Courtney, "Drama as a Generic Skill," *Youth Theatre Journal*, 1: 1 (Summer 1986): 5–10, 27.

64 Richard Courtney, *Re-Play: Studies of Human Drama in Education* (Toronto: Ontario Institute for Studies in Education Press, 1982).

65 Joseph Lee, *Play in Education* (New York, 1915).

66 Robert W. Witkin, *The Intelligence of Feeling* (London: Heinemann, 1974).

67 Popper, *Objective Knowledge*.

68 Courtney, *Re-Play*.

69 John E. Cowen, ed.,*Teaching Reading through the Arts* (Newark, Del.: International Reading Association, 1983).

70 Courtney, *Re-Play*.

71 Richard Courtney, "The Victoria Project," 1988. The findings of this project were confirmed with students of Chinese origin in Toronto by Jay Peng.

72 Polanyi, *Personal Knowledge*, 6.

73 Dorothy Heathcote, "Drama," *English in Education*, 3 (Summer 1969); repr. in *Dorothy Heathcote: Collected Writings on Education and Drama*, ed. Liz Johnson and Cecily O'Neill (London: Hutchinson, 1984), 62.

74 Robert E. Stake, *Evaluating the Arts in Education* (Indianapolis: Charles E. Merrill, 1974).

75 Courtney and Park, *Learning through the Arts*.

76 Richard Courtney, David W. Booth, John Emerson, and Natalie Kuzmich *Teacher Education in the Arts*, research report (Jackson's Point, Ont.: Bison Books, 1985).

77 Richard Courtney, David W. Booth, John Emerson, and Natalie Kuzmich, *No One Way of Being: The Practical Knowledge of Elementary Arts Teachers*, research report (Toronto: Ministry of Education, 1987).

78 Courtney, *Aesthetic Learning.*
79 B.G. Glaser and A.L. Straus, "Discovery of Substantive Theory: A Basic Strategy Underlying Qualitative Research," in *Qualitative Methodology,* ed. W. J. Filstead (Chicago: Markham Publishing Co., 1970).

CHAPTER EIGHT

1 This chapter relies heavily on James W. Flanagan's *David's Social Drama* (Sheffield: Almond Press, 1988). His exposition of hologramic methods is exemplary. See also David Bohm, *Wholeness and the Implicate Order* (London: Routledge and Kegan Paul, 1980); Karl H. Pribram, *Languages of the Brain* (Englewood Cliffs, NJ: Prentice Hall, 1981).
2 The extreme difference between the two fields shows that when there are parallels they are highly significant.
3 Romano Harré, *The Philosophies of Science* (Oxford: Oxford University Press, 1972), 174.
4 Harré, *The Philosophies of Science,* 172. The model is homologous according to A.-J. Greimas, *On Meaning: Selected Writings in Semiotic Theory,* trans. Paul J. Perron and Frank H. Collins (Minneapolis: University of Minnesota Press, 1987).
5 Harré, *The Philosophies of Science,* 174–5.
6 Harré, *The Philosophies of Science,* 179–80.
7 Mario A. Bunge, "Phenomenological Theories," in *The Critical Approach to Science and Philosophy,* ed. Mario A. Bunge (New York/London: Free Press/Collier-Macmillan, 1964), 236.
8 Flanagan, *David's Social Drama,* 26.
9 Edmund Leach, "Against Genres," in *Structuralist Interpretations of Biblical Myth,* ed. Edmund Leach and D. Alan Aycock (Cambridge: Cambridge University Press, 1983), 89–112.
10 Flanagan, *David's Social Drama,* 72.
11 But the comparisons that are made can inject pragmatism and positivism that both expect *and* suspect consistencies in human behaviour.
12 This is discussed in various places in my *Drama and Intelligence: A Cognitive Theory* (Montreal: McGill-Queen's University Press, 1990). See also Victor W. Turner, "Social Dramas and Stories about Time," *Critical Inquiry,* 7 (1980): 141–68.
13 John M. Ziman, *Reliable Knowledge* (Cambridge: Cambridge University Press, 1978), 185.
14 Leach, "Against Genres."
15 Courtney, *Drama and Intelligence,* 140–3.
16 "Adequately" is used here instead of "truly" or "correctly" because the interpretations of holists are not objectively testable assertions.
17 Otto Weininger, "'What if' and 'As if': Imagination and Pretend Play in

Early Childhood," in *Imagination and Education*, ed. Kieran Egan and Dan Nadaner (New York: Teachers' College Press, 1988), 141-52.

18 Robert R. Wilson, *Sociological Approaches to the Old Testament* (Philadelphia: Fortress, 1984), 4.

19 Lewis R. Binford, *For Theory Building* (New York: Academic Press, 1977).

20 Ontological and epistemological problems remain, but the combination of categories of information illuminates the combinations and makes them manageable.

21 A laser beam is a highly coherent monochromatic radiation, a single-phase beam of light. It is split in two when it passes through a partially silvered mirror known as a "beam splitter." By using filters, mirrors, and spreading lenses, the two portions of the beam are directed onto a plate. This plate is emulsion-backed and it captures the amplitude and phase of the two beams: [1] The object beam is diffracted off an object; its waves are thrown partially out of phase by the contours of the object. [2] The reference beam falls directly, unaltered and in phase, onto the plate. The wave patterns of the two portions interfere to produce a wave front of partly coherent and partly incoherent crests and troughs. The fringe patterns of constructive and destructive interference, as it is called, are encoded. When the plate (the hologram) is struck by an illuminating beam, the pattern – and hence the object's image (also called a hologram) – is reconstituted.

See, Nils Abramson, *The Making and Evaluation of Holograms* (New York: Academic Press, 1981); Graham Saxby, *Holograms* (New York: Focal Press, 1980); Joseph E. Kasper and Steven A. Feller, *The Hologram Book* (Englewood Cliffs, NJ: Prentiece-Hall, 1985).

22 The coherence of the object and reference beams must be only partial. If the crests and troughs of the two beams are either totally congruent or totally incongruent, no interference pattern, and therefore no image, is encoded and none can be reconstituted.

23 Courtney, *Drama and Intelligence*, 4-7.

24 I am grateful to my colleague Dr David E. Hunt for his comments, which have enriched this figure.

25 Research strategies of this kind are also reversible. The process of making holograms from master holograms (the functional equivalent of making photographic copies from negatives) can also be used as a model for the two-step process required to combine studies in specific disciplines into interdisciplinary studies.

26 Without the pattern, educational researchers would be either reduced to knowing very little, which would force them to trust a simple source, or strongly tempted to accept previous interpretations by simply paraphrasing sources – again trusting a single source. Unfortunately one or other of these substitutions is often made in educational research.

27 As every point of light from the object is spread across the complete surface of the plate, when the plate is broken or divided, each part retains the whole image but lacks perspectives contained in the larger plate.

28 The analogy is appropriate even when no new information is discovered, because researchers, like viewers looking through a shuttered window or small hologram, try constantly to peer beyond the limits of the information in order to gain a view of a bigger scene.

29 When the illuminating beam strikes the interference pattern encoded in the plate, the beam reconstitutes one of the original light waves, usually the object beam.

30 This is because the light reconstituted by the illuminating beam is the actual light that was diffracted from the object.

31 The actual = warmth, beauty, vibrancy, dimensionality, proximity. The fictional = inaccessibility, beyond, past, "here and non-here."

32 Leach, "Against Genres," 98.

33 Robert Wilson, "The Old Testament Genealogies in Recent Research," *Journal of Biblical Literature*, 94 (1975): 169–89. Robert Wilson, *Genealogy and History in the Ancient World* (New Haven: Yale University Press, 1977); Robert Wilson, *Sociological Approaches to the Old Testament* (Philadelphia: Fortress Press, 1984).

34 G.E. Wright, "What Archeology Can and Cannot Do," in *The Biblical Archeologist Reader IV*, ed. E.F. Campbell and D.N. Freedman ([1971]; Sheffield: Almond Press, 1983), 65–72.

35 The examples from Wilson and Wright (see 33 and 34 above) used only two information sources. To add a third brings the complexity of requiring that relationships [a] between two ancient sources and [b] between ancient and alien sources (either ancient or modern) must both be examined before [c] a plausible causal explanation can be offered. In order to accomplish [a] and [b] in educational research, we can appeal to holography; or [c] we can turn to ritology and developmental drama, as below.

36 The laser beam is split into three or more parts; i.e., at least two object beams and one reference beam. Instead of diffracting off objects, however, the object beams pass through the master holograms, projecting their pseudoscopic images onto a plate where the reference beam interferes with them. The pseudoscopic images from the master(s) are encoded as parts of a composite information source. When the composite hologram is lighted by an illuminating beam, viewers can see one or other image or both – actually a composite of both – depending on their angles of vision, i.e., their perspectives. Additional generations of images would lead to a composition so complex that computer analysis and enhancement would be needed in order to sort and view any of the images.

37 David Bohm, *The Special Theory of Relativity* (New York: W.A. Benjamin, 1965); Bohm, *Wholeness and the Implicate Order*.

38 David Bohm, quoted in Martin Curd, review of Bohm, *Wholeness and the Implicate Order*, in *Physics Today*, 34 (1981): 58.

39 Michael Polanyi, *Personal Knowledge* (New York: Harper and Row, 1962).

40 Bohm, *Wholeness and the Implicate Order*, 150–7.

41 Renée Weber, "The Enfolding-Unfolding Universe: A Conversation with David Bohm," in *The Holographic Paradigm*, ed. Ken Wilbur (Boulder, Colo.: Shambala New Science Library, 1982), 97.

42 Bohm, *Wholeness and the Implicate Order*, 210.

43 Turner, "Social Dramas."

44 Peter L. McLaren, *Schooling as a Ritual Performance* (London: Routledge and Kegan Paul, 1983)

45 Terence S. Turner, "Transformation, Hierarchy, and Transcendence: A Reformulation of Van Gennep's model of the Structure of *Rites of Passage*," in *Secular Ritual*, ed. Sally F. Moore and Barbara G. Meyerhoff (Amsterdam: Van Goprcum, 1977), 60.

46 Richard Courtney, *Dictionary of Developmental Drama* (Springfield, Ill.: Charles C. Thomas, 1987).

47 Roy A. Rappaport, *Pigs for Ancestors* (repr. New Haven: Yale University Press, 1984), 299–496.

48 Richard Courtney, *Play, Drama and Thought: The Intellectual Background to Dramatic Education* (4th rev. ed. Toronto: Simon and Pierre, [1968], 1989), 171–3.

49 David W. Booth and Alistair Martin-Smith, eds.,*Re-Cognizing Richard Courtney: Selected Papers in Drama and Education* (Markham, Ont.: Pembroke Press, 1989), 192–200.

50 Holistic studies and their distinctions act like beam splitters in holography. Domains are separated so that they can be clarified and eventually reintegrated according to other relationships. In turn, the new relations can be illumined in order to see different holistic images.

CHAPTER NINE

1 Douglas A. Roberts, "Science as an Explanatory Mode," *Main Currents in Modern Thought*, 26: 5 (May-June 1970): 131–9.

2 Developmental drama as an academic discipline is defined as "the study of the developments (or transformations) that result from dramatic action." The two complementary sides of theory are the personal and the social. The practical fields include education, therapy, ritual, and other cultural forms. See my *Dictionary of Developmental Drama* (Springfield, Ill.: Charles C. Thomas, 1987).

3 Even the most formal dramatic act (i.e., within the director-oriented theatre of the West End or Broadway) is still inherently spontaneous. For degrees of

dramatic spontaneity, see my "Theatre and Spontaneity," *Journal of Aesthetics and Art Criticism*, 31: 1 (Fall 1973): 79–88.

4 Educational drama based on creative spontaneity ("creative drama") began in Britain and the United States in the early years of the twentieth century and continued by isolated teachers thereafter. By the 1950s it had expanded considerably in the UK and the USA, and had begun in the Commonwealth. It spread rapidly: by the 1970s to Europe, and by the 1980s to the Third World (e.g., Tanzania, Thailand, etc.)

   The rapidity of its growth can be illustrated by the case of Ontario. In 1967 there may have been three teachers of "creative drama" in the province. By 1987 there were over fifty thousand students registered in drama programs in grades 8–12 following official guidelines issued by the Ministry of Education; other elementary students following the curriculum supplement *Drama in the Formative Years*, by David W. Booth (Toronto: Ontario Ministry of Education, 1984); and hundreds of "specialist" teachers of drama. See Richard Courtney and Robert Campbell, *Educational Drama: A Modern International History* (London: National Drama, in press).

5 The structures and dynamics of dramatic thought are discussed in my "The Dramatic Metaphor and Learning," in *Creative Drama in a Developmental Context*, ed. Judith Kase-Polisini (Lanham, Md.: University Press of America, 1985), 39–64.

6 Being a midwife to others is famous as a statement of the Buddha. It is also a common existential phrase amongst leaders in educational drama; e.g., Rt. Rev. E.J. Burton, Dorothy Heathcote. There is a clear indication that the field of developmental drama operates differently from the predominant ethos of Occidental society (e.g., conflict/competition/war) and, parallel with some Oriental thought, operates through similarity/co-operation/peace.

7 E.J. Burton, *Reality and "Realization": An Approach to a Philosophy* (London: Drama and Education Fellowship, 1966).

8 These intrinsic learnings are shown in Richard Courtney and Paul Park, *Learning through the Arts*, research report, 4 vols. (Toronto: Ministry of Education, 1980).

9 Robert W. Witkin, *The Intelligence of Feeling* (London: Heinemann, 1974).

10 In educational drama this view is specifically held by Peter Slade, who describes it as "spitting out evil in a legal framework": *Child Drama* (London: University of London Press, 1954).

11 Courtney, "The Dramatic Metaphor and Learning." See also my *Play, Drama and Thought: The Intellectual Background to Dramatic Education*, (4th rev. ed. Toronto: Simon and Pierre, [1968], 1989), part 2.

12 Martin Buber, *I and Thou* (New York: Scribner's, 1958). Buber came to this

notion as a student attending the theatre in Vienna. See Maurice Friedman, ed., *Martin Buber on Theater* (New York: Funk and Wagnall, 1969).

13 For intuition, see Richard Courtney, David W. Booth, John Emerson, and Natalie Kuzmich, *No One Way of Being: The Practical Knowledge of Elementary Arts Teachers*, research report (Toronto: Ministry of Education, 1987).

14 Howard Gardner, *Frames of Mind: The Theory of Multiple Intelligences* (New York: Basic Books, 1983).

15 For commentary, see my *Re-Play: Studies of Human Drama in Education* (Toronto: Ontario Institute for Studies in Education Press, 1982).

16 Viola Spolin, *Improvisation in the Theater* (Evanston, Ill.: Northwestern University Press, 1963); Keith Johnstone, *Impro* (London: Faber and Faber, 1979).

17 Glynne Wickham, *Early English Stages, 1300–1600,* 3 vols. (London: Routledge and Kegan Paul, 1966–72).

18 Colin Skinner and M.D. Faber, "The Spanish Tragedy: Act IV," *Philological Quarterly,* 49: 4 (October 1970): 444–59.

19 Johnstone, *Impro.*

20 Brian Way, *Development through Drama* (London: Longman, 1968).

21 *Dorothy Heathcote: Collected Writings on Education and Drama*, ed. Liz Johnson and Cecily O'Neill (London: Hutchinson, 1984).

In Conclusion

1 H. Caldwell Cook, *The Play Way* (London: Heinemann, 1917), 1.

2 Harriet Finlay-Johnson, *The Dramatic Method of Teaching* (London: Nisbet, n.d.).

3 Werner Heisenberg, *Physics and Beyond: Encounters and Conversations* (New York: Harper and Row, 1971). For Shannon, see Charles Hampden-Turner, *Radical Man: The Process of Psycho-Social Development* (New York: Doubleday, 1981).

Index